SEX AND FAMILY IN THE BIBLE AND THE MIDDLE EAST

By Raphael Patai

SEX AND FAMILY IN THE BIBLE AND THE MIDDLE EAST

KINGDOM OF JORDAN

ISRAEL BETWEEN EAST AND WEST: A STUDY IN HUMAN
RELATIONS

THE SCIENCE OF MAN: AN INTRODUCTION TO ANTHROPOLOGY
2 *vols.* (*In Hebrew*)

MAN AND TEMPLE IN ANCIENT JEWISH MYTH AND RITUAL

ON CULTURE CONTACT AND ITS WORKING IN MODERN PALESTINE

MAN AND EARTH IN HEBREW CUSTOM, BELIEF, AND LEGEND: A
STUDY IN COMPARATIVE RELIGION 2 *vols.* (*In Hebrew*)

JEWISH SEAFARING IN ANCIENT TIMES: A CONTRIBUTION TO
THE HISTORY OF PALESTINIAN CULTURE (*In Hebrew*)

WATER: A STUDY IN PALESTINOLOGY AND PALESTINIAN FOLKLORE
IN THE BIBLICAL AND MISHNAIC PERIODS (*In Hebrew*)

SEX and FAMILY
in the Bible
and the Middle East

BY

Raphael Patai

1959

DOUBLEDAY & COMPANY, INC.

Garden City, New York

This book, while not written from a religious angle, treats the Bible with reverence, and it is the author's hope that it does not contain anything that could be offensive to the religious-minded reader.

The references, by chapter and verse, follow the Masoretic text of the Hebrew Bible from which the King James and subsequent English versions occasionally deviate to the extent of one verse. In general, the English translation published by the Jewish Publication Society of America was used. On several occasions, however, the author felt that he would prefer a different rendering, in which case he retranslated the passage in question from the Hebrew original.

The scriptural references (to the Old Testament, the Apocrypha, the New Testament, and the Koran) are inserted in parentheses into the text of the book. Other references are listed at the end of the volume under the heading "Sources and Notes." These are arranged according to the pages on which they are utilized in the book and within each page heading, according to the order in which they appear.

Contents

SEX AND FAMILY IN THE BIBLE
AND THE MIDDLE EAST

Chapter 1

INTRODUCTION

WE of the Western world, born and bred in the big cities of modern Euro-American culture, find it increasingly difficult to identify ourselves with the characters of the Bible, to recognize the common element in their lives and in ours, and to apply to our own situation solutions found by them when they grappled with problems of their world. The ostensible differences between Biblical life, and especially its early pastoral-tribal phase pictured in the book of Genesis, and our own complex existence are so great that they tend to block out the underlying, all-human, common factor. We live, not in open tents pitched on wind-swept hillsides, but in tall and tight apartment houses; our daily work leads us, not out onto the fields and the flocks, but into our offices and factories; unannounced guests come to us but rarely, but if they do, we don't run out to slaughter a sheep, but suggest that we all go to the nearby restaurant for dinner; we don't go to our cousins or neighbors to arrange for the marriage of our children, but make polite conversation with the strange young men who come to take our daughters out on a date, and hope that the young folk will find their way and settle down sooner or later. We do not lift up our eyes in prayer to God for deliverance when faced with adversity, but run to our doctor, lawyer, psychiatrist. We do not look forward to a mature age of increasing leisure utilized for contemplation, but engage in what has been termed "frantic activism" to escape boredom; we idolize youth and fear aging. In fact, in the majority of cases our behavior, both the expected and the actual, is the exact opposite of that of the Biblical characters in analogous situations. Thus, much that is contained in the Bible—the main source and fountainhead of our religion—has become in our eyes a mere collection of genre pictures describing a strange and remote world with which we have little if anything in common.

This means that also the ethical teachings of the Bible, which, after all, are but the quintessence of Biblical society's experience with God, nature, and fellow men, appear to us to be strange and remote, and not easily applicable in our own lives. We pay lip service, to be sure, to the moral ideals contained in the Old and New Testaments, but when it comes to concrete details the strangeness of style and thought, of idiom and idea, impel us more often than not to dismiss the Biblical lesson as irrelevant for our own problems.

The strangeness and remoteness of Biblical values, ethics, and attitudes are often accentuated by one specific circumstance. This is the brevity of reference, the allusive style which takes for granted knowledge of context and background not possessed as a rule by the twentieth-century Westerner. Therefore, nuances are lost on us almost in every case, and even basic meanings often. With all its appeal and occasionally patent charm, beauty, power, and loftiness, much of the Bible thus remains either entirely closed to us or, at best, allows only a veiled glimpse of its true and full significance.

One way to overcome this handicap is to view the Bible against its contemporary background. Written documents, pictures, statues and monuments unearthed in Egypt, Mesopotamia, Syria, and Palestine herself, and dating back into the very days in which various books of the Bible were written, greatly enrich our understanding of the Book of Books. This approach has been extremely rewarding and has been and is still being diligently followed by hundreds of scholars whose work has to date resulted in a truly panoramic view of the Biblical world.

The other path, equally rewarding but much less frequently followed, leads to a better understanding of the Bible by viewing it against the background of the nineteenth- and twentieth-century folk life of the Middle East. The advantage of this approach against the first one lies primarily in the much greater richness of the informative material which it can adduce. When drawing upon the ancient Near East, the student is confined to pieces of documentary evidence which by lucky chance have been preserved through millennia and found or unearthed in excavations. By its very nature this evidence is limited, sporadic, and fragmentary. When utilizing, on the other hand, recent source material, one enjoys the advantage of having full, or at least fairly complete, descriptions of the manners and customs of peoples, their sayings and proverbs, their folklore and mores, their values and attitudes. One also has the possibility of initiating inquiries into hitherto unexplored areas and topics, and of gathering firsthand information based on field observations. Thus there is available, either actually or potentially, a wide basis of detailed data against which to view practically any Biblical passage or statement.

This approach is predicated on one basic premise: namely, that folk life in the nineteenth- and twentieth-century Middle East is essentially comparable to the life of the ancient Hebrews as reflected in the Bible. No student of culture would, of course, assume that life in the Middle East has not changed in the three and a half millennia which passed since the days of Abraham. Changes have occurred, as they must, in every century and every generation. But in the Middle East, possibly more than in any other world area, changes have been slow. The way of life and even the physical appearance of a village in Palestine or in Syria of the twentieth century are consequently very similar to what they were in the days of David. The same holds good for the nomads of the Syrian desert who greatly resemble the nomads among whom was the ancestral family group of the Hebrews. All folk society exhibits the trait of conservatism beneath superficial and insignificant change.

Middle Eastern folk society is characterized to a remarkable degree by the persistence of the basic underlying pattern. Thus it is completely legitimate, from a methodological point of view, to seek a fuller understanding of what the Biblical characters did and said and thought through observing how the folk societies in "Bible lands" behave and speak and think thirty to thirty-five centuries later.

It has to be stated that the folk life upon which the comparative material in this book draws is fast fading in the Middle East of the mid-twentieth century. "Westernization," that is, the pervading influence of Western culture—material and technological as well as attitudinal and emotional—has largely overrun the cities and is rapidly radiating from them into the surrounding countryside. It is in the more remote villages and in nomadic tribal society that one can still encounter the atmosphere, the forms of individual and family life, reminiscent of the Biblical world. But even here, it is merely a question of another few years, decades at the utmost, until millennial tranquil traditions will be supplanted by the new ways of the West. This book, comparing and bringing together as it does Biblical life with that of the traditional Middle Eastern world of the nineteenth and twentieth century, is thus something of a monument to this waning world as well.

While a general study, along the lines indicated, of Biblical Hebrew life would be highly desirable, it would be a tremendous undertaking requiring possibly a lifetime of study and resulting, not in a book, but in a series of volumes. I therefore felt that it was more practicable to confine myself to a discussion of the family which is central, focal, and pivotal in both Biblical society and in the life of the tradition-bound strata of the Middle Eastern peoples in the present time. Inextricably interlaced with all aspects of family life is sex, hence the subject of the book: sex and family in the Bible in the light of present-day folk life in the Middle East. I sincerely hope that, by thus elucidating sex and family in the Bible, a basis is created for the better understanding, not only of the folk life of the ancient Hebrews, but also of their moral ideas which are contained in the most valuable, most lofty, and most permanent parts of the Bible.

THE FAMILY

THE race of man was conceived of by the ancient Hebrews as a widely furcated family. God created the first man and woman, who begot children who, in turn, became the ancestors of all mankind. This is the explicit story told in the book of Genesis. In addition, the idea is reflected in the two terms for "man" in Hebrew: *Adam* and *Enosh*, the first of which was the name of the first man, the second that of his grandson.

The concept of humankind as a family has survived in the Middle East to the present day. Every kin group and, in fact, most other social groups as well, trace their ancestry back to a single individual. This individual, in turn, had relatives who are believed to have been the ancestors of other kin groups. The more remote the common ancestor the more remote the relationship among the kin groups, but ultimately all of mankind finds its source in the original, God-created man, Adam.

Structurally the Biblical family—as well as the modern Middle Eastern family—consists of the male head, his wife or wives, his sons with their wives and children, and his unmarried daughters. In anthropological parlance, this family is usually referred to as "extended," in contradistinction to the "nuclear," or "immediate," or "biological" family predominant in Western civilization, which consists of the father, mother, and minor children only.

In the extended family the choice of marriage partners is a prime concern, and whom a man is forbidden to marry, allowed to marry, expected to marry, required to marry has greatly occupied the Middle Eastern mind from Biblical times down to the present day.

In the Biblical story relating the origin of mankind, we are told that "Cain knew his wife and she conceived and bore Enoch . . ." (Gen. 4:17); that to Seth, the third son of Adam and Eve, "there was born a son . . ." (Gen. 4:26); and that after Adam begot Seth he "begot sons and daughters . . ." (Gen. 5:4). The unspoken implication therefore is clear enough: the sons of Adam and Eve married their own sisters. From the laconic, terse statement it would appear that neither the narrator of this story nor his audience regarded brother-sister marriages as incestuous. One has, however, to take into account that folk belief is willing to countenance and to accept as historical reality events, deeds, and features which would not be tolerated in actual life. According to a legend contained in the Talmud—that vast post-Biblical repository of Palestinian and Babylonian Jewish lore, law, and learning—a girl, destined to be his wife, was born together with each of the sons of Adam, thus to ensure the propagation of the human race. Yet, of course, brother-sister marriage was regarded as incestuous by the Jews of the Talmudic period (first to fifth centuries A.D.), just as it was in the days of the Hebrew monarchy when the Levitical code was written (Lev. 18:9; 20:17). It is interesting to note that the same folk belief is still current among the Egyptian fellahin: according to their stories, too, whenever Eve gave birth to a son she also gave birth to a twin sister, and later Adam married them to one another. Needless to say that brother-sister marriage has disappeared from Egypt with the introduction of Islam.

But, to return to the Biblical account of the origin of the human family, ten generations after Adam, the Deluge reduced mankind again to a single man and woman and their descendants. The Noah story names only Noah and his three sons, Shem, Ham, and Japheth, their wives remaining nameless. This is not unusual in other Biblical and later Middle Eastern genealogies either: only descent in the paternal line is considered important and worthy of mention. The male descendants of the three sons of Noah are enumerated (Gen. 10), and again their wives are nowhere mentioned, but since the only women available to the grandsons of Noah were his grand-daughters, it follows that they could have married no one else. In the third Noahide generation all the individuals were either full siblings or paternal cousins. Therefore any grandson of Noah must have married either his sister or his father's brother's daughter. These two types of marriage were, in fact, common in Biblical times, and the latter of the two has remained the preferred marriage in the Middle East to the present day.

The stories about the origins of mankind, as embodied in the first chapters of the Book of Genesis, represent age-old traditions which were current in the ancient Near East in several variants. But they were more than that: they were also the projection back into the past of actual conditions. What these stories do is to attribute to the original human family the traits characterizing the structure and the functioning of the family as known to the storytellers themselves. And what is equally interesting is the fact that the same features have remained the characteristic traits of the Middle Eastern family down to the present day. Let us have a closer look at them.

The Biblical and the Middle Eastern families are characterized by six basic traits. The full complement of these six traits is found nowhere else outside the Middle East. In the Middle East itself, on the other hand, all the six traits are found everywhere—with a few minor exceptions which are due to specific cultural influences—and in every epoch from the most ancient times down to the present. In anthropological terms, which serve as a kind of convenient shorthand in place of more cumbersome and lengthy descriptions, the Biblical and Middle Eastern families are (1) endogamous, (2) patrilineal, (3) patriarchal, (4) patrilocal, (5) extended, and (6) polygynous.

Endogamous means that there is a preference for marriage of close blood relatives. According to the Biblical narrative, in the first generations following Adam, and again after Noah, endogamy was a sheer necessity; later it became a traditional preference. This trait and its implications for the Biblical and

Middle Eastern family will be discussed at greater length in the following chapter.

Patrilineal means that descent is reckoned in the father's line and not in the mother's line. Each man is regarded as belonging to the family to which his father belongs. According to the Book of Genesis, as we have seen, early mankind followed this rule. The same rule retained its validity throughout the Biblical epoch and thereafter, down to the present-day Middle East. As a current Arabic proverb phrases it: "In descent people rely on the father and not on the mother; the mother is like a vessel that is emptied." In a quarrel or a feud between the father's and the mother's family, a man is expected to support his father's side against that of his mother.

Patriarchal means that the father is lord and master of his family. As we shall see in a subsequent chapter dealing with the patriarchal power, in the Biblical family as well as in the families belonging to the traditional sectors of the Middle Eastern peoples today, the head of the family has the right even over life and death of the members of his family.

Patrilocal means that when a man marries he brings his bride into the family and household of his father of which he continues to remain a member. The classical Biblical example of this is the family of Jacob. The sons of Jacob remained living with their father even after they had married and had children and even grandchildren of their own. Such a family is *extended*, that is, it consists of the elderly male family head, his wife or wives, his sons and their wives and children, and his unmarried daughters. The extended family can be observed as a fully developed well-established institution among the Hebrew patriarchs as described in the Book of Genesis, and can be found functioning in precisely the same manner to this very day in the Middle East. Such a family, as a rule, lives either in the same house, or in a number of adjoining houses, or, in the case of the nomadic groups, in a cluster of tents pitched next to one another. All property is held in common by the extended family and is controlled by its head. The extended family functions as an economic unit: the men of the family work together in animal husbandry, agriculture, artisanship, business, or in any other occupation that constitutes the basis of its livelihood. From the common income or profit the expenditures of each member of the family are defrayed.

The sixth and last trait of the Biblical and Middle Eastern family is that it is *polygynous*, that is to say, a man can have more than one wife. Since a subsequent chapter will treat of polygyny and concubinage in considerable detail, nothing more has to be said here on this subject.

In addition to the family head, his wives and concubines, his descendants and their womenfolk, the Biblical family also included slaves. Slavery was a feature of Middle Eastern social life whose last remnants in countries like Yemen and Saudi Arabia survive to the present day. The number of slaves has depended at all times on the wealth of the family. Poor families —which have always been the overwhelming majority in the Middle East—could never afford slaves. Rich families, on the other end of the economic scale, and especially rulers and princes, had veritable armies of them, males and females, used for work, armed service, household duties, and concubinage. The slaves, while not, strictly speaking, members of the family, have always been regarded as quasi members, and especially when they were not acquired by purchase but were born in the house to slave parents who themselves were the property of the family. Such a "house-born" slave—as the Biblical Hebrew phrase has it (Gen. 14:14)—was in Biblical times, and remained down to the twentieth century, often as close to his owner as a son or brother, and not infrequently even more loyal and faithful.

As a result of this great variability in the number of slaves, as well as in the number of the actual genealogical family members, no generally valid single statement can be made as to the average number of persons in a household. From the Biblical accounts and from the observation of nineteenth-century and present-day conditions in the Middle East, it would appear that practically no upper limit exists to what constitutes a household. Abraham is said to have had 318 trained arm-bearing servants, all born in his house (Gen. 14:14–15). Considering that young men usually have mothers who are still alive, as well as sisters in about the same numbers (unless, of course, these are sold and removed within a few years after their birth), we must assume that Abraham's household must have consisted of at least a thousand persons if not more. At first glance this figure seems to be greatly exaggerated, but if we consider that even today there are Bedouin sheiks and chiefs whose households consist of a similar number of persons, all we can legitimately conclude from the Biblical narrative is that Abraham must indeed have been a very powerful sheik in his day.

Jacob's family at the time of their migration to Egypt consisted of sixty-six males (Gen. 46:26). If we add the wives of the adult males, as well as Jacob's daughters and his sons' daughters (Gen. 46:7), we reach an estimated figure close to two hundred. How many slaves this huge family had cannot even be guessed, but their total number must have exceeded a thousand. Already in his early years Jacob had acquired many male and female slaves (Gen. 30:43), and their number must have increased in proportion with the increase of his family and their livestock.

It is of course difficult for us, conditioned as we are by our own social experience, to think of such a huge human aggregation as a "family." The Biblical and later Middle Eastern outlook, however, finds no difficulty whatsoever in applying the same terms to a nuclear family of three, to an extended family of thirty, to a tribal wandering unit of three hundred, and even to a huge tribe of three or thirty thousand. Meticulous research could probably detect some differences in preferential usage of these terms, but by and large the same names (such as *bayit* [literally house], *mishpāḥāh* [family], in Hebrew; or *bayt* [tent], *ahl* [family] in Arabic) are used indiscriminately when referring to both very small and very large units.

Chapter 2

MARRIAGE BETWEEN FIRST-DEGREE RELATIVES

WE are conditioned by our upbringing and early socialization to regard with horror the idea of sexual relations between first-degree relatives. A study of other cultures, however, reveals that this is by no means universal in mankind. The early history of mankind contains many instances indicating that first-degree blood relationship was not regarded an impediment to marriage.

In ancient Egypt, for instance, the Pharaohs married their sisters or half-sisters as did the later Ptolemies. Under Roman rule marriage between full siblings and half-siblings occurred frequently among Egyptian peasants and artisans. According to Diodorus, sibling marriage was not only permitted but was considered an obligation for Egyptians.

In certain Pehlevi texts of ancient Iran, dating in their present form from the sixth to the ninth centuries A.D., marriages between siblings, as well as between parents and children, are defended and advocated, as they are in the later years of the Sassanian dynasty and in subsequent centuries. By the fifteenth century A.D., however, marriage between first-degree relations is mentioned in Iranian sources only as a long-extinct practice of the past.

In ancient Palestine, marriages between half-siblings were both legally permitted and actually practiced. Among the Phoenicians, King Tabnith is recorded to have married his father's daughter (by another mother), Am Ashtoreth, a type of marriage which remained legal in Tyre to the times of Achilles Tatius. This was true also in ancient Mecca, and traces of it are found in the Bible, both in patriarchal times and in the reign of King David.

Abraham and his wife Sarah were half-siblings, children of the same father by two different mothers. This revelation is made tangentially in one of the two otherwise very similar stories which tell about Abraham's adventures under the rule of foreign kings. In both instances, before entering the territory ruled by the potentate, Abraham was fearful that the king, in his desire to acquire Sarah for his harem, would kill him, and therefore he asked Sarah to say that she was not his wife, but sister.

What Abraham foresaw came to pass. Both Pharaoh (Gen. 12:15) and Abimelech (Gen. 20:2) took Sarah into their harems and did not harm Abraham, whom they believed to be the beautiful woman's brother. Evidently the Biblical narrator presupposed that the mores of both lands (Egypt and Gerar) adjudged it a far graver crime to take the wife of a living husband than to kill the husband beforehand. In both cases God was said to punish the inadvertent offender and to reveal to him in a dream that the woman was in fact the wife of Abraham. It was in response to Abimelech's indignant reproach that Abraham revealed Sarah's true identity as his wife and half-sister (Gen. 20:12).

The legality of half-sibling marriage was evidently maintained to the days of King David. One of David's wives bore him a son, Absalom, and a daughter, Tamar. Another son of David by another wife, Amnon, desired Tamar and by a clever ruse cornered her in his room. Upon perceiving Amnon's intent, Tamar entreated: "Nay, my brother, do not force me . . . do not thou this wanton deed . . . I pray thee, speak unto the king, for he will not withhold me from thee" (2 Sam. 13:12–13). The meaning, of course, is clear: if Amnon were to ask David for Tamar in marriage the king's consent would be forthcoming. Amnon, however, disregarded Tamar's plea and raped her. Two years later Tamar was avenged by her full brother, Absalom, who killed Amnon—for the wanton violation and subsequent rejection of Tamar by Amnon, not for his desire for her (2 Sam. 13:23–29).

Marriage between paternal half-siblings, which, according to the evidence of the story quoted above, was legal in Israel down to the tenth century B.C., was regarded in subsequent centuries as incestuous. In the sixth century we find the prophet Ezekiel (22:11) bitterly accusing Jerusalem of a number of sexual transgressions—among them union between a man and "his sister, his father's daughter." The Levitical law forbids marriage between half-siblings under the penalty of death: "If a man shall take his sister, his father's daughter, or his mother's daughter, and see her nakedness, and she see his nakedness; it is a shameful thing, and they shall be cut off in the sight of the children of their people: he has uncovered his sister's nakedness, he shall bear his iniquity" (Lev. 20:17; cf. 18:9, 11).

There is no evidence in the Bible as to marriage between father and daughter, although there is one story describing sexual relations between a father and his daughters. After Lot and his two daughters escaped from Sodom, the daughters, under the impression that the whole of mankind was annihilated and that they were doomed to childlessness, plied their father with drink and when he was in his cups cohabited with him. Both conceived and bore sons, who became the ancestors of the Moabites and Ammonites (Gen. 19:30–38). What is significant in this story—aside from the highly exceptional circumstances—is that there is in it no expression at all of disapproval. Irregular as the union was, it served a commendable purpose, the propagation of the race, and reached full fruition in the emergence of the people of Moab and Ammon to the east of Biblical Israel.

Separated by many centuries, but in direct continuum with the Lot story, comes a South Arabian tale concerning Bu Zaid, the greatest medieval legendary hero of the Bani Hillal tribe.

In tone and intent the two stories closely parallel each other: both tell of the procreation of a desired heir in an irregular union and regard the act as justified by the noble purpose it served. The Bu Zaid story is summarized by Bertram Thomas as follows:

"Bu Zaid had a wife but did not allow himself complete coition with her, and so he suspected that the two sons she had borne were not his but another's. The tribe perceived that they did not resemble him and also had their suspicions, so came privily to Bu Zaid's sister and said that Bani Hillal must have a son from the loins of Bu Zaid. Wherefore one night she went secretly to her brother's bed and he, not knowing her in the darkness from his wife, lay with her. And as he was about to withdraw himself prematurely, according to his habit, she jabbed him with the bodkin that she had kept in her hand in readiness for this moment. The shock achieved its intent and in the fullness of time she bore a son, who came to be known as 'Aziz bin Khala, 'Aziz, son of his uncle. And 'Aziz grew up into a strong youth, endowed with courage and other virtues."

While the medieval Arab mentality thus saw no sin in an occasional union of brother and sister, in pre-Islamic Arabia it was legal for a man to marry his half-sister or his own daughter. According to Rizkallah, there were four types of marriage among the pre-Islamic Arabs, and one of them was that of a man with his own daughter or daughter-in-law.

'Auf, the father of the famous companion of Muhammad, 'Abd al-Rahmān, married his paternal sister, al-Shafā. A trace of this type of marriage has survived to modern times at Mirbat.

The available Biblical evidence is insufficient to form an opinion as to the frequency of marriage between first-degree relatives. There can be no doubt that it occurred, that it was legal, and that it fell into disuse by the end of the period of the Hebrew monarchy, but we have no way of gauging the extent to which it was practiced while it was still regarded as legal and after it became regarded as an incestuous union.

COUSIN MARRIAGE

ON THE other hand, ample evidence contained in the Book of Genesis indicates that in the patriarchal family of Abraham and his descendants marriage between uncle and niece, between nephew and aunt, and especially between cousins, was practiced frequently and was indeed preferred to marriage with non-related women. Abraham's brother, Nahor, married a daughter of a third brother, Haran (Gen. 11:27, 29). Isaac, the son of Abraham, married his father's brother's son's daughter (Gen. 22:23; 24:47). Isaac's son, Esau, married his father's brother's daughter, Mahalath (or Basemath, Gen. 28:9; 36:3). Isaac's other son, Jacob, married his mother's brother's two daughters, Leah and Rachel (Gen. 29), who were related to him also on his father's side.

Such close in-family marriage was practiced by the Hebrews in later times as well. Amram (the father of Moses) married Jochebed, his father's sister (Ex. 6:20; Num. 26:59). Hezron, a grandson of Judah, married a paternal second cousin (1 Chron. 2:4–5, 21; Gen. 50:23). King Rehoboam, Solomon's son, married his father's brother's (Absalom's) daughter, Maacah, and he loved her "above all his wives and concubines" (2 Chron. 11:20–21). The hero of the Book of Tobit married his father's brother's daughter, and, according to the angel who accompanied Tobias, it would have been a mortal sin for Reuel, Tobias' uncle, to give his daughter to anybody else but to Tobias, who had the right to inherit his sonless uncle (Tob. 6:9ff.; 7:2, 10–12).

The last example answers the question why cousin marriage should have been preferred to marriage with unrelated individuals. It seems that the preference for such a marriage had something to do with the endeavor to preserve property within the family. This motivation is brought out clearly in the case of the daughters of Zelophehad (Num. 27:1–11; 36:1–12). According to the story, the traditional rule of inheritance was that the property of a man who died without sons was inherited by his lateral relatives. The man Zelophehad died without leaving a male heir, but he had five daughters. The daughters came with a request to Moses: "Give us a possession among the brethren of our father" (Num. 27:4). The God-inspired decision of Moses was that the daughters of Zelophehad should indeed inherit his land but should be allowed to marry only members "of the family of the tribe" of their father (Num. 36:6, 8). In this manner provision was made to prevent the land of Zelophehad from passing into the hands of future grandsons who would belong to other tribes. As it eventually transpired, all the five daughters of Zelophehad were married to sons of their father's brothers.

This motivation has survived in the Middle East to this day, together with the institution of cousin marriage itself. All over the Middle East cousin marriage has remained the most favored and most frequent marriage. In fact, the few studies which have been made on the frequency of marriage between a man and his father's brother's daughter indicate that such marriages take place whenever suitable marriage partners are available among the offspring of two brothers. The preferred status of a wife who is also a cousin is indicated by the term "my cousin," which is used by marriage partners in addressing each other even if they are not thus related. The law of Islam prescribes that a man's estate upon his death be divided as follows: sons get twice the share of daughters. Upon the death of the daughter her children, of course, will receive her property. If she is married to a non-related man, her children belong, in accordance with the prevalent Middle Eastern rules of patrilineal descent, to the tribe or descent group of her husband. Thus a share of the property would become alienated from the original family, respectively its male descendants. This problem is eliminated if the rule is followed which, according to the Biblical account, was established for the daughters of Zelophehad. If paternal cousins marry, their children are the offspring of the same grandfather both through their father and their mother, and thus whatever the daughter inherits from a man is passed on by her to her children, who are also the patrilineal grandchildren of the same man. In this case, therefore, even that part of the family property which is inherited by the daughters remains in the family.

A glance at the Middle Eastern world supplies information as to additional motivations which may have made cousin marriage preferred in the eyes of the ancient Hebrews as well. The strengthening of kinship ties is one of them. Kinship in Middle Eastern culture, both in Biblical days and today, was, and has remained, pivotal, and has had a much greater importance than in modern Western civilization. Not only the man's status and prestige depended almost exclusively on the kin group to which he belonged, but often his very life could be preserved only if his kin group stood by him. In accordance with patrilineal rules of descent, the unquestioning loyalty of each man was to his own brothers, father, grandfather, and other paternal relatives. In these circumstances, if a man's daughter was married to a non-related individual she became incorporated into the family of her husband, and both she and her future sons became lost as far as the strength of her own family was concerned. If, on the other hand, the daughter was married to her father's brother's son, such a union strengthened the man's family by tying his nephew to himself with the bonds of matrimony.

A third motivation for cousin marriage is that such marriages are more stable than marriages between two non-related partners. From the early Middle Ages and down to the nineteenth century the opinion was frequently voiced that the tie of blood is likely to attach husband and wife to each other more strongly, that affection conceived in years of childhood when the boy and girl were brought up together in one home is the best basis for a lasting conjugal love upon reaching maturity.

Yet another motivation for cousin marriage is the desire that the marriage partners should be equal in status. No one is closer in status than children of two brothers, therefore they are the most suitable mates.

To this we may add that the prevalent custom of establishing a home for the young couple in the house of the groom's parents (the so-called "patrilocal" residence) also greatly favors marriage between cousins. A girl who was brought up in an unrelated family may have difficulty in fitting into the home life of her groom's parents. In the case of paternal cousins both young people grow up in the same home, and the problem of the bride's adjustment into the groom's family does not arise.

For all these reasons cousin marriage is preferred and is regarded as the ideal marriage. Many proverbs from all parts of the Middle East express this sentiment. A Moroccan Arabic proverb says, "He who marries his *bint 'amm* [father's brother's daughter] celebrates his feast with a sheep from his own flock." Another Moroccan proverb states: "Marrying a stranger is like drinking water from an earthenware bottle (that is, one does not see what one drinks), but marriage with a *bint 'amm* is like drinking water from a dish" (that is, one can see what one drinks). The English saying, "Marriages are made in heaven" has its counterpart in a Persian proverb which, however, refers only to cousin marriage: "The marriage of cousins is tied in heaven."

To sum up, in the Middle Eastern patrilineal kinship system it is of extremely great importance for the head of the family to be assured of the unwavering support of his brothers and their sons. The greater the number of the male kin on whose unquestioning loyalty the head of the family can count, the greater his influence, power, security, and prestige. One of the time-proven methods of strengthening the ties of kinship and common interests between the head of a family and his patrilineal kinsmen is to give them his daughters in marriage. These considerations in most cases outweigh by far the financial loss resulting from the reduced bride price paid by a brother's son. The same considerations hold good also from the point of view of the young man about to choose a wife.

If the wife is from a different family, and even more so if she is from a different village or tribe, the husband cannot be sure that the interests of his father-in-law will always harmonize with his own. Contrary interests, especially if they lead to mutual raiding or warfare, place the wife in a difficult, and at times tragic, situation whereby the inner cohesion in the nuclear family of the husband and also in the extended family of which he is a member may be weakened. On the other hand, if his wife is a *bint 'amm*, a daughter of his father's brother, the likelihood of the occurrence of such disharmony and tension is greatly reduced, and in general the community of interests between a man and his father-in-law is enhanced.

Close in-group or in-family endogamy is to this day the prevalent practice in all social strata of the Middle East, with the exception of those exposed to modern Western influences. Endogamy still seems to satisfy most young men and women, because young people who grow up in the large and protective framework of the extended family seem to be conditioned by their upbringing to have a preference for continuing their lives in the same environment and atmosphere; given this preference, close in-group marriages, such as between a man and his father's brother's daughter, have all the advantages as against marrying a non-related outsider. Two young people who grow up in the same extended family (or at least in two closely related extended families) have in general a pre-existing similarity in outlook and personality determinants, and can therefore look forward to a much smoother adaptation to each other in the extended family than can be the case in an out-group marriage. As Chapple and Coon put it: "The marriage of cousins is a convenient system of mating bringing together two individuals who, in most cases, already know each other, and two families which already have some form of adjustment."

IN-GROUP AND OUT-GROUP MARRIAGE

THE sentiment complementary to the preference for close in-family marriage is the objection against marrying non-related, and especially foreign, men or women. This feeling, amply attested in the Bible and powerfully alive in conservative sectors of the Middle Eastern peoples to this very day, is expressive of the conviction and the experience that a person with foreign mores must be a disturbing factor in the extended family setup. The foreign bride who upon marriage becomes incorporated into the extended family of her husband is felt by the latter as an intruder and as a disruptive force.

Isaac's son, Esau, married two Hittite girls, "and they were a bitterness of spirit unto Isaac and to Rebekah" (Gen. 26:34–35). This resentment was so strong in both parents that upon Rebekah's urging, "I am weary of my life because of the daughters of Heth; if Jacob take a wife of the daughters of Heth, such as these, of the daughters of the land, what good shall my life do me?" (Gen. 27:46.) Isaac "called Jacob and blessed him, and charged him, and said unto him: 'Thou shalt not take a wife of the daughters of Canaan; arise, go to Paddan-Aram, to the house of Bethuel thy mother's father, and take a wife from thence of the daughters of Laban thy mother's brother'" (Gen. 28:1–2).

When Esau saw how strong was his parents' disapproval of his Canaanite wives, he too contracted, in addition, an endogamous marriage: he took a daughter of Ishmael, Isaac's brother, to be his wife (Gen. 28:8–9).

Of Judah the son of Jacob it is told that, after he separated from his brothers, he "took and went in unto" the daughter of a Canaanite named Shua (Gen. 38:2). No open criticism of this action is voiced in the narrative, but the story of the unfortunate fate of the issue of this union definitely contains a hidden or implied censure. Two of Judah's sons born to him by Shua's daughter died, the third one remained without off-spring (Gen. 38:3–11; 46:12).

Several generations later, Moses himself had to suffer because of the persistent anti-foreign sentiment with regard to marriage. He married a Cushite woman, and his own siblings, Miriam and Aaron, "spoke against Moses because of the Cushite woman whom he had married" (Num. 12:1).

While Moses, however, was exonerated by God for his marrying a non-Hebrew woman, an Israelite prince of his days paid with his life for a similar offense. "Zimri, the son of Salu, a prince of a father's house among the Simeonites," brought a Midianite woman, "Cozbi, the daughter of Zur . . . head of the people of a father's house in Midian," into his tent. He did this publicly (Num. 25:6), and this circumstance, as well as the fact that both were of princely houses of their respective peoples, leaves little if any doubt that this was an actual marriage. Yet an outraged priest, Phinehas, a grandson of Aaron, drove into the wedding tent and killed both Zimri and Cozbi (Num. 25:8).

In the same generation there was also intermarriage between Israelite women and Egyptian men (Lev. 24:10). The offspring of one such union is represented as a blasphemer put to death by stoning (vv. 14, 23).

After the conquest of Canaan, when the Israelite tribes settled down in the midst of a considerable number of tribes and peoples, the objection against intermarriage with them continued to be strong for several generations. When Samson fell in love with a Philistine woman in Timnah and asked his father and mother: "Get her for me to wife," his parents objected, using the time-honored argument: "Is there never a woman among the daughters of thy brethren, or among all my people, that thou goest to take a wife of the uncircumcised Philistines?" (Judg. 14:1–3.)

However, the close contact with the nations whose remnants continued to inhabit Palestine in the very midst of the Hebrew tribes, and with the neighboring peoples, resulted in an in-

creasing trend to intermarry with them. Prohibitions of marrying foreigners, and especially of intermarriage with the seven
nations of Canaan (the Hittites, Girgashites, Amorites, Canaanites, Perizzites, Hivites, and Jebusites), continued to remain on the books, the official reason given being the danger
of being led astray into idolatry by the foreign women (Deut.
7:2–4). But in practice these prohibitions were ignored, and
intermarriage with the peoples of Canaan became practically
general, as stated in a woeful admission by the author of the
Book of Judges (3:5–6). The practice was not confined to the
simple folk; the leaders of the tribes, and later of the whole
Israelite nation, also took foreign wives. The changing attitude
is reflected in the fact that no longer is any deprecatory comment or active opposition recorded in the narratives which contain the accounts of these intermarriages.

Gideon had a concubine in Shechem who became the
mother of Abimelech (Judg. 8:31). Elimelech's sons married
Moabite women (Ruth 1:4). David and Solomon married several foreign women (2 Sam. 3:3; 1 Ki. 3:1; 11:1–2). Ahab married Jezebel, the daughter of King Ethbaal of Sidon (1 Ki.
16:31).

The two servants of Joash who conspired against him and
murdered him, and who undoubtedly belonged to the court
nobility, were the sons of Israelite men and an Ammonite and
Moabite woman respectively (2 Chron. 24:25–26). In all these
cases only Solomon and Ahab come in for censure, not because
of the fact of intermarriage itself, but because of the subsequent establishment of idolatrous practices in the royal court
introduced by the foreign princesses (1 Ki. 11:1–8; 16:31–33).

In the same period also marriages of Israelite women to foreign men occurred frequently enough. Bath-sheba was the wife
of a Hittite (2 Sam. 11:3). The famous artisan of Tyre, Hiram,
was the son of a Tyrian father and a Hebrew woman from the
tribe of Naphtali (1 Ki. 7:13–14). According to one of the two
versions which tell about the parents of Amasa, Absalom's general, his father was Jether the Ishmaelite (1 Chron. 2:17),

while his mother was, according to both versions, Abigail, daughter of Nahash, a Hebrew woman of a high-ranking family (2 Sam. 17:25; 1 Chron. 2:17).

The practice of intermarriage continued among the Hebrews until the exile and was resumed after their return from Babylonia. At this time, however, it was objected to by their own princes and by Ezra, the scribe, who had the authority of Persian King Artaxerxes to issue decrees and pass laws. The objection in that period was based on an ethno-religious conviction: "The people of Israel, and the priests and the Levites, have not separated themselves from the peoples of the lands . . . For they have taken their daughters for themselves and for their sons; so that the holy seed have mingled themselves with the peoples of the lands . . ." (Ez. 9:1–2). Thereupon Ezra issued a proclamation calling upon all those who had married foreign women to separate themselves from them. This was carried out within three months (Ez. 10).

To sum up the evolutionary course described by the ancient Hebrew attitude to intermarriage, we found that in the patriarchal nomadic stage of early Hebrew history it was strenuously objected to. Following the conquest of and settlement in Canaan the attitude softened, and several generations of settled agricultural life in close proximity to other peoples resulted in the adoption of the permissive attitude to intermarriage which characterized the Canaanites even in the patriarchal period (cf. the Shechem-Dinah story, and especially Gen. 34:9). Still later, religious objection arose to intermarriage and the ancient endogamous practice was restored, this time underpinned by a divine commandment.

The ethno-religious practice of in-group marriage is recommended in the apocryphal Book of Tobit:

"Beware, my child, of all whoredom, and take first a wife of the seed of thy fathers, and take not a strange wife, which is not of thy father's tribe: for we are the sons of the prophets. Noah, Abraham, Isaac, Jacob, our fathers of old time, remember, my child, that they all took wives of their brethren, and were blessed in their children, and their seed shall inherit the land. And now, my child, love thy brethren, and the sons and the daughters of thy people, to take a wife of them . . ." (Tob. 4:12–13).

A very similar range of attitudes to intermarriage can be found to this day in the Middle East. The nomads still follow rather rigid endogamous rules; the average villagers are much more lax in this respect; while the religious townspeople and the few learned among the villagers substitute the rules of religious endogamy in place of the old ethnic occupational ones.

The typical attitude of the nomads is that, failing marriage between children of two brothers, a man should marry within his wider kin group, then within his tribe. Where nomads live in proximity to settled people, they disapprove of intermarriage with them, just as Jacob's sons did with the Shechemite townsfolk. A South Arabian proverb attributes the origin of this rule to Noah: "Said Father Noah: the ploughman to the ploughwoman, the retainer to the retainer woman, the slave to the slave woman."

In general it can be stated that each nomadic group in the Middle East tends to behave as an endogamous unit. Marriage outside one's own group is frowned upon, discouraged, forbidden, and not infrequently severely punished, occasionally even with the death penalty. These endogamous restrictions prevail everywhere in one form or another, and they apply usually with much greater strictness to women than to men. Groups which countenance, or accept with disapproval, marriage between their own men and women from groups of inferior status, often make it completely impossible for their women to marry men of inferior-status groups. Fulanain tells the tragic story of a sheik of the noble Bani Sabah tribe of the Quraysh, who, after having sojourned for twenty years as a fugitive among the marsh Arabs of lower Iraq, noticed that his only daughter was harboring tender feelings toward one of the youths of a marsh tribe. Although the two young people never met face to face, and the youth asked for the girl's hand in marriage, the old sheik preferred to kill his only daughter rather than let her marry into a low-status tribe.

The so-called noble (aṣīlīn) Bedouin tribes of the Syrian and Arabian deserts guard most jealously their purity of blood and do not permit either their men or their women to marry members of an inferior tribe. In choosing a marriage partner for either a son or a daughter, satisfactory descent is regarded by them an indispensable prerequisite. Members of the noble Rwala, one of the leading tribes of the Syrian Desert, cannot marry persons belonging to the Sleyb, Hawāzim, Fheyjāt, Shararāt or 'Āzim tribes, which, although camel breeders like the Rwala themselves, are low-status groups, since they are unable to defend themselves and have to pay khuwwa, protection money, to the more vigorous tribes. The Rwala hold themselves aloof even from other free Arab tribes and discourage, though they do not absolutely forbid, intermarriage with them. As to marriages with male slaves or slave girls, such occurrences are a legitimate reason for putting the offender to death. A Rweyli marrying a slave girl would be killed by his own kin, whom he defiled by his act. Intermarriage is forbidden for the Rwala also with the ṣāni' (pl. ṣunna') groups, those blacksmiths and tinkers who from time to time attach themselves to Rwala (and other Bedouin) camps, and of whom it is known to the Rwala that they have no marriage restrictions.

The same restrictions exist also among the powerful Shammar tribes of Iraq and the Syrian Desert. No son of a Shammar tribe can marry a slave girl or a girl from an inferior tribe. If he did, his own people would kill him. If a noble tribesman takes up such trades as blacksmithing, salt making or carrying, lime burning, charcoal burning, skinning animals and curing the skins, he makes himself dishonorable and the Shammar and other noble tribes will refrain from intermarrying with him and his.

Similar limitations prevail in southern Arabia where, for instance, the Qara mountain tribesmen do not intermarry with the Shahara, whom they regard as no better than slaves. The Shahara, again, do not marry outside their own people.

The villagers are much less strict in following rules of endogamy. The ideal remains among them, too, to marry close relatives in the first place, and girls from the same locality in the second. But marriages with outsiders are neither forbidden nor actually rare. In the South Palestinian (now Jordanian) Muslim Arab village of Artas, studied by Miss Hilma Granqvist in the 1920s and 1930s, she found that 42.8 per cent of the married men had out-of-the-village wives, and about 30 per cent of the married women were married to out-of-the-village men and lived with their husbands outside the village. Most of these exogamous marriages were with men or women from neighboring villages or from the nearby small town of Bethlehem. Many wives were taken from the Ta'āmre semi-Bedouins, the neighbors of Artas in the east, but no Artas women were married to that tribe, or to any other semi-nomadic or nomadic group.

In the towns one finds, as one would expect to, a greater variety in the choice of marriage partners. Some circles are very conservative and follow strict endogamous rules. These include newly settled elements among whom the old social customs are still observed. On the other hand one finds modern groups where even religious differences begin to be disregarded. Among leading families in the cities family endogamy is frequently practiced, as a rule for prestige and status reasons.

The official traditional Muslim marriage regulations follow the ancient Biblical rule that marriages should be concluded only among co-religionists. Muslim women are flatly forbidden to marry any non-Muslims, while Muslim men are forbidden to marry pagan women, and allowed to marry women belonging to the "peoples of the Book," that is Christians, Jews, or Zoroastrians. The prevailing sentiment, however, is still very strongly opposed to such interfaith marriages.

Where different ethnic groups meet, even though all of them be Muslims, marriage limitations often restrict the choice of a mate within one's own group. In Afghanistan, e.g., it seems that it is unlawful for a down-country man (i.e., one from India) even though he be Muslim, to marry an Afghan. Cases are reported where such a marriage was concluded, and the Afghan authorities kept the offender in jail for about a year. At the other, Western, end of the Middle East, in the town of Timbuctoo, which is inhabited by three distinct ethnic elements of differing statuses, men of high-status groups can acquire wives or concubines from any status group, but the men of low status are limited by the fact that the high-status women do not marry inferiors.

A comparison of the attitude of the ancient Hebrews with regard to in-group marriage with the one prevalent in Middle Eastern folk societies in recent times clearly points up the presence throughout thousands of years of a basically identical outlook. Marriage between equals remains the ideal, and the concept of equality is ideally confined to close relatives in the first place, and to other members of one's own in-group in the second.

POLYGYNY AND CONCUBINAGE

FROM the earliest times down to the present day the Middle East has remained a world area where the simultaneous marriage of a man to two or more wives was permitted and occasionally, but not too frequently, practiced. To have more than one wife was (and remained in traditional circles) a mark of high status, of prestige, and of wealth. In a polygynous society, moreover, it is a matter of distinction also for a woman to be married to a man who can afford more than one wife, not to mention the fact that where there are two or more wives the burden of household chores is lighter for each one of them. For these reasons women in the Middle East do not always object if their husband wants to marry a second wife. In most cases there is, of course, jealousy between co-wives, competition for the favors of their husband, and juggling for a position of advantage for the sons.

When a man has two wives, it often happens that he loves one of them and hates, or at least dislikes or is indifferent to, the other. An example of this "marital triangle" can be found in the Biblical story of Jacob and his two wives, Leah and Rachel. In spite of the many sons Leah bore to Jacob, he hated and neglected her (Gen. 29:31) and loved only Rachel, to the point where Leah burst out in bitterness, turning on her sister: "Is it a small matter that thou hast taken away my husband?" (Gen. 30:15.)

The pain and the anguish of a first wife upon having to share her beloved husband with a second new and younger wife are expressed in many proverbs, sayings, and songs. The first wife complains: "In the night of the co-wife I was embittered." Or: "The co-wife is bitter, even if she were honey in a jar." She knows only too well that the husband can "subdue a woman with another woman." As against these feelings of the first wife, the husband says (according to the women):

"Sleeping by the old wife is to me like an oven filled with dung. Sleeping by the new wife is to me like the night of Allah's feast."

The terms "beloved" and "hated" (Gen. 29:31; 1 Sam. 1:5) were applied so often to the two co-wives that they entered the legal terminology (Deut. 21:15). The same terms, in their Arabic equivalents, survive in the Arab East to this day, together with many other features of the ancient polygynous family. The very name by which a co-wife is called today in Arabic, ḍarrah, is the same by which she was called in Hebrew in Biblical times (ṣarah; e.g., 1 Sam. 1:6; Lev. 18:18), and by which she was called in the Laws of Hammurabi (ṣerritu), a term originally meaning "enemy" (in the female form of the noun).

Polygyny continued to be practiced in Israel throughout the Biblical period, but it seems to have been restricted to men who occupied leading positions, who were rich, or had some other claim to distinction. This is the general rule in the Middle East to this day, while the simple people, both in Biblical times and today, had (and have) to be satisfied with one wife, or at least with one at a time.

Gideon, the Israelite judge, had many wives who bore him seventy sons (Judg. 8:30). Judging from the number of sons, Jair with thirty sons (Judg. 10:4), Ibzan with thirty sons and thirty daughters (Judg. 12:9), Abdon with forty sons (Judg. 12:14), all judges in Israel, must have had several wives each. King David had several wives (1 Sam. 25:39f., 43; 2 Sam. 3:2ff.; 5:13), and King Solomon, of course, had a huge number of them (1 Ki. 9:16; 11:3; cf. S. of Sol. 6:8). Also of King Rehoboam, Solomon's son, it is stated that he had eighteen wives and sixty concubines (2 Chron. 11:21). Each of Rehoboam's twenty-eight sons also had many wives (2 Chron. 11:23). The frequency of marriage with two women necessitated legislation with reference to the rights of their children (Deut. 21:15).

In spite of the Biblical commandment warning the king against taking many wives (Deut. 17:17), the kings and rulers in Israel have always kept large harems, in accordance with the general Middle Eastern customs which prevailed from the earliest times down to the present. These harems always included a larger number of concubines than regular wives.

In the stories of Genesis we see that several of the patriarchs had, in addition to regular wives, also one or more concubines. Abraham, Jacob, Gideon, Saul, David, Solomon, Rehoboam, etc., all had concubines (Gen. 16:1, 2, 5, 8; 25:6, 12; 30:3, 9; 32:23; Judg. 8:31; 2 Sam. 3:7; 5:13; 15:16; 1 Ki. 11:3; S. of Sol. 6:8; 1 Chron. 1:32; 3:9; 2 Chron. 11:21). The difference between a wife and a concubine has remained the same from Biblical times down to the present day in the Middle East. A free man could acquire a slave girl for the purpose of sexual gratification, just as he could purchase a male or female slave for the purpose of doing any kind of work in the home. Such a slave girl retained her slave status but her master was not supposed to sell her, and especially not if she bore him a child. The children of a concubine had the same status as the children of full wives. They inherited in the same proportion, and if a man had no child by a wife, the child of his concubine inherited his status, position, and occupation as well.

While the taking of many wives was often motivated by sensuous desires, the taking of concubines served in many cases primarily the purpose of begetting sons when a man's wife remained barren.

When Sarah saw that she bore no children to Abraham, she asked him to "go in unto her handmaid" Hagar, the Egyptian, in the hope that she, Sarah, "shall be builded up through her" (Gen. 16:1–4). The idea expressed in this phrase is that when the handmaid becomes pregnant, her powers of fertility would pass on to her mistress and she, too, would become pregnant. To ensure this, the handmaid gave birth to her child upon the knees of her mistress (Gen. 30:3). With the same motivation, Rachel gave Bilhah, her handmaid, to Jacob (Gen. 30:3), and Leah did the same when she stopped bearing (Gen. 30:9). In all these cases the handmaid who became the concubine of a man was the slave girl of the man's wife. However, a man could acquire also directly a concubine by buying a free girl from her father, either for himself or for his son (Ex. 21:7–10). Or a man could take a woman captured in war as a concubine (Deut. 21:10–14).

Since a woman's status in the family depended to a large extent on her fruitfulness, barrenness in a wife resulted occasionally in quarrels between her and her husband, whom she would be inclined to accuse of being the cause of her childlessness (Gen. 30:1–2), and in jealous tension between co-wives or between a wife and a concubine. The childless Sarah was despised by her fruitful handmaid Hagar; Sarah, in turn, dealt with her so harshly that Hagar fled from their home (Gen. 16:5–6). Of Elkanah's two wives, one, Penninah, had children, but the other, Hannah, had none: "And her rival vexed her

sore, to make her fret, because the Lord had shut up her womb"
(1 Sam. 1:6).

The same situation continued to result in the same tensions
three millennia later, as observed in Palestine and in Egypt:

"If the first wife has no children, the husband marries another or takes a slave. And it not unfrequently happens that
the fortunate slave, when the mother of a son, is promoted to
the post of honor and authority, and, of course, she becomes
insolent towards her mistress."

"If the chief lady be barren, and an inferior, either wife or
slave, bear a child to her husband or master, it commonly results that the latter woman becomes a favorite of the man, and
that the chief wife or mistress is 'despised in her eyes' as Abraham's wife was in the eyes of Hagar on the same account."

If a man had no wife but only a concubine, her status ap-
proximated that of a wife. In the tragic story of a man and his
concubine to which we shall have occasion to refer again later,
the man is alternatingly called the "husband" and the "master"
of the woman, and the "son-in-law" of her father, who, in turn,
is called his "father-in-law" (Judg. 19:3, 4, 5, etc., 26, 27;
20:4).

THE CO-WIVES' RIGHTS

THE co-wives' rights with respect to the marital attentions of
their husband are indicated in the Book of Genesis in connection with the mandrakes incident. We cannot go here into all
the folkloristic details of the beliefs centering around this plant,
fascinating as these would be. Let it be enough to state in passing that the belief that, by eating it, barren women can become
fertile and impotent men potent has existed in the Middle East
from antiquity to the present time, and is shared also by many
other peoples in the world.

Now Reuben, Leah's first-born, probably a lad of eight to
ten years, wandering about in the fields during the wheat har-

vest season, found some mandrakes and brought them back to his mother. The find must have caused quite a stir in Jacob's encampment, for Rachel heard of it and immediately went to her sister, asking her to give her the mandrakes. The two sisters struck a bargain. Leah gave Rachel the mandrakes, and in return Rachel promised Leah: "Therefore he [Jacob] shall lie with thee tonight for thy son's mandrakes" (Gen. 30:15). When Jacob came home from the field in the evening, "Leah went out to meet him and said: 'Thou must come in unto me for I have surely hired thee with my son's mandrakes.' And he lay with her that night" (Gen. 30:16), and Leah duly conceived and bore Jacob a fifth son. As to Rachel, the mandrakes achieved their purpose and she, too, conceived and bore a son, Joseph (Gen. 30:22–24).

Several features strike us in this story. First there is the anger of Leah over Rachel's having taken away her husband (Gen. 30:15). Evidently Jacob, in his excessive love for Rachel, did not abide by the rules which govern a man's marital relations with his two wives to this day among the tribes of the Syrian-Arabian Desert. He must alternately spend one night with one and one with the other. Each of the wives cooks for him a day in turn, and on that day it is the woman's right to have the husband spend the night with her, whether he cohabits with her or not. This rule must have been in existence in Jacob's time, and it was its violation which embittered Leah. According to the custom of the desert, if the husband spends a night with one wife out of turn, he must compensate the other with a sheep or a goat as the price for her night.

In reading of the mandrakes incident, it seems peculiar that the two wives should have been able to decide between themselves with whom their husband should spend the night. Had Jacob himself nothing to say in the matter? Was he, the patriarch, the absolute ruler over his family, obliged to obey the decisions of his wives? The answer to these questions is definitely yes. A glance at the present-day desert tribes may help us to understand the situation. Among these tribes the position of the husband in relation to his wives and the other members of his family is largely the same as it was in Biblical times. And among them, too, the two co-wives of a man may strike a bargain, one of them buying the night from the other whose turn it is.

Among the Rwala Bedouins, for instance, a man who has two wives must share his time equally between the two. Each wife cooks for him on alternating days, and he is supposed to spend the night with her. This is the woman's right, and even if a man does not love his wife he is expected to spend the night with her. He may lie down next to the wife in her tent and say, "Tonight I wish for nothing," and the woman has to acquiesce. Or, if he acutely dislikes the wife, he may even sleep in his own tent, or in the men's compartment of the family tent, but he definitely must not sleep with the wife he loves if it is not her turn.

Sometimes the two wives will haggle among themselves, duplicating, not only the spirit that agitated Rachel and Leah, but the very words used by those Biblical matrons. "Let me have the man tonight!" one wife will say to the other, who then will ask: "What will you give me for it?" If they come to an agreement, the wife who sold her night's right to her co-wife will say to the husband: "I grant you furlough; go to your wife over there!" However, in spite of these mandatory rules of the customary law, if a man chooses to ignore them, in his exceeding love for one of his two wives, the neglected wife can do nothing but rage and complain, much as poor Leah must have done.

Among the Hejāya of Transjordan, the neglected wife can take possession of a sheep or a goat as compensation for the night the husband should have spent with her. Among other tribes, the neglected wife can complain to her own family, who then will make representations to the husband, and the latter must pay for the night. In one tribe at least, the Tarābīn, the matter is brought to the attention of the tribal sheiks, who then question the husband and, if he is found guilty, hold him to the payment of a fixed sum to the wife.

In the case of Rachel and Leah it did not come quite to this. But, according to the Biblical narrator, God, who is the Supreme Judge of all, "saw that Leah was hated" by her husband "and he opened her womb; but Rachel was barren" (Gen. 29:31). Evidently Jacob did not neglect Leah completely, but cohabited with her occasionally at least, as a result of which she gave birth in succession to four sons, and thereafter "she left off bearing" (Gen. 29:35). Once she stopped bearing, Jacob ceased altogether to have relations with her, and this was the situation up to the incident with the mandrakes.

Chapter 3

ROMANTIC LOVE

In view of the prevalence of arranged marriages and the custom of the parents' choosing marriage partners for their children, one might form the opinion that romantic love did not and does not exist in the Middle East, at least not where traditional circumstances obtain. Nothing, however, could be farther from the truth than such an assumption. Romantic love can blossom amidst the most adverse circumstances, and does, in fact, play a considerable role in the Middle East, even in the most restrictive tradition-bound sectors of society. In spite of the greater or lesser segregation of the sexes, a boy and a girl do find opportunities to see each other, to exchange glances and words at the well or in the fields while tending the flocks, and to arrange for secret trysts. The danger of being discovered by the girl's father or brothers can no more keep them apart than can parental disapproval in our own society hinder the young people from meeting.

In the Bible we have ample evidence of romantic love, both premarital and marital. Between Jacob and Rachel it was a matter of love at first sight which endured until Rachel's untimely death in childbirth. "Jacob served seven years for Rachel, and they seemed unto him but a few days for the love he had to her" (Gen. 29:20)—nowhere in world literature can one find a more succinct and more touching description of enduring passion. Jacob transferred his love from Rachel to her sons, both during her lifetime and after her death (Gen. 33:2; 37:3,

35; 42:38; 45:27–28). Shechem's "soul did cleave unto Dinah
the daughter of Jacob and he loved the damsel," (Gen. 34:3)
after he raped her. Samson loved the woman of Timnah
(Judg. 14:1–3); King Rehoboam loved Maacah (2 Chron.
11:20–21). Love must have motivated David to take Uriah's
wife (2 Sam. 11:2ff.), and Adonijah to ask for Abishag (1 Ki.
2:17). The entire Song of Songs is a paean to love, epitomized
in the immortal words, "For love is strong as death, jealousy is
cruel as the grave; the flashes thereof are flashes of fire, a very
flame of the Lord" (S. of Sol. 8:6). Likewise, the oft repeated
prophetic comparison of the love of God for Israel with the
love of husband for wife indicates that passionate love between
spouses was so well known in ancient Israel that a reference
to it in poetic simile could create the most powerful response
the prophets wished to evoke in their audience.

Love trysts, illicit affairs, jealousy—all these are well known
in the Arabian Desert to this day. Side by side with the formalized aspect of marriage as a family affair, we find frequent
manifestations of the power of love that breaks through barriers of custom. "Love comes from Allah," says a proverb current among the Rwala. In fact, in the relatively free social
atmosphere of the desert tribes, a boy may join his sweetheart
where and whenever he wishes to. He even may visit her in the
evening, or they may meet in a vacant tent, sitting there by the
fire all night and whispering endearments into each other's ears.
If the two lovers are well matched, their parents usually allow
them to marry. Also in southern Arabia marriage is as often
as not a genuine love match, for there is no complete segregation of sexes and young people have plenty of opportunities
to see each other. Among the nomadic tribes of the Libyan
Desert even greater freedom prevails: the boys are allowed
openly to court the girls, to visit them in their camps, and to
sing to them of their love in verses of their own composition
as a preliminary to marriage.

Also in the northeastern parts of the Middle East tribal societies have preserved much of that ancient freedom of women

which prevailed in pre-Islamic Arabia. Among the Kurds and the Lur tribes of western Iran, young men and girls meet freely, they join in the old folk dances, and the courting of the marriageable girls goes on in the old forms, in which quick wit and repartee are combined with spontaneous or traditional poetical expression of feelings.

In general, it can be stated that romantic love is more prevalent and receives more emphasis in the nomadic tribes than in settled society. Among the Bedouins love is generally recognized as a stage preceding marriage, while among the villagers the prevalent view is that love will come during marriage. The love songs sung by Bedouin lovers resemble to a remarkable degree those contained in the Song of Songs: much attention in both is paid to the physical beauty of the beloved, her hair, her eyes, her teeth, her neck, her breasts, her hips, her waist, comparing them to a great number of familiar objects held beautiful in popular view. Even a married woman's falling in love with another man—the situation which underlay the similes used by the Hebrew prophets in speaking of Israel's unfaithfulness to God—occurs not infrequently in the desert where married women have plenty of opportunity to make the acquaintance of other men.

CHOOSING A WIFE

SINCE the wife of a son became incorporated into his father's family, the choice of a wife was, under usual circumstances, made, not by the son, but by the father or one of his trusted representatives. This was the rule in Biblical times and has remained the prevalent custom in tradition-bound circles in the Middle East to the present day. Only the disobedient son, the recalcitrant and rebellious one, would marry a woman of his own choice without the prior consent of his father, and in this case he would either move completely out of the family circle or at least occupy a merely peripheral position in it (Gen. 26:34–35).

When Isaac became of marriageable age, his father, Abraham, sent his trusted servant Eliezer to find a wife for him among his kinfolk in Mesopotamia (Gen. 24:4, 37–38). Jacob, being away from his family, had to choose a wife for himself but in strict accordance with explicit instructions he received from his father. Isaac said to him: "Take thee a wife of the daughters of Laban thy mother's brother" (Gen. 28:2), which he did. On the bridal side, it was the girl's father who made the marriage agreement with him (Gen. 29:19). When Shechem violated Dinah and wanted to marry her, he asked his father, Hamor, "Get me this damsel to wife" (Gen. 34:4), whereupon Hamor went to the girl's father, Jacob, to ask her in marriage for his son (Gen. 34:6). In the fraudulent agreement which Jacob's sons made with Hamor and his people, several times reference is made to "giving and taking daughters" as wives (Gen. 34:9, 16, 21). When Judah, son of Jacob, became the head of his own extended family, he himself chose wives for himself and for his sons (Gen. 38:2, 6). When Samson fell in love with a Philistine woman, he asked his father and mother to "get her for him to wife" (Judg. 14:2).

In the law prohibiting intermarriage with the seven nations of Canaan, only the taking and giving of daughters for the sons is mentioned. That a man may take a wife for himself is not envisaged (Deut. 7:2–3).

In the tradition-bound Middle Eastern nomadic tribe, village, or urban quarter the same customs persist to this day. When the parents of a young man think that the time has come for him to marry, or when they feel that they finally can spare the amount they have to lay out for his bride price, they decide which of the daughters of their nearest or more remote relatives is the most suitable match for their son and start sending out feelers to find out whether the girl's parents are agreeable to a match. The first contact is usually made either through a neutral intermediary or between the young man's mother and the girl's mother, and the paternal consent is the formal closing of the preliminary negotiations.

The consent of the son to a match arranged by his parents is usually obtained without difficulty. The chances for finding normal premarital heterosexual outlets are as slight for a young man as they are for a girl. To procure a wife for himself without the payment of the bride price by his father is well nigh impossible for a young man in the traditional Middle Eastern family setup where all the property is controlled by the head of the family. This being the situation, there is no intrinsic need to consult the young man himself: he can be assumed to be amenable, driven as he is by his biological urges to marriage, and dependent as he is on his father economically.

As to the consent of the daughter, there is a wide variety of customs both in the Bible and in the modern Middle East. In some cases and places the girl's consent is obtained beforehand, in others it is completely disregarded. There is no mention at all of the sentiments of Leah and Rachel when they were given in marriage to Jacob. In negotiating with Hamor, the wishes of Dinah were disregarded, or at least no mention of them is made in the text. The tenor of the Shechem-Dinah story implies that the daughters who were to be "given" and "taken" in marriage by both sides had nothing to say in the matter.

Reuel gave his daughter Zipporah to Moses (Ex. 2:21). Thus Caleb, too, disposed of the hand of his daughter Achsah, offering her as a prize to him "that smiteth Kiriath-sepher and taketh it" (Josh. 15:16–17). Saul offered his daughter to David (1 Sam. 18:17). Similarly, it was "the men of Israel" who swore, saying, "There shall not any of us give his daughter unto Benjamin to wife" (Judg. 21:1)—as a result of the wanton behavior of the Benjamites at Gibeah (Judg. 19:24ff.; 20:10). Thereafter, in order not to have a "tribe blotted out from Israel" (Judg. 21:17), the 400 virgins left alive after the extermination of Jabesh-gilead were given by the "whole congregation" to the Benjamites (Judg. 21:12–14). When these

women proved insufficient, the men of Israel arranged that the
Benjamites be enabled to "catch" and carry off girls at the annual dance feast in the vineyards of Shiloh (Judg. 21:19–23).
In all this, the giving and taking of girls in marriage is purely
a matter for the menfolk to decide upon; the girls themselves
play a completely passive role.

Between the "arranged" marriage by capture, as it occurred
in Shiloh, and genuine marriage by capture without the consent of the girl's parents or even without the consent of the
girl herself, there is no distinct dividing line. While the Bible
contains no record of the latter, one can assume that it must
have occurred, occasionally at least. In the Middle East this
primitive form of obtaining a wife has survived, side by side
with the more peaceful methods, in a number of places, e.g.,
in southern Arabia and among the nomadic inhabitants of the
Sinai Peninsula.

The prevalent custom remains to this day in the Middle East
that the daughter is disposed of; she has no say at all in the
matter of her marriage. In some places, e.g., in some of the
Hadhramaut mountain tribes in southern Arabia, the rule is
for a father to provide a husband for his daughter without con-
sulting her, and in neighboring Oman it is regarded as actually
being shameful for a father to consult the wishes of his daughter or even to tell her of his visit to the cadi concerning the
nuptials, so that she knows very little until the night she is
conducted to her new home.

On the other hand, both in the Bible and in the modern
Middle East we find examples of the opposite custom as well.
When Eliezer asks for Rebekah's hand for Isaac, Bethuel—
Rebekah's father—and her brother Laban first agree in principle, but then when the time of departure arrives, they say:
"We will call the damsel and inquire at her mouth," and they
ask Rebekah, "Wilt thou go with this man?" (Gen. 24:51,
57–58.) This custom of asking the girl whether she consents to
the marriage discussed by her father with the father of the
young man or his representative is still practiced by several no-

madic tribes in and around the Syrian Desert. These tribes not only allow their girls to accept or reject a proposal, but they are proud of this custom and look upon it as a distinction which proves their superiority over the settled inhabitants of the villages and towns. The Manāhil and some other tribes of the Hadhramaut in southern Arabia, go to the extreme of requiring *only* the consent of the girl herself for her marriage, while the father says that it is of no concern to him.

The Rebekah episode, however, may represent a special case. In several places in the Middle East it has remained the custom to this day for the girls (or their parents) to require of the husband, if he is a stranger, to settle with them. Where such a *matrilocal* marriage is practiced, the father of the girl cannot decide that his daughter should leave the parental home or its immediate vicinity and follow the husband to his own country. This was the situation in the city of Zabid in Yemen in the fourteenth century. Ibn Battuta reports of the women of this city that they did not refuse to marry strangers, but if an out-of-town husband wished to move away from their city, the wife did not follow him. The wives remained in the city, took care of their children, and supplied all their wants until their husbands' return. "Even if one were to offer them the most precious things in order to persuade them to leave the city, they would not do it," remarks Ibn Battuta, who was clearly impressed by the obstinacy of that town's women.

The same custom prevailed in southern Arabia down to the nineteenth century when Burton observed that those "wild men do not refuse their daughters to a stranger, but the son-in-law would be forced to settle among them." Also in Egypt a girl would seldom consent, or her parents allow her, to marry an outsider, unless he promised to reside with her in her native town or village. The same custom prevailed also among the people of the Palestinian Arab village of Artas.

In the light of these parallels it would seem that had Bethuel found a husband for his daughter among the local men, he could have, and probably would have, disposed of his daughter's hand without asking her for her consent. This is exactly what Bethuel's son, Laban, did, when his turn came to marry off his daughters, Leah and Rachel. The bridegroom, Jacob, in this case agreed to abide with Laban for seven years, and then for another seven; therefore the consent of the girls for this matrilocal marriage was not required. Note also in this connection the long and detailed argument Jacob gave to his wives when after twenty years of connubium with them in their father's place he asked them to go with him to Canaan. He accused Laban of having cheated him, of having become inimical to him; and, in addition, he related to them that God had appeared to him and commanded him to go back to Canaan. Thereupon the women agreed, and the flight began (Gen. 31:1–18).

To return now to the previous generation: when Eliezer, as Abraham's representative, asked for the hand of Rebekah, her father and brother gave their own consent (Gen. 24:50–51), but they also had to ask Rebekah herself, because the proposed match meant that Rebekah had to leave her home and journey to join a husband in a foreign land. Eliezer, knowing the custom, foresaw that the girl to be chosen by him might refuse to follow him into Canaan and insist that her husband settle with her in her father's home or home locality (Gen. 24:5). This, however, was ruled out by Abraham (Gen. 24:6, 8). The "happy end" of the story is well known: in spite of the custom, Rebekah consented, followed Eliezer to Canaan, and became Isaac's wife.

One more detail in the story of Eliezer's mission needs to be elucidated. Eliezer's behavior upon his arrival in the house of Bethuel apparently contrasts with what was, and is to this day, regarded in the Middle East as good manners. Customarily, when a guest arrives in the home of a host he is expected to enjoy three days of hospitality. The first day is supposed to be spent with greetings and inquiries about each other's health and family. The second day is supposed to be devoted to feasting, and only on the third day is the guest supposed to state his errand or the purpose of his visit. Accordingly, the three days of hospitality are aptly called in Arabic *Salām*, *Ṭaʿām*, and *Kalām*, that is to say, greeting, eating, and talking.

In contrast to this customary behavior we find that as soon as Eliezer entered Bethuel's house, ungirded his camels, and washed his feet, he said, "I will not eat until I have told mine errand" (Gen. 24:33). Thereupon, with the consent of his hosts, he launched into the story of his mission and ended by asking for the hand of Rebekah for his master's son Isaac (Gen. 24:34–49). Eliezer thus appears to have behaved in a manner not consistent with the traditional rules of accepting and enjoying hospitality. But, again, a comparison with modern Arab life shows that Eliezer's behavior, far from being unseemly or unmannered, was strictly in accordance with the best etiquette. When on a mission of obtaining the hand of a daughter of the family in marriage, the bridegroom's representative has the prerogative, and, in fact, is expected, to demand that he be allowed to state his errand before he tastes any food or drink. Among the Arabs of Palestine exactly the same custom has survived to the present day. When the representative of the bridegroom arrives in the house of the bride's parents the latter, of course, set some food before him but he says: "I will not taste anything until I know that I shall have what I want," or, "I will not enjoy your salt or taste your food until you give me what I have come for." Upon receiving an affirmative answer, phrased very similarly to the words spoken by Laban and Bethuel (Gen. 24:50–51), the guest partakes of the meal, and at a later hour negotiations about bride price begin.

THE BRIDE PRICE

THE bride price is one of the oldest and most venerable features of the matrimonial institution in the Middle East. Already in the days of the Biblical patriarchs it was an ancient and firmly established tradition which was maintained and continued by the family of Abraham unquestioningly, as a matter of course. Today, the great majority of Middle Eastern people still regard it as a precondition of marriage.

In essence, the bride price is a payment rendered by the family of the bridegroom to the father or to the family of the bride. Its origin must be sought in a family setup in which a young girl was an economic asset for her father's family. The departure of the girl from her own family was an economic loss, and this was compensated by the bride price. From the point of view of the bridegroom's family the acquisition of a wife meant the addition of a pair of working hands in exchange for the amount paid over to the bride's family. It is a testimony to Middle Eastern conservatism that bride price is still being demanded and paid even in those circles (such as the urban middle class) in which a daughter has long ago become an economic liability for her father's family, and in which the acquisition of a wife by a man means that he has to defray the not inconsiderable expenses of an additional, economically unproductive, person in his household.

Over and above the purely economic considerations there has always been, of course, the procreative factor. In the patrilineal family children belong only to the families of their fathers. A new union, therefore, holds out the promise of increasing the numbers and the strength of the bridegroom's father's family, enabling him to gain status and prestige through the birth of grandsons. No comparable advantage accrues from the birth of children to the mother's family, of which they will not be members. Therefore, it is regarded as proper by all concerned that the bride's father, who loses, not only a daughter, but all her future progeny, should receive material compensation for her in the amount and up to the limit allowed by local tradition.

The payment of a high bride price increases the prestige of the husband and of his father. This expenditure is one of the few recognized manifestations in traditional Middle Eastern society of Thorstein Veblen's "conspicuous consumption." A

family which in housing, clothing, and eating habits can deviate but very little from the accepted norms of its society can
show in the one act of paying a high bride price that it is better off economically than its neighbors.

Over and above all this, in some cases the payment of a large
bride price may be the expression of the love of the bridegroom
for his bride. It is assumed that the young man must love the
girl very much in order to be able to prevail upon his father
to pay an inordinate bride price for her.

Only when cousins marry is the bride price reduced and
fixed usually at one half of the amount required in the same
group for a non-related bride. The several motivations which
make cousin marriage preferred contribute to the customary
acceptance of such a cut-rate bride price from a brother's son.

The payment of a bride price is not regarded as degrading
by either party. On the contrary, the value and esteem of a
woman are directly contingent upon the size of the bride price
paid for her. It is easily understandable that the more noble
the family and the more beautiful the girl, the higher the bride
price asked for her. Also her strength, age, ability, and character influence the bride price. It is less apparent, but equally
true, that, the higher the bride price paid for the girl, the more
she is esteemed by her husband and his family. If a man ob-
tains a wife for a small bride price he has little respect for her.
If much was paid for her, he feels that he has something valuable, a person who has to be treated well and respected.

The status of a woman in her husband's home is affected
by the size of the bride price in yet another way. Part of the
bride price, and occasionally all of it, is spent by the father of
the girl on her trousseau. Silver and gold jewelry—earrings, nose
rings, bracelets, anklets—form an important part of the outfit
received in this manner by a girl from her father. These orna-
ments are worn constantly by the Middle Eastern woman, and
their number and quality serve as status indicators within the
permissible narrow range of variation allowed by local custom.

The importance of the bride price is indicated by the length of negotiations leading to the fixation of the exact amount. The agreement in principle between a girl's parents and the youth's representatives concerning the marriage is a mere preliminary. After the two parties reach a general understanding that a match between their children is mutually agreeable, they settle down to a protracted series of meetings and discussions about the bride price. At the beginning the amount asked for by the bride's side and the one offered by the bridegroom's side are so far apart that the situation would appear hopeless to an inexperienced outsider. In patient negotiations, conducted with much aplomb, beseeching, and rendering of impressive oaths, the gap is successively narrowed until finally a bargain is struck.

The amount agreed upon is usually not paid out in full. As a rule, only two thirds of the bride price is paid over prior to the wedding. One third is retained by the bridegroom and becomes payable only if and when he divorces his wife. This amount, in fact, constitutes a kind of a reserve on which the wife can count, should she be divorced by her husband and find herself without financial support. On the other hand, the obligation to pay out this last third of the bride price is an important restraining consideration which keeps the husband from divorcing his wife on the spur of a moment in a sudden flash of anger.

In nomadic society the bride price is paid in kind: in the Qara Mountains, in the Hadhramaut region of southern Arabia, the bride price varies from twenty cows down to one cow; among the Rwala, the usual bride price is one or two she-camels and the first mare captured after the wedding. In addition to these animals, jewelry is also given by the bridegroom. The more the youth and his family desire the marriage, the more bride price and gifts they offer; the less the girl's family is interested in the match the more they demand. In one case, reported from the Rwala by Alois Musil, the father of the girl demanded, in addition to the customary number of camels, also earrings, a necklace, pendants to the necklace, and a huge amount of silk and cotton. This case is reminiscent, in reverse,

of the Shechem-Dinah story, where the anxious suitor said to
the family of his beloved: "Ask me never so much bride price
and gift, and I will give according as ye shall say unto me; but
give me the damsel to wife" (Gen. 34:12). The Biblical Hebrew word for bride price, *mohar*, used in this verse, is the same
by which the bride price is designated to this day among the
Arabs, *mahr*. In the pastoral society of the Biblical patriarchs
this was paid in animals, just as it is done among the Middle
Eastern nomads to this day.

In urban society the bride price is given in money, as is
done mostly also among the villagers. The amount varies
greatly from place to place and from period to period but is,
as a rule, kept within strict limits in each locality, at each given
time, and within each socioeconomic group. Thus in the city
of Mecca, for instance, in the nineteenth century, the *mahr*
used to be a few hundred dollars in the middle class, but only
a few dollars among the poor people. Among the Karab and
neighboring tribes in southern Arabia the bride price varies
from 200 to 50 riyals, while in the Asir mountains it is con-
siderably smaller. In Yemen the *mahr* was in the nineteenth
century 8 to 10 girsh. In the Hadhramaut mountains, among
the Bait Kathir, the bride price of a virgin bride varies between
20 and 300 Maria Theresa dollars (or 6.66 to 100 U.S. dollars), according to her family, face, and fortune. In Oman, to
the east, among the Janabah, it is only 12 to 60 Maria Theresa
dollars (4 to 20 U.S. dollars).

In several places, in order to prevent exorbitant demands, attempts have been made to set a fixed amount as bride price.
This was done, e.g., among the Jedīd al-Islām, the Marrano-
Jewish community, of Meshhed, Iran, in the nineteenth century; in some Arab villages in Palestine in the 1920s; and
among some tribes of Morocco and Tunisia. In the Mzab in
North Africa, the egalitarian custom fixes the bride price at
150 duros (750 francs) for rich and poor alike. However, in
many cases these regulations are soon discarded or disregarded,

and the traditional procedures of haggling over the bride price resumed.

The same vacillation between free negotiation and fixed bride price can be found in the Bible. The Shechem-Dinah story clearly points to a situation where the bride price was a matter to be discussed and agreed upon. On the other hand, certain Biblical passages presuppose that the bride price was fixed. Exodus 22:15–16 states that "If a man entice a virgin that is not betrothed, and lie with her, he shall surely pay a bride price for her to be his wife. If her father utterly refuse to give her unto him, he shall pay money according to the bride price of virgins." The exact amount of a "virgin's bride price" is mentioned in Deuteronomy 22:29: fifty shekels of silver.

Just as in the modern Middle East, in Biblical times, too, the bride price was paid over to the bride's father (Gen. 34:12; 1 Sam. 18:25; Ex. 22:15–16; Deut. 22:28–29). All over the Middle East the custom demands that the father give part of the bride price to his sons, to the bride's mother, and to other next of kin. This explains the great eagerness with which Laban, Rebekah's brother, participated in the negotiations with Eliezer (Gen. 24:29–31, 50, 55).

Only the stingy father keeps all the bride price for himself and uses it for his own purposes—"eats it up," as both the modern Arabic and the Biblical phrases (Gen. 31:15) have it.

SERVING FOR A WIFE

IN HEROIC times the performance of dangerous military exploits could take the place of the bride price. Caleb offered his daughter Achsah to him "that smiteth Kiriath-sepher and taketh it" (Josh. 15:16–17; Judg. 1:13); King Saul offered his daughter to "the man who killeth" Goliath (1 Sam. 17:25). When Michal, Saul's daughter, fell in love with David, Saul asked for a hundred foreskins of the Philistines in place of a bride price (1 Sam. 18:20, 25). Similar occurrences are recounted to this day in Bedouin camps. The hero who thus wins his lady is a familiar figure in the folklore of many nations.

However, if a man is not of heroic bent and, moreover, has no money, or animals, or other property which he could give in consideration for a girl to her father, he still has one way of acquiring a wife. This is by rendering service to the girl's father and receiving the girl in place of payment. Among the Arabs of Palestine (today: Jordan) this custom has been reported especially in cases when a young man, for one reason or another, had to leave his family and seek his fortune among strangers.

A young herdsman from the village of Ḥalḥūl, 'Abd il-Nebī by name, came to the village of Artas and said to Aḥmed Jēdallah: "O my uncle Aḥmed, will you give me one of your daughters? I will serve you for her bride price." Aḥmed replied: "There are three girls. You are the wolf of them, whichever you wish, name her to me!" The young man said: "I will have Nijme, I will be your herdsman and serve you for her bride price . . ." And he served his years and when the time was finished he took her.

Another young man, from the Ta'āmre Bedouins, served as a shepherd an Artas man and after eight years of service received his daughter as a wife.

These cases closely parallel the Biblical story of Jacob. Jacob, too, arrived as a stranger in Mesopotamia and entered there into the service of his kinsman Laban. In place of wages Jacob asked to be given Laban's daughter Rachel for wife: "I will serve thee," he said to Laban, "seven years for Rachel thy younger daughter" (Gen. 29:18). When the seven years were up, Laban deceived Jacob by introducing his older daughter, Leah, into the wedding chamber. Although Jacob did not receive the bride chosen by him, his wages for the seven years' service were paid when he received a wife. Thereafter Jacob entered into a second agreement with Laban to serve him an additional seven years for Rachel.

Chapter 4

FROM BETROTHAL TO WEDDING

ONCE the parents agree that they will have their children marry each other, the youth and girl are not supposed to see each other. It is especially up to the girl to make every effort not to be seen by her future husband. This premarital avoidance has to be observed even if the two young people are paternal cousins and live in the same house, or the same courtyard, or in two tents customarily pitched one next to the other. If the girl should inadvertently encounter her affianced, she must hide, or, if this be impossible, at least cover her face with a veil; this latter custom is observed even in tribes or other social aggregates among whom the veiling of women is not practiced.

This custom explains the otherwise puzzling behavior of Rebekah when she encountered Isaac in the open field. When Rebekah noticed a man in the distance whom she recognized from his clothing as being what in modern Middle Eastern parlance would be called a "notable," "she alighted from her camel" (Gen. 24:64), thereby observing the decorum customary in Biblical times (Josh. 15:18; 1 Sam. 25:23; 2 Ki. 5:21) as well as in present-day rural Middle Eastern society in encountering and greeting persons of high standing. However, she remained unveiled. But when, in answer to her question, "What man is this that walketh in the field to meet us?" Eliezer said: "It is my master," Rebekah immediately "took her veil and covered herself" (Gen. 24:65): the bride is not supposed to be seen by the bridegroom until the moment they are left alone in the wedding chamber.

THE WEDDING

WE NOW come to the wedding itself. Those who read the stories of the patriarchs in the Book of Genesis most probably ask themselves the question: what was the actual wedding ceremony which legally united the youth and the maiden and made them man and wife? At first glance, no clue seems to be contained in the Biblical text. At least in the case of the marriage of Isaac and Rebekah, or of Jacob and Leah and Rachel, there was no obvious formalized act which could be construed as the ritual solemnization of the wedding. Could it then be that there was actually no wedding ceremony at all in the days of the Biblical patriarchs? A scrutiny of present-day Middle Eastern marriage customs may supply the solution.

In the Middle East today there are found many variations of wedding customs. The urban wedding is a ritualized legal-religious ceremony; the village wedding has less of the ritual element in it; while the wedding in the nomadic sector is the simplest one, probably the oldest one in the area, and it is this variant therefore which holds out the promise to contain some clue to the better understanding of the Biblical patriarchal wedding.

A close scrutiny of the wedding ceremonies among the nomadic tribes of the Syrian Desert discloses the following facts: once an agreement has been reached by the two families, the wedding takes place soon after. Among the Rwala, a special small round tent is pitched by the women toward evening, and the bridal bed is made in it. Among the poor, merely a corner of the tent inhabited by the groom's parents is partitioned off for the young couple. Toward sunset, a few of the groom's female relatives go to the bride's parents' tent to fetch the bride and bring her to the prepared tent. A little later the groom also enters, after which the tent is closed. There are no additional wedding ceremonies. Among the Montafiq the special tent or hut erected for the bridal couple for the wedding night is made of reed mats; among the Sulabāt, of gazelle's skins. The erection of a special wedding tent is an old Arab custom which was practiced already in the days of Muhammad in the seventh century.

The same custom prevailed in Biblical times as well. The small tent or hut, erected for the consummation of the marriage, was called by different names (*qubbah*, Num. 25:8; *ohel*, 2 Sam. 16:22; *ḥuppah*, Ps. 19:6; *ḥeder*, Jo. 2:16; *'eres*, S. of Sol. 1:16). This can be taken as an indication of the same local diversity in the shape and construction of the bridal tent which characterizes it in the present-day Middle Eastern folk usage.

Depending on the economic standing of the families involved, and on the locality—where urban influences may be stronger or weaker—the simple basic ceremony of escorting the bride from her parents' home to the wedding tent may undergo elaborations to varying degrees. The unostentatious walk may burgeon until it assumes the character of a festive and pompous procession, with torchlight, musicians, many porters and animals carrying the bride's trousseau, gunfire, racing, mock fights, and the like. But the common core in all this remains evident: it is the public escorting of the bride into the groom's home. This is the only wedding ceremony known among the Middle Eastern nomads (and even among many villagers) on the simplest level.

The same act, performed likewise under the eye of public approbation, was the only wedding ceremony known to the Biblical patriarchs. Thus Isaac brought Rebekah into his mother Sarah's tent and thereby he "took" her and "she became his wife" (Gen. 24:67). Thus Laban, after he feasted "all the men of the place" took Leah "in the evening . . . and brought her" to Jacob "and he went in unto her" (Gen. 29:23). Incidentally, Laban's fraudulent exchange of Leah for Rachel was only possible because prior to the induction of the bride into the wedding chamber Jacob was not allowed to see her, because she was veiled when she was conducted to him, and because inside the wedding chamber at night there was complete darkness. This custom has survived to this day in various Middle Eastern folk societies. In Persia, for instance, there is no light at all in the marital chamber, and a man does not see his wife until he has consummated the marriage.

The simple act of conducting the bride into the groom's tent or chamber has, in the later Biblical period, developed into an elaborate ceremony. The bride and the groom, in their separate processions, were led in the street to the accompaniment of songs and music (Jer. 7:34; 16:9; 25:10); or they were carried in palanquins, dressed up as king and queen, perfumed with myrrh and frankincense, and surrounded by swordsmen (S. of Sol. 3:6–11).

This elaboration of the wedding procession is characteristic to this day of those Middle Eastern classes among whom the possession of material goods beyond the barest minimum gives the impetus to making a wedding the most memorable event (or, better: period) in the family's life. The display of swords in the procession still continues, although more often nowadays it is supplanted by guns which are wildly fired into the air or at the flag carried in the procession. The bride and groom are still frequently styled queen and king, half in mock and half in earnest, and are seated on a threshing board which is referred to as their "throne." Among the Egyptian fellahin the bridegroom is addressed as *"yā emīr,"* O Prince.

In several Middle Eastern communities, and especially among those belonging to the Eastern Christian Churches, the bride and the groom are actually crowned for the wedding ceremony. The wearing of a crown as a symbol of the royal status of the bride and the groom is a very old custom in the Middle East, which left its traces already in the Bible. In the Song of Songs the bridegroom is not merely called "king" but is identified with the greatest of the kings of Israel, renowned for his riches, wisdom, and his love of luxury and women: "Go forth,

O ye daughters of Zion, and gaze upon King Solomon, even upon the crown wherewith his mother hath crowned him in the day of his espousals, and in the day of the gladness of his heart" (S. of Sol. 3:11). Toward the end of the first Israelite kingdom it was customary to crown also the bride (Ezek. 16:12).

Another important feature of the wedding is the feast, the festive meal to which as many guests are invited as at all possible; often an entire tribe or village. Typical of these feasts is the circumstance that only the menfolk are invited to participate in them. The women, including the bride, are absent, or have a feast of their own in the bride's parents' home. Thus we read that "Laban gathered together all the *men* of the place and made a feast" (Gen. 29:22) when he gave his daughter in marriage to Jacob. At the wedding feast of Samson he was surrounded by thirty companions (Judg. 14:10-11). Marriage feasts with large gatherings were indulged in by kings, according to St. Matthew's parable (Matt. 22:2ff.). This feasting usually lasted for seven days (Gen. 29:27-28; Judg. 14:12, 17), just as it does to this day in most places in the Middle East where the age-old traditions are still honored.

THE BLOODSTAINED GARMENT

WITH the great emphasis placed on female chastity in Biblical times, one would expect that some ritual or ceremony should surround the establishment of a bride's virginity upon the consummation of the marriage. It so happens that no direct record of such proceedings is contained in the Bible. That nevertheless some traditional form of obtaining and preserving proofs of the bride's virginity did exist in Biblical times can be concluded from a legal passage which refers to the preservation of the bloodstained garment worn by the bride during her defloration. In Deuteronomy 22:13-19 we read: "If any man take a wife, and go in unto her, and hate her, and bring up an evil name upon her, and say: 'I took this woman, and when I came nigh to her, I found not in her the tokens of virginity'; then shall the father of the damsel, and her mother, take and bring forth the tokens of the damsel's virginity unto the elders of the city in the gate. And the damsel's father shall say unto the elders: 'I gave my daughter unto this man to wife, and he hateth her; and, lo, he hath laid wanton charges, saying: "I found not in thy daughter the tokens of virginity"; and yet these are the tokens of my daughter's virginity.' And they shall spread the garment before the elders of the city. And the elders of that city shall take the man and chastise him. And they shall fine him a hundred shekels of silver, and give them unto the father of the damsel, because he hath brought up an evil name upon a virgin of Israel; and she shall be his wife; he may not put her away all his days."

This Biblical law evidently presupposes that upon the consummation of each marriage the bloodstained garment, the "tokens of virginity" of the bride, were carefully preserved by her parents. For the garment to serve as a conclusive proof of the bride's virginity, it had to be delivered into her parents' hands, not only immediately upon the consummation of the marriage, but also under public surveillance; otherwise the parents could produce, at a later date, any bloodstained garment when confronted with an accusation of lack of virginity in their daughter.

The public ascertaining of the bride's virginity has continued to be the practice in the Middle East in tradition-bound social strata down to the present day. Several variants of the custom have been reported, both from Palestine and the neighboring countries. In Mecca it has been the custom on the morning following the wedding night, when the newlyweds leave their chamber, for the bride's mother to hurry to the bridal bed, gather up the bloodstained *sharshef,* and show it to all her women friends who used to spend the night with her. In the older form of the custom, as reported by Leo Africanus in the sixteenth century from Fez in Morocco, a woman used to be stationed in front of the wedding chamber, and as soon as the bridegroom has deflowered his bride he handed to her the bloodstained napkin, which she thereupon showed to all the assembled guests, proclaiming in a loud voice that the bride was found to have been a virgin. The public exhibition of the bloodstained garment is practiced to this day in Morocco.

In Egypt, down to the nineteenth century, the bloody garment was carried by the female relatives of the bride in triumph to the houses of the neighbors, or hung over the door of the peasants' house.

In the Kuwait area it is the custom to this day that the young girl puts up a struggle on her wedding night in an attempt to save her virginity. Female relations of both sides listen to the sounds of the struggle and the screams of the bride from outside the tent or the door of the room. After cohabitation, the bridegroom takes out the bloodstained bed sheet to the bride's female and male relatives, displays it to them, and calls out in pride and pleasure: "God whiten your faces, you have indeed kept your daughter pure!"

Among the Jews of Kurdistan, an old man, or an old man and an old woman, both from the bride's family, used to be stationed in front of the nuptial chamber. As soon as he consummated the marriage, the bridegroom opened the door of the room so that all should be able to see the bloodstained sheet. It was especially important that women from the bride's family should be present, so that they should be able to bear witness in case the bridegroom, at a later time in a moment of anger, should calumniate his bride. When the women satisfied themselves that the bride was a virgin, they started their joyous "kilili" triller, and this sound, as well as the music of the band which was also started, made it public knowledge in the middle of the night that the bride was found to be a virgin. Thereupon a relative of the bride carried the bloodstained sheet to the house of her father.

In Persia, the bloodstained white cloth is sent to the groom's parents or to the bride's parents. Also among the Jews of Persia the women used to wait in front of the nuptial chamber and then enter to observe the blood on the couch. The sheet was shown to all present and then deposited in the home of the bride's parents.

In some places the compulsive need to ascertain, without a shadow of a doubt, the bride's virginity was so strong that witnesses were required to be present in the nuptial chamber during the act of defloration. This was practiced by the Arabs of Upper Egypt down to the nineteenth century: "On the wedding night, the bridegroom, when he approaches his bride, is accompanied by two women, who, on coming out from the nuptial chamber, bear witness to the virgin state in which he found the new-married girl . . ."

Among the Egyptian fellahin today, acting under the same compulsive motivation, the women test the bride's virginity "in the most primitive manner" immediately preceding the consummation of the marriage. In Cairo, about a hundred years ago, yet another peculiar custom existed which, too, must have grown out of the desire to ascertain the virginity of the bride at the time of the consummation of the marriage. Burckhardt reports that on the wedding night the bridegroom would convince himself that the bride was a virgin, and then proceed to deflower her. However, he continues in Arabic (my translation), "there are many men who forego cohabiting with the girl at this time and deflower her with their finger. The simple people also use a wooden key for this purpose, while the fellahin and the low-class people deflower the girl only with the key, and even deride those who do not do likewise."

Defloration of the bride with the finger is practiced by Egyptian fellahin to this very day. The bridegroom wraps a piece of cloth around his index finger, deflowers with it the bride, usually in the presence of the village midwives, who occasionally actively help him in the performance of the act, and then the bloodstained kerchief is shown to the relatives. The first cohabitation often takes place only the next day.

One or another variant of the custom of preserving the bloodstained garment has been reported from many Middle Eastern societies from antiquity down to the present. Closest to the Biblical tradition is the form of the custom as it used to be practiced among the fellahin in Palestine. They used to preserve the bloodstained piece of cloth in the bride's hope chest (ṣanduqa), so that if she should subsequently be accused of not having been a virgin, she should be able to produce the proofs of her virginity.

According to the Biblical law, if the girl was, in fact, found to have been unchaste, her punishment was death: "But if this thing be true, that the tokens of virginity were not found in the damsel; then they shall bring out the damsel to the door of her father's house, and the men of her city shall stone her with stones that she die; because she hath wrought a wanton deed in Israel, to play the harlot in her father's house; so shalt thou put away the evil from the midst of thee" (Deut. 22:20–21).

Extreme punishment for premarital unchastity of a girl in her father's house has continued in the Middle East in various places well into the nineteenth and even twentieth centuries. In Syria, among the fellahin, if the bride was found not to be a virgin, she was killed by her father, brothers, or their representative. The same rule is adhered to by the Rwala Bedouins and in some sectors of the population of Iraq. These parallels seem to indicate that in Biblical times, too, the kinsmen of the bride must have had the major responsibility in putting to death the unchaste girl, although the text only states that her stoning is being carried out at the door of her father's house by the men of her city. In any case, it is clear that both in the Biblical view and in modern times, the lack of virginity in a girl was (and is) regarded as a disgrace for her father's family which can be expiated only by her death.

Chapter 5

THE IMPERATIVE OF FRUITFULNESS

THE first words spoken by God to Adam and Eve were "Be fruitful and multiply" (Gen. 1:28). These words, although clearly a command, are characterized in the Biblical text as a blessing. Thus the ancient Hebrews projected the imperative of fruitfulness back into the very first day on which man was created. Later Jewish lore and learning, in assembling the positive and negative injunctions of the religion, listed "fruitfulness and multiplication" as the first of the 613 commandments.

The legendary and legal expressions of the idea reflect faithfully the actual feelings of the Middle Eastern peoples from pre-Biblical to modern times. The entire atmosphere in which individuals in the Middle East grew up throughout the ages was saturated with the imperative of fruitfulness. A man's status and stature, prestige and progress through life were deeply affected by the number of his progeny. Only a man who had many sons could count, with advancing age, on becoming an important member of his community whose voice is hearkened to in council. Only a man who had many sons could hope to become the head of his extended family and of the larger kin group of which this family formed part. Only such a man could feel secure in a social environment where might meant right, and where might in the final count depended on the number of males whose unquestioning loyalty he could command. For these and many other reasons, economic, political, strategic, sentimental, "be fruitful and mul-

tiply" was indeed, and has remained to this day, the greatest
of blessings.

This blessing, first pronounced by God over the newly
created animals (Gen. 1:22) and the first human pair, was subsequently repeated by him and by his flesh-and-blood spokesmen whenever the promise of supreme bliss and boon was
imparted to an individual. "Be fruitful and multiply" was the
thrice repeated blessing given by God to Noah after the deluge
(Gen. 8:17; 9:1, 7). The first time God spoke to Abraham he
promised him a rich progeny: "I will make of thee a great nation" (Gen. 12:2). This blessing of Abraham is repeated in
Genesis several times with an insistent and unrelenting monot-
ony that could stem only from the conviction that numerous
progeny is the highest of all human aspirations. After Abraham
separated from Lot, God blessed him: "I will make thy seed
as the dust of the earth . . ." (Gen. 13:16). When the childless, aging Abraham complained, God reassured him: "Count
the stars, if thou be able to count them—so shall thy seed be!"
(Gen. 15:5). In the dreadful night scene of the covenant between the sacrificial pieces it was again the promise of a rich
seed which allayed Abraham's fears and was held out to him
by God as the supreme reward of man: "Unto thy seed have
I given this land . . ." (Gen. 15:18). And again, when Abraham was ninety, he heard the divine promise: "I will multiply
thee exceedingly. . ." "Thou shalt be the father of a multitude
of nations . . ." "I will make thee exceedingly fruitful . . ."
(Gen. 17:2–3, 5, 6). Again, by the terebinths of Mamre, the
Lord said: "Abraham shall surely become a great and mighty
nation" (Gen. 18:18). After the birth of Isaac, the divine
promise was repeated: "In Isaac shall seed be called to thee,
and also of the son of the bondwoman will I make a nation
because he is thy seed" (Gen. 21:12–13). After Abraham
demonstrated his unquestioning obedience to God by his willingness to sacrifice Isaac, the reward is again couched in the
same terms: "In blessing I will bless thee, and in multiplying

I will multiply thy seed as the stars of the heaven and as the sand which is upon the seashore . . ." (Gen. 22:17).

Stars and sand—these two great symbols of fruitfulness return again and again in the Biblical narrative which carries on the story of the Hebrew patriarchal family: the promise and the blessing of a seed as numerous as stars and sand is repeatedly given by God to Isaac (Gen. 26:4, 24) and to Jacob (Gen. 28:14; 32:13), and it is reiterated in later Mosaic and prophetic utterance (Ex. 32:13; Deut. 1:10; 10:22; Hos. 2:1; Isa. 48:19; Neh. 9:23; 1 Chron. 27:23). Numerous seed is promised also to Ishmael (Gen. 17:20; 21:18), Abraham's first-born by Hagar; to Sarah, the mother of all Hebrews (Gen. 16:10; 17:16), and to Rebekah (Gen. 25:23). "Our sister, be thou the mother of thousands of ten thousands" (Gen. 24:60) is the blessing given to Rebekah by her family.

It is a peculiar feature of the patriarchal story that in the midst of all this pressure for fecundity three out of the four traditional mothers of the Hebrew nation were barren for long periods before, by the special grace of God, they were able to conceive and thus ensure the future of the promised seed. Sarah, we are told, was an old woman, far beyond her menopause (Gen. 18:11–12), when she miraculously conceived to her centenarian husband and bore Isaac, her only child (Gen. 21:5). Rebekah, Isaac's wife, was barren, and conceived her twins only after Isaac entreated the Lord for her (Gen. 25:21–22). In her case, too, this was her only pregnancy. Rachel, Jacob's beloved wife, was barren, and her desire to have children was so great that she burst out in a moment of despair and said unto Jacob: "Give me children, or else I die" (Gen. 30:1). As a consequence of the birth of her second son Rachel died (Gen. 35:18–19). The only truly fruitful one among the ancestral mothers of the Hebrews was Leah, who gave birth to six sons and a daughter (Gen. 35:23). Even the handmaids enjoyed only a diminished fertility: Hagar had only one son, Bilhah two, and Zilpah two. This record compares rather unfavorably with the averages found to this day in those Middle

Eastern societies where uncontrolled fertility is still practiced and where the average number of children born to a woman during her lifetime ranges from six to eight. Barrenness remained the greatest single affliction that could befall a couple in later times as well. About a thousand years after Abraham, when Elisha wanted to repay the Shunammite woman her hospitality, the prophet's servant, Gehazi, knew what was uppermost in her mind: "Verily, she hath no son, and her husband is old" (2 Ki. 4:14).

Several centuries later, the story of the childless old couple to whom an angel announces the impending birth of a son is told about the parents of John the Baptist (Luke 1:5–13).

The belief that it is God who "opens" or "closes" the wombs of women is well attested both in the Bible and in the modern Middle East. It was God who "restrained Sarah from bearing" (Gen. 16:2). It was He who "shut up" Hannah's womb (1 Sam. 1:5–6). When the childless Rachel demanded sons of Jacob, he answered her in anger: "Am I in God's stead who hath withheld from thee the fruit of the womb?" (Gen. 30:2.) It was only when God "remembered" Sarah that she was able to conceive (Gen. 21:1–2). Only when "the Lord let himself be entreated" (Gen. 25:21) did Rebekah conceive. When God saw that Leah was hated by her husband, "he opened her womb" (Gen. 29:31). After having given birth to four sons, Leah "left off bearing" (Gen. 29:35), and thereafter God had to hearken unto her before she conceived again (Gen. 30:17). After telling the story of the mandrakes—the love-apples which were believed to make barren women fertile—the Biblical narrator hastens to reassure us that it was God's direct intervention which resulted in Rachel's conception: "God remembered Rachel, and God hearkened unto her, and opened her womb, and she conceived (Gen. 30:22–23). Hannah conceived only when "the Lord remembered her" (1 Sam. 1:19). Also according to the later Hebrew view, it is God who gives children (1 Chron. 28:5; Isa. 8:18; 66:9; Hos. 9:14; Ps. 127:3).

The same belief persists in the Middle Eastern world to this day. It is God who gives children to a woman or withholds them from her. The expression used in this connection in Arabic is very significant: God "feeds" the woman with a child. That is to say, God puts the child into the woman's womb, as a person puts food into his mouth.

The idea that God gives children as a reward of piety is coupled with a paean to the fruitful wife and to the value of sons in two Psalms.

> Lo, the heritage of the Lord are sons
> A reward is the fruit of the womb.
> Like arrows in a hero's hand,
> So are the sons of youth.
> Happy the man who filled his quiver
> They shall not be put to shame
> When they speak with enemies in the gate.
>   (Ps. 127:3-5)
>
> A Song of Ascents.
> Happy the God-fearing man
> Who walketh in His ways.
> When thou eatest the labor of thy hands
> Happy art thou and it is well with thee.
> Thy wife—like a fruitful vine in thy house
> Thy sons—like olive plants around thy table.
> Behold, thus is the man blessed
> That feareth the Lord.
> The Lord bless thee out of Zion,
> And see thou the good of Jerusalem
> All the days of thy life.
> And see the sons of thy sons,
> Peace be upon Israel.
>   (Ps. 128)

When a woman is barren, she will not shy away from any means or measure to achieve conception. The means resorted to range from purely magical methods to religious vows and prayers. The mandrake, which, according to the Genesis story, was regarded as a remedy for barrenness (Gen. 30:14ff.) was still used in the nineteenth and even in the twentieth century by Arab women in Transjordan and in Syria, and by Sephardi Jewish women in Jerusalem: they either ate mandrakes or tied them around their body in order to conceive. Samaritan women in the seventeenth century used to place mandrakes beneath their beds for the same purpose. Among the many other plants and fruits eaten by Middle Eastern women as a remedy for barrenness, let us mention only one: dates from a palm tree at the Mar Saba Monastery in Jordan are believed to be the best cure for sterility. The diseases for which the powers of the saints and of their holy places are most frequently invoked to this day among the Arab villagers in Jordan are sterility and fevers.

The birth of Samuel constitutes the classical Biblical example for the religious vow made in order to obtain the desired pregnancy. The childless Hannah went to the temple in Shiloh, and "vowed a vow and said: 'O Lord of Hosts, if Thou wilt indeed look on the affliction of Thy handmaid, and remember me, and not forget Thy handmaid, but wilt give unto Thy handmaid a man-child, then I will give him unto the Lord all the days of his life, and there shall no razor come upon his head'" (1 Sam. 1:11). In due time a son, Samuel, was born to her.

The circumstances of Samuel's birth are duplicated to some extent by the prenatal history of Samson. Manoah's wife was barren, too, and although it is not related that she prayed for a son or made a vow, we must assume that, like every barren woman in the Bible and in the Middle East, she greatly and even desperately desired a son, and was ready to make any vow in order to obtain her desire. An angel then announced to her that she would conceive and bear a son who must become a Nazirite unto God from the womb: no razor shall come upon his head (Judg. 13:2ff.). Presumably, Manoah's wife became pregnant only after she undertook, that is, vowed, to dedicate to God the son that would be born to her. The Samson and Samuel stories are duplicated by the account of the annunciation of John the Baptist's birth to his childless elderly parents (Luke 1:5–15).

The imperative of fruitfulness motivates Middle Eastern women to this day to make vows at local shrines which in themselves are the lineal descendants of the Shiloh sanctuary where Hannah prayed for a son. Barrenness is still considered the greatest misfortune and disgrace that can befall a woman. Why this should be so will be discussed in the following section. Many a barren woman seeks to obtain a son from local saints or *welis* whose tombs are found near many villages in all Middle Eastern countries. The vows made occasionally still involve the dedication of the hoped-for son to the service of God for a certain period of time.

A Palestinian Arab childless woman would vow: "If you, O man of God, grant me a child, I shall let him serve you one month." Such vows, more frequent among Christians than among Muslims, are fulfilled by helping the *qandalaft* (sexton) in his work, sweeping the shrine, lighting lamps, etc. This is what probably the child Samuel did for Eli in the Shiloh sanctuary when he "ministered unto the Lord before Eli the priest" (1 Sam. 2:11, 18; 3:1).

When a twentieth century Christian Arab woman who is childless makes a vow offering the son whom she desires to St. Antonius (*Mār Anṭon*), the fulfillment of the vow means that the boy must wear the garb of the order of St. Antonius for one year. The parents provide the cloth for the garb which is cut by the priest or in the convent; the convent presents the child with a girdle-rope, a rosary, and a cap. The priest puts the garments on the child and takes them off a year later. It is remarkable how closely these details follow the story of the child Samuel. He too was girded with "a linen ephod" and his mother made him a little robe which he wore for a year, then to be replaced by a new one (1 Sam. 2:18–19).

In another type of vow practiced by barren Arab women, they undertake to sacrifice a sheep to the saint, or a sheep every year, or to give the saint the child's weight in silver coins.

The means and methods utilized by Middle Eastern women to rid themselves of the curse of sterility are innumerable. A study of these constitutes a most fascinating field in the folklore of the Middle East. But we must refrain from entering it at present, and have to confine ourselves to quoting a statement by Chardin, who observed in the eighteenth century in Persia: "I have seen women who did not know what saint to make their vows to next, and they even made pilgrimages to Christian churches."

Probably even more difficult than for a Muslim woman to go to a Christian church for help is for the sterile wife to lead another woman to her husband's bed. But even this was done at all times and is being done to this day in the Middle East. The motivation which in patriarchal times was powerful enough to overcome the reluctance of the wife to share her husband with another woman was the belief that, by having the other woman give birth to her child on the knees of the sterile wife, the latter, too, would become fertile and begin to bear children.

Thus when Sarah was childless, she gave her handmaid Hagar to Abraham, saying: "Go in, I pray thee, unto my handmaid; it may be that I shall be builded up through her" (Gen. 16:2). Similarly Rachel said to Jacob: "Behold my maid Bilhah, go in unto her; that she may bear upon my knees, and I also may be builded up through her" (Gen. 30:3). Also Leah thereupon gave her handmaid Zilpah to Jacob to wife (ib. v. 9). The procedure referred to in these passages has been interpreted as a form of adoption: the barren wife adopts the child born to her husband by her handmaid. However, in view of the fact that in each of the three cases the wife herself ultimately conceived following the union of her husband with her handmaid, it seems probable that the intended purpose was to achieve fertility. Bodily contact can transfer something of the powers of the fertile woman unto the sterile woman. This is in strict accordance with the principles of contagious magic which still have world-wide currency in folk societies. One of

the traditional methods to make a sterile woman fertile, practiced in certain Jewish communities down to recent times, was
to let her sit on the birthstool immediately after it was used
by a woman in parturition. Another method, used in Safed,
Palestine, down to the twentieth century, was to take a piece
from the dress of a woman who had just become a mother,
to soak it in water, and then to pour the water over the body
of the sterile woman. Also the navel cord and the afterbirth
were used for the same purpose. It thus seems likely that a
sterile woman was believed to become fertile if the birth of
a child of her own husband and of her handmaid took place on
her knees.

The intense desire for children motivates sterile Middle
Eastern women to this day to induce their husbands to "go
in unto" another woman, that is, to take a second wife. It may
no longer be consciously hoped that the fecundity of the second wife can produce fertility in the first, sterile, wife as well.
But the entire upbringing of the woman and the social atmosphere in which she lives make her want children to such an
extent that if she must resign herself to childlessness, she wants
at least her husband to have children, the house to have children, the family as a whole to have children—even if it be at
the price of a second wife.

Père Jaussen, in describing the customs of the people of
southern Transjordan, mentions that such cases are known
even among the Orthodox Christian Arabs whose religion prohibits polygyny. An Orthodox Christian couple of the town of
Madeba had only one child, a son. The boy died, and in the
very midst of the funeral rites, his mother cried out to her
husband: "Take yourself a young wife to give you children,
since I am too old." The insistence of a childless woman that
her husband take a second wife can also stem from the appre-
hension lest, upon the death of her husband, his estate be inherited by his lateral relatives and she lose her right to stay
in his house. On the other hand, if her husband has sons by
the second wife, her right to stay in the house is secured.

ADULTERY AND STERILITY

In a society which regards numerous progeny as the supreme good which man can achieve, barrenness must needs be considered as the greatest of calamities. In fact, sterility is felt to be such a misfortune, such a crushing blow, that the religious Middle Eastern mind is involuntarily driven by it to soul searching, to self-examination, and to the inevitable conclusion that some heinous sin must have brought it about. The overall idea pattern into which this trend of thought fits is the general assumption that all calamities are caused by sins, that all misfortune is a proof of misconduct, that all suffering has its ultimate roots in the sufferer himself. The simpler folk belief regards the sin as the direct cause of the calamitous effect; it presupposes a sympathetic connection between the human act and the behavior of the natural forces which affect the state and condition of man. The more sophisticated religious mind recognizes that human action can have no direct influence on nature, but is watched by God, and it is he who visits every deviation from the straight and narrow path by retributive punishment. In both views it is assumed that the punishment fits the crime, and that the nature of the misfortune under which a person suffers contains a clue as to his sin which brought it about.

In this outlook, it is almost inevitable that a causal connection be predicated between adultery and other sexual transgressions on the one hand and sterility on the other. Sexual sin, whether committed intentionally or inadvertently, must result—in this view—in an impairment of the powers of fertility: an illicit sexual act prevents conception, which is the aim and purpose of all licit sexual activity.

The Biblical example of this belief is contained in the story told in the Book of Genesis about Abraham, Sarah, and Abimelech. Abimelech, king of Gerar, believing that Sarah was the sister (and not the wife) of Abraham, took her into his harem. Thereupon, even before he actually "had come near her," "the Lord fast closed up all the wombs of the house of Abimelech, because of Sarah Abraham's wife." After Abimelech restored Sarah to Abraham, "Abraham prayed unto God, and God healed Abimelech, and his wife, and his maidservants, and they bore children" (Gen. 20:17-18). It can be safely assumed that, when Pharaoh committed the same unwitting transgression, the "great plagues" which the Lord brought on him and his house (Gen. 12:17) also included the supreme calamity of barrenness. Incidentally, it can be observed here that the time which must have elapsed between Sarah's induction into the royal harems and her release must have been considerable: it must have taken several months at least before it became evident that "all the wombs" in the palace were closed.

Several years later, Abimelech almost repeated the same mistake. This time it was Abraham's son and heir, Isaac, who came to sojourn in Gerar with his beautiful wife, Rebekah. Isaac, like his father before him, was afraid "lest the men of the place should kill him for Rebekah," and so he said, "She is my sister." When, a long time after, Abimelech looked out the window and saw Isaac and Rebekah have marital relations, he reproached Isaac: "What is this thou hast done unto us? One of the people might easily have lain with thy wife, and thou wouldest have brought guiltiness upon us" (Gen. 26:6–10). Again the context makes it probable that what Abimelech feared was the "shutting up of the wombs" of the womenfolk in Gerar. Such a consequence of an inadvertent sexual sin would indeed have been a calamity for Gerar. One cannot assume that a society which was known to kill strangers in order to take their wives would have recoiled from adultery with the wife of a stranger on purely moral grounds.

The notion underlying the full version of the Abraham-Sarah-Abimelech story, namely that adultery causes sterility, is expressed more specifically in the laws of Leviticus. In Chapter

20 of that book, prohibitions of adultery, sodomy, homosexuality, and incest are enumerated, together with the punishment prescribed for their transgression. In most cases the penalty is death, even for such a minor sin as having intercourse with a menstruating woman—"both of them shall be cut off from among their people" (Lev. 20:18). In two cases, however, the punishment is not death but the curse of sterility: if a man lies with his uncle's wife or takes his brother's wife, "they shall be childless" (Lev. 20:20–21). This is clearly the religio-legal expression of the more ancient popular view that illicit sex relations result in barrenness. "They shall die childless" (Lev. 20:20) is a penalty almost as severe as being actually put to death; it is a deferred death sentence. Abraham in his desperate outcry, "O Lord God, what wilt Thou give me, seeing I go hence childless" (Gen. 15:2), uses the same word ('arīrī), which appears twice in the Levitical law referred to above.

The very same idea recurs in the Book of Job. To commit adultery with a neighbor's wife, says the suffering Job, "is a fire that consumeth unto destruction, [which] would root out all mine increase" (Job 31:9–12). The Hebrew term for "increase"—t'bhu'ah—usually means "crop"; but the context and especially the reference to another punishment invoked by Job —that if he is guilty of the vice of adultery then let his wife be violated by other men—indicate that the phrase "root out all mine increase" means simply destroy my progeny, make me childless.

The very same idea is dwelt upon at greater length and more explicitly in another passage in the Book of Job. This time it is Bildad the Shuhite, one of Job's three friends, who is speaking. He describes in considerable detail the terrible consequences of sinning. He states that the sinner, whom he calls the "wicked," loses his sexual power (ōn), is ensnared by his own misdeeds, others shall occupy his tent, "his roots shall dry up beneath, and above shall his branch wither . . . his remembrance shall perish from the earth . . . he shall have neither son nor son's son among his people, nor any remaining in his dwelling" (Job 18:5–21). Also Zophar the Naamathite, the second friend of Job's, expresses similar ideas (Job 20), and Job himself repeats them (Job 27:14).

Later Jewish lore was even more outspoken on the subject of sin and sterility. In the apocryphal Book of Enoch it is stated that women are afflicted with barrenness only as a result of their own misdeeds (1 Enoch 98:5). A second century A.D. midrash embellishes the Biblical account of Sarah's barrenness: when women of the neighborhood came to pay a visit to Abraham's womenfolk, Hagar said to them: "Sarah, my mistress, seems to be a righteous woman, but she is not; were she righteous would she not have conceived all these years? And I, I conceived in one single night." And when the "nations of the world" saw that Abraham had no offspring they said, "Were he righteous, would he not beget?"

This belief, that sins cause sterility, has remained alive in Palestine down to the present. Elihu Grant, who studied the fellahin of Palestine in the early decades of the twentieth century, was told about a Christian Arab in a village who had accumulated a fortune through thievery, and as a result of this he was cursed by God: he was childless, although, in defiance of the church, he lived in bigamy with two wives. Also in the village of Artas (today in Jordan), a man whose sons by his two wives died was said to be under a curse, since he caused the death of his father's brother's widow. From the southern outskirts of the Middle East comes an example which closely parallels the Biblical view that sexual transgression causes barrenness. The Dinkas of the Upper Nile believe that incest angers the ancestral spirits, who punish the girl by making her barren. Even should she marry, she will have no children until she has confessed her sin and atonement has been made for it.

Since sterility is caused by sins in general and by the sin of adultery in particular, it is an overt manifestation of a sinful state. Therefore, while we regard sterility as a misfortune for which the afflicted woman or her husband can certainly not be blamed, in the Biblical and Middle Eastern view it is a shame and a disgrace. While Rachel was barren, it was a "shame" (ḥerpāh) for her; when she finally conceived and gave birth to a son, she greatly rejoiced because "God hath taken away my shame" (Gen. 30:23). Also Elisabeth, when she became pregnant with John, exclaimed: "Thus hath the Lord dealt with me in the days wherein he looked on me to take away my shame among men" (Luke 1:25).

The same Hebrew term for shame is used in the Bible also in connection with famine, another calamity caused by adultery and fornication. In a phrase very similar to the one used by Rachel and Elisabeth, the prophet Ezekiel talks about the glorious days of grace: "I will multiply the fruit of the tree and the increase of the field, that ye may receive no more the shame of famine among the nations" (Ezek. 36:30). Famine is a "shame" because—just like human barrenness—sterility in the trees and the fields is caused by sin, the sin of fornication, adultery, and other sexual transgressions. In the Book of Leviticus, following a long and detailed list of incest prohibitions, and after warnings against intercourse with women during their menstruation, there comes the threat: if you commit these abominations, the land will become "defiled" and "vomit you out" (Lev. 18, 20:10–22). When the land becomes defiled it ceases to yield fruit and crops; it becomes barren and the sinful people "perish quickly from off the good land" (Deut. 11:17). This is why the drought which plagued the land in the days of Jeremiah evoked the feeling of shame among the inhabitants of Judah and Jerusalem (Jer. 14:3–4): it made them aware of the sins they had committed.

That adultery was indeed regarded as the arch sin or the original sin which can cause the people to "perish from off the good land" (Deut. 11:17) can be further substantiated by reference to the constant use in Biblical language of sexual terminology and imagery when speaking of the second great sin, that of idolatry. In fact, all through Biblical literature, idolatry is spoken of as a collective adultery or whoredom of the people of Israel. At Mount Sinai, God is said to have cautioned the people lest "they go awhoring" after the gods of the Canaanites as a result of intermarriage (Ex. 34:15–16). The verb "to go awhoring" appears in the great adhortative peroration in which Moses cautions the people against sins in general (Num. 15:39; cf. also Deut. 31:16).

In the general synopsis which opens the Book of Judges and which presents the recurrent pattern of the tribal history of Israel in the premonarchal period, the sin of idolatry is couched in the same terms: "The Lord raised up judges . . . and yet they hearkened not unto their judges, for they went awhoring after other gods and worshiped them . . ." (Judg. 2:16–17). All the three major prophets, and three of the twelve minor prophets whose writings are preserved in the Bible, use this phrase. All of them use it repeatedly, sometimes with an unrestrained, almost pornographic bitterness, like Ezekiel, who describes how the harlot Jerusalem opened her legs to everyone that passed by (Ezek. 16:25).

Just as adultery results in sterility, idolatry too has the same dreadful consequence. In a passage in the Book of Exodus (23:24–26) this view is expressed clearly although it talks, not of the penalty of idolatry, but of the rewards for serving only the Lord: "Thou shalt not bow down to their gods . . . And ye shall serve the Lord your God . . . none shall miscarry nor be barren in thy land . . ."

The sin of idolatry was thus almost indistinguishable in Biblical mentality and phraseology from the sin of adultery. Both resulted in the same punishment: barrenness among the humans and the disruption of the normal course of nature, the malfunctioning of its powers, drought, other natural catastrophes, and, ultimately, famine and the destruction of the people.

Judaism has always been a religion with a completely positive attitude toward life. Human life was valued by it above all. According to a Talmudic rule, if a man is given the choice by an inimical temporal power to transgress a Biblical commandment or to suffer death, he is allowed to transgress any and all, in order to save his life, with the exception of three:

idolatry, fornication, and bloodshed. The view that of these three cardinal sins fornication is the gravest is expressed in the Book of Jubilees which was compiled close to the beginning of the Christian era. There we read: "There is no greater sin than fornication . . ." (Jub. 33:20). In the first post-Christian centuries the same view was held and repeatedly expressed by many of the sages and scholars of Talmudic Judaism.

Fornication has remained the archsin which causes drought and consequent famine, according to the views of the Middle Eastern folk down to recent times. The tacit assumption is that whenever drought occurs, it comes as a punishment for some sexual transgression which was committed by one or more persons without the knowledge of the community. Therefore, according to popular logic, if a ceremony is to be performed for the purpose of putting an end to a drought, it is well that the principals participating in it should be persons whose innocence in matters sexual is beyond the shadow of a doubt. Such persons can call upon God to have pity on the people by emphasizing their innocence and thus counterbalancing, as it were, the pernicious influence of the sexual sin that caused the drought in the first place.

Accordingly, children who cannot yet commit sexual sins, or old women who no longer can commit them, used to have the chief roles in rain processions held in the Palestine-Trans-jordan-Syria area as late as the 1930s. In northern Palestine, in the village of Tibnin, for instance, boys and girls would walk about in the streets, each carrying a stick to which was attached a rag dripping with water. The adults would sprinkle water on the children, who sang:

> "O our Lord, O our Lord,
> Give rain to our seed.
> They are big, those who sinned,
> We are small, what are our sins?"

In other Arab villages in Palestine the children used to sing:

"O our Lord, O our Lord,
We are small, what are our sins?
We asked bread from our mother,
She hit us on our mouth."

In Beit Jala near Bethlehem (today in Jordan), the Christian
Arab children sing:

"O our Lord, do not punish us,
Everything [bad comes] from our elders.
Our elders, the great ones,
O my Lord, burn them in fire."

Among the semi-Bedouins of Sawāherah al-Wad, in the Judean Desert (today in Jordan), the oldest woman is placed on
the back of a donkey with a hand mill in front of her which
she keeps turning. She is led through the fields, accompanied
by a troop of village children carrying a cock, which they tor-
ment in order to make it cry aloud. The old woman sings a
rain song and the children shout the response, words which
stress their innocence. Similar ceremonies take place, or used
to take place until recently, in many localities.

Although the children's words do not mention the particular
sin of which they are innocent, the very fact that small children
and old women well past their menopause (qaṭʻa) take part in
the ceremony indicates that the reference must be to freedom
or purity from sexual sin. After all, small children and old
women can commit all kinds of sins; they can lie, cheat, steal,
even kill. The only sin they are incapable of committing is
fornication, and it is precisely this circumstance which quali-
fies them as principals in the rain request ceremony.

The sexual mores of folk societies differ, of course, from
place to place. But whatever is regarded as a transgression by
local tradition is believed to result in a disruption of the orderly
functioning of the natural forces and to cause drought. Among
the Merekede, for instance, in southern Arabia, sexual hospitality was regarded as an honorable, quasi-religious practice.
When the Wahhābīs subjugated the Merekedes, they forced

them to renounce this custom which was regarded by the Wahhābīs as immoral. For two years thereafter there was a scarcity of rain, and the Merekedes saw in this misfortune a punishment from on high for having abandoned the laudable rites of their forefathers. They petitioned 'Abd el-'Azīz, the Wahhābī chief, who thereupon granted them the permission to resume honoring their guests as before.

The complementary side of the belief that adultery causes sterility is the view that a woman accused of adultery and proven innocent will become fertile, conceive, and bear children. This view is expressed in connection with the Biblical law concerning the *Sōṭāh*, the woman accused of adultery which, incidentally, is the only example in the Bible of institutionalized ordeal proceedings:

If any man's wife go aside, and act unfaithfully against him, and a man lie with her carnally, and it be hid from the eyes of her husband, she being defiled secretly, and there be no witness against her, neither she be taken in the act; and the spirit of jealousy come upon him, and he be jealous of his wife, and she be defiled; or if the spirit of jealousy come upon him, and he be jealous of his wife, and she be not defiled; then shall the man bring his wife unto the priest, and shall bring her offering for her, the tenth part of an ephah of barley meal; he shall pour no oil upon it, nor put frankincense thereon; for it is a meal-offering of jealousy, a meal-offering of memorial, bringing iniquity to remembrance. And the priest shall bring her near, and set her before the Lord. And the priest shall take holy water in an earthen vessel; and of the dust that is on the floor of the tabernacle the priest shall take, and put it into the water. And the priest shall set the woman before the Lord, and let the hair of the woman's head go loose, and put the meal-offering of memorial in her hands, which is the meal-offering of jealousy; and the priest shall have in his hand the water of bitterness that causeth the curse. And the priest shall cause her to swear, and shall say unto the woman: "If no man have lain with thee, and if thou hast not gone aside to uncleanness, being under thy husband, be thou free from this water of bitterness that causeth the curse; but if thou hast gone aside, being under thy husband, and if thou be

defiled, and some man have lain with thee besides thy husband"—
then the priest shall cause the woman to swear with the oath of
cursing, and the priest shall say unto the woman—"the Lord make
thee a curse and an oath among thy people, when the Lord doth
make thy thigh to fall away and thy belly to swell; and this water
that causeth the curse shall go into thy bowels, and make thy belly
to swell and thy thigh to fall away"; and the woman shall say:
"Amen, Amen." And the priest shall write these curses in a scroll,
and he shall blot them out into the water of bitterness. And he
shall make the woman drink the water of bitterness that causeth
the curse; and the water that causeth the curse shall enter into her
and become bitter. And the priest shall take the meal-offering of
jealousy out of the woman's hand, and shall wave the meal-offering
before the Lord, and bring it unto the altar. And the priest shall
take a handful of the meal-offering, as the memorial part thereof,
and make it smoke upon the altar, and afterward shall make the
woman drink the water. And when he hath made her drink the
water, then it shall come to pass, if she be defiled, and have acted
unfaithfully against her husband, that the water that causeth the
curse shall enter into her and become bitter, and her belly shall
swell, and her thigh shall fall away; and the woman shall be a curse
among her people. And if the woman be not defiled, but be clean;
then she shall be cleared, and shall conceive seed. This is the law
of jealousy, when a wife, being under her husband, goeth aside,
and is defiled; or when the spirit of jealousy cometh upon a man,
and he be jealous over his wife; then shall he set the woman before
the Lord, and the priest shall execute upon her all this law. And
the man shall be clear from iniquity, and that woman shall bear
her iniquity (Num. 5:12–31).

This passage contains a number of highly interesting details
whose analysis, however, would lead us too far afield. Concentrating on the adultery-fertility aspect of the proceedings,
we find that already the earliest students of the Bible, like the
philosopher Philo of Alexandria and the historian Josephus
Flavius (first century A.D.) emphasized that innocently accused
barren women who underwent the Sōṭāh proceedings conceived and gave birth to children. A century or so later

(second century A.D.) the famous Talmudic sage, Rabbi Akiba, interpreted the passage in exactly the same way. Akiba's contemporary, Rabbi Ishmael, however, objected to this interpretation. "If so," he said, "could not all the barren women hide themselves (so as to be suspected and accused of adultery by their husbands), and thereupon, after undergoing the Sōṭāh ceremony, conceive? And if there is one who does not hide, she be the loser? Nay, what is the true meaning of the words 'If the woman be not defiled but be clean, then she shall be cleared and shall conceive seed' (Num. 5:28)? If she gave birth painfully, from now on she will bear easily; if she bore females—now she will bear males; if ugly ones—beautiful ones; if black ones—white ones; if short ones—long ones; if one by one—two by two."

The sages of the Talmud attributed such importance to the fertilizing (or fertility-improving) aspect of the "bitter water" that they stated that a woman who is beyond the childbearing age, or who for some physical reason could under no condition bear children, cannot be subjected to the Sōṭāh ceremony.

They also found a symbolical reference to the two possible outcomes of the ceremony in the use of the dust which was mixed into the "bitter water" (Num. 5:17): "Why did the Torah say, 'take dust for the Sōṭāh'? If she is cleared, she will have an offspring like unto our father Abraham of whom it is said, 'I am but dust and ashes' (Gen. 18:27); if she is found guilty, she returns to her dust [i.e., dies]."

Dust or earth mixed in water is used in ordeals among several peoples who possibly could have received cultural influences from the ancient Near East. Among the Ewe-speaking people of southern Togo, a province to the east of Ashanti, when a wife is childless she goes with her husband to the priest of the Earth. The husband gives certain presents to the priest, who instructs him to inquire of his wife whether she has committed any secret sin. If the woman hides anything she will die as a result of the ceremony; if not, she will conceive. In the course of the ceremony the priest pours holy water over the woman; the water contains palm kernels and pebbles which consecrate it.

The parallel between this Togo ritual and the Biblical *Sōṭāh* ceremony is very close. In both, the childless woman, suspected of a sin, undergoes an ordeal; if she is sinless, she conceives; if guilty, she dies. In the ordeal, water and dust (Bible) or water and pebbles (Togo) are administered. The swallowing of dust or earth without an ordeal, as straight fertility magic, has been practiced by barren women in many places in and around the Middle East: among the Egyptian fellahin, on Sumatra, in southern India, etc.

Ordeal in connection with accusations of adultery has been retained by Islam in a mitigated form. No longer is the wife subjected to the drinking of "bitter water"; a mutual swearing of fivefold oaths is all that the Koran requires of the husband and the wife:

"As for those who accuse their wives [of adultery] but have no witnesses except themselves; let the testimony of one of them be four testimonies, (swearing) by Allah that he is of those who speak the truth; and yet a fifth [testimony], involving the curse of Allah on him if he is of those who lie. And it shall avert punishment from her if she bear witness before Allah four times that the thing he saith is indeed false, and a fifth [time] that the wrath of Allah be upon her if he speaketh truth" (Koran 24:6–9). In this procedure the wrath or the curse of God is substituted for the destructive power of the "bitter water." No reward (such as conception) is indicated for the innocently accused wife. On the contrary, the marriage is in any case annulled, and the woman is separated by a perpetual divorce from her husband, who may never in any circumstances resume cohabitation.

THE LEVIRATE

THE problem of the levirate in the Bible is an intricate one, interwoven as it is with regulations concerning the redemption of the landed property of a man who dies without heirs. In the present context we shall examine only the essence of levirate itself, that is, the law according to which it is a man's duty to marry the childless widow of his brother. In a Middle Eastern society, where there has always been such a great emphasis on progeny and where for a man not to leave his seed behind meant a death almost as personal as his own bodily demise, such a law was bound to exist, its purpose being to "raise up seed" to the childless deceased brother.

Several additional factors, however, had to be present in the social mores of the society in order to make levirate both possible and necessary. One of these was polygyny. Only in a society where a man was allowed to have several wives could he be expected to marry his childless brother's widow irrespective of his own marital status. Secondly, the family had to be patrilocal and extended—only where brothers dwell jointly in one household, together with their father, can one count on the availability of a brother to fulfill the law of levirate. It also had to be patrilineal, because only in that case did it make any sense that a brother should substitute for a deceased brother to "raise up seed" for him. And, finally, only in a patriarchal family order, where the women were disposed of by their fathers and, upon marriage, came under the *patria potestas* of their husbands, respectively their husbands' fathers, could the law function without having to countenance objection or even refusal on the part of the widow. All these conditions obtained in the Biblical patriarchal period, as well as in traditional Middle Eastern society down to the present.

The earliest Biblical reference to the levirate shows it to have been an old-established law, or, better, a binding custom, in the days of the Hebrew patriarchs. Judah, the son of Jacob, had three sons, we read in Genesis 38. He took a wife, named Tamar, for his first-born son, Er. But Er died childless, and thereupon Judah ordered his second son, Onan, to fulfill the duty of the levirate: "Go in unto thy brother's wife, and perform the duty of a husband's brother unto her, and raise up seed to thy brother" (Gen. 38:8). These instructions contain all the essential features of the levirate. Onan's subsequent act shows both the compulsory nature of the custom and the way in which it was expected to be carried out. Onan evidently did not want to fulfill the duty of the levir, yet he had no option to refuse. He had to cohabit with Tamar. He knew that if, as a result of that union, Tamar should conceive and bear a son, the child would be called, not "So-and-so son of Onan," but "So-and-so son of Er." He would be regarded in all legal and family respects the son of Er. This he objected to, and since open refusal in view of his father's instructions was impossible, he practiced *coitus interruptus*, so as "not to give seed to his brother" (Gen. 38:9). The duty of the levirate, however, was regarded as a divinely sanctioned family custom. Its evasion had to bring about severe punishment, and thus the subsequent death of Onan was attributed to an act of God: "The thing which he did was evil in the sight of the Lord; and He slew him also" (Gen. 38:10).

This ancestral story definitely establishes the levirate as a typical, divinely sanctioned duty. The sequel, describing the subsequent incident between Tamar and Judah, shows that, as far as a childless widow was concerned, it was her right to be married to a brother of her deceased husband, or failing this, to one of his other next of kin, such as her father-in-law.

The Deuteronomic codification of the law of levirate recapitulates all the essential features of the old folk custom: "If brethren dwell together, and one of them die and have no son, the wife of the dead shall not be married outside to a stranger; her husband's brother shall go in unto her, and take her to him to wife and perform the duty of a husband's brother unto her.

And it shall be that the first-born that she beareth shall succeed in the name of his dead brother that his name be not blotted out of Israel" (Deut. 25:5–6).

Between the patriarchal days when the levirate was a mandatory obligation and the period of the Deuteronomic code, the original nomadic tribes of Israel became settled agriculturists and town dwellers among whom the old family cohesion underwent a definite weakening. Accordingly, while the levirate was still upheld as an ideal duty, the brother-in-law was now given an alternative which enabled him to refuse marrying his brother's widow: "And if the man like not to take his brother's wife, then his brother's wife shall go up to the gate unto the elders and say: 'My husband's brother refuseth to raise up unto his brother a name in Israel; he will not perform the duty of a husband's brother unto me.' Then the elders of the city shall call him and speak unto him; and if he stand and say, 'I like not to take her,' then shall his brother's wife draw nigh unto him in the presence of the elders, and loose his shoe from off his foot and spit in his face and she shall answer and say, 'So shall it be done unto the man that doth not build up his brother's house.' And his name shall be called in Israel 'The house of him that had his shoe loosed'" (Deut. 25:7–10).

A comparison between this law and the rule followed in Judah's patriarchal family gives us a clue as to the social development that took place among the Hebrews in the intervening centuries. In patriarchal times the nomadic or semi-nomadic extended family was master of its own fate; the head of the family ruled; whatever he decided was unquestioningly followed by his dependents, it being understood that his decisions always conformed to age-old customary law. In this society, levirate was a duty, and there was no other choice left to the brother of a man who died childless. The society reflected in the Deuteronomic law is one of settled agriculturists. They live in villages or in towns with walls and gates. The elders of the place constitute a formalized court of justice which sits at the gate. A disagreement arising between two members of a family is no longer decided by the family head but is brought before the elders to the gate. Even a woman has the right to appeal to them. The consequent weakening of family cohesion now makes it possible for a man to refuse to live up to the old duty of levirate. He still has to undergo a humiliating ceremony administered in the presence of the elders and under their supervision, but after its performance he is free from the levir's obligation.

The story of Ruth and Boaz is placed against a social background similar to the one reflected in the Deuteronomic passage quoted above. Also the legal procedure as described in the Book of Ruth largely conforms to the Deuteronomic law of the levirate. Ruth is a childless widow. Her deceased husband had no living brother, and thus the duty of the levirate devolved upon the next nearest kinsman whose precise relationship to Ruth's husband is not specified. Boaz, a wealthy landowner, was a more remote relative of Ruth's husband. Following her mother-in-law's advice, Ruth washes and anoints herself, and at night, when Boaz is well in his cups, lies with him. Later at night, when Boaz awakens, Ruth, up to that moment unknown to Boaz, asks him, as a near kinsman, to marry her. Boaz, who evidently likes Ruth, is willing, but first the nearest kinsman, who has both the obligation and the right of the levir, has to declare publicly whether he wishes to perform to Ruth the part of a kinsman, or not.

Next day the two men meet at the gate, and Boaz demands of the next of kin in the presence of ten of the elders of the city to declare himself. The man thereupon states that he is not in a position to redeem Ruth's land and to marry her, and, according to the then and there prevailing variant of the custom, he draws off his shoe. Thereupon Boaz declares that he would buy the land left by Elimelech, Ruth's father-in-law, and marry Ruth, "to raise up the name of the dead upon his inheritance that the name of the dead be not cut off from among his brethren and from the gate of his place" (Ruth 4:10).

Before going on to examples which show how the law of

levirate functions in ancient and modern Middle Eastern folk societies, it should be mentioned here that the later Levitical law forbade marriage between a man and his brother's wife (Lev. 20:21; cf. 18:16), and that the Talmudic law, codified in Babylonia circa A.D. 500, tended to discourage levirate marriage and to make instead the performance of the ceremony of the loosening of the shoe obligatory.

Laws of levirate in the wider sense, that is, provisions of marriage between a widow and her husband's next of kin, had existed in the ancient Near East a long time prior to the emergence of the Hebrew tribes, among the Sumerians, the Assyrians, and the Hittites. The closest ancient parallel to the Biblical law is found among the old Iranians of whom Al-Biruni, quoting Tansar, reports that "if a man dies without leaving male offspring, people are to examine the case. If he leaves a wife, they marry her to his nearest relative. If he does not leave a wife, they marry his daughter or the nearest related woman to the nearest related male of the family. If there is no woman of his family, they woo, by means of the money of the deceased, a woman for his family, and marry her to some male relative. The child of such a marriage is considered as the offspring of the deceased. Whoever neglects this duty and does not fulfill it kills innumerable souls, since he cuts off the progeny and the name of the deceased to all eternity." Both the provisions of this ancient Iranian law and its motivation bear a striking resemblance to the Biblical law of the levirate.

Overlapping with the end of the Talmudic period was the pre-Islamic Arab age preceding the appearance of Muhammad, usually referred to as the "Days of Ignorance" (*Jāhilīya*). Tabari, the great Koran commentator, reports that "In the days of ignorance, when a man's father or brother or son died and left a widow, the dead man's heir, if he came at once and threw his garment over her, had the right to marry her under the bride price of her lord [i.e., paid for her by her late husband], or to give her in marriage [to somebody else] and take her bride price. But if she anticipated him and went off to her own people, then the disposal of her hand belonged to herself."

While this is undoubtedly a form of levirate, it lacks the basic motivation of the Biblical law, the raising up of seed to the deceased kinsman. However, the act which in this pre-Islamic Arab custom symbolizes the taking of the woman, the throwing of the garment over her head, is virtually the same as the one which in the Ruth episode is said to have signified marriage: "Spread thy skirt over thy handmaid . . ." (Ruth 3:9) is what Ruth asked Boaz to do. Also in the famous allegory of Ezekiel, God betrothes the maiden Jerusalem unto himself by spreading his skirt over her (Ezek. 16:8). The throwing of an 'abā, or man's cloak, over the head of the bride is part of the marriage ceremony among the Bedouins of the Sinai Peninsula. The groom's father or other relative covers the bride with a cloak saying: "Nobody but so-and-so will be your husband," or, "None shall cover thee but such a one." Among the Arab villagers of Palestine the bridegroom sends a mantle to the bride's father; when, on the wedding day, the bride is conducted to the bridegroom's house, sitting on a camel, she is wrapped in this mantle. A ceremony with a mantle figures also in connection with levirate marriage in Artas, contracted between a man and his brother's widow during the burial of the deceased. Miss Granqvist found six cases of levirate in the village of Artas. Of these, in four cases the first husband had left no child behind. In several cases the motivation of the levirate marriage was not to let the widow be taken by a stranger for wife.

In southern Transjordan, if a married man dies, his brother asks for his widow at his grave at the burial. He turns to her relatives and says: "Give me a substitute in her, let me be cheered up through her." This request is fulfilled. After the burial, the widow's relatives purchase a mantle and present her with it.

Among the Bedouins of Arabia Burckhardt found that "If a young man leaves a widow, his brother generally offers to marry her; custom does not oblige either him or her to make this match, nor can he prevent her from marrying another man. It seldom happens, however, that she refuses, for by such a union the family property is kept together." Even King Ibn Saud of Arabia practiced levirate: he married his brother's widow and adopted his children "as a duty."

In Afghanistan, too, levirate marriage used to be practiced until recently, and it was a grievous affront not to ask the brother's consent if the widow was to be married to somebody else. If the deceased had children, it was considered more honorable for his widow to remain unmarried. In neighboring India—as well as in some parts of Melanesia—only the younger brother of the deceased has the right to marry his widow. In Abyssinia, when a man dies or is emasculated—as so often used to happen in African wars—his brother has to marry his widow, respectively wife.

The closest modern parallel to the Biblical levirate is reported by T. Ashkenazi from the semi-Bedouins of northern Palestine. Among them, in order to insure the continuity of the family, a widow's brother-in-law must marry her, even if she is much older than he, in case the deceased husband left no children behind. Cases were known in which the widow had to wait eight to ten years until her brother-in-law, who was too young, was able to marry her. If he refuses to marry her, she becomes free to marry anybody, but in most cases it is then the turn of another near kinsman, such as her own father-in-law, to marry her. However, if the deceased husband was killed, the duty of levirate becomes strictly obligatory.

MARRIAGE WITH THE FATHER'S WIVES

FROM one point of view, the levirate is merely one specific example of a general type of marriage in which the heir of a deceased man inherits his wife or wives together with his other property. If the man leaves no son behind, it is his brother who inherits him and has both the right and the duty to marry his widow. This is clearly indicated in the story of Ruth where the inheritance of the property and the taking of the wife in marriage are listed as two complementary parts of one and the same right and duty of the nearest kinsman who functions as the *goel*, the redeemer (Ruth 4:5, 9–10).

If the deceased leaves a son, it is, of course, the latter's right to inherit his property. From the point of view of inheritance, the women—that is the wives and concubines—of the deceased constitute part of his property and are inherited, together with the rest of it, by his son. In fact, the taking possession of the wives of the deceased was regarded as the most important act which established the right of the son to the inheritance of his father. To take possession of a man's womenfolk was done in the one obvious manner: by marrying them. This was the custom in early Arab society, in Mecca, in Medina, and in Yemen, as attested by numerous historical cases. The son married his father's wives, with the exception, of course, of his own mother, and thereby demonstrated that he succeeded his father.

This old Semitic custom explains several incidents related in the Bible as isolated cases and not easily understood otherwise. The first mention of such an occurrence—extremely brief and fragmentary—is found in Genesis 35:22. Jacob, now renamed Israel, was encamped at Migdal Eder, when his first-born son Reuben "went and lay with Bilhah, his father's concubine." The text breaks off abruptly with the words "and Israel heard . . ." What happened after Jacob heard of Reuben's act can be gathered from the last words and blessings Jacob pronounced, many years later, on his deathbed: "Reuben, thou art my first-born," the dying patriarch is reported to have said, "my might and the first fruit of my manhood. Thou werest the strongest and the wildest of all my sons. But thou acted shamelessly, therefore thou shalt not be the first any more. Because thou wentest up to thy father's bed, then thou defiledst my couch . . ." (Gen. 49:3–4). From these words of Jacob it appears that his reaction when he heard that Reuben had slept with Bilhah was to curse him and to take away the rights of the first-born from him. This punishment, however, happened to be in keeping with the tradition in the family of Abraham: in every generation, the right of the first-born was lost, or forfeited, by the first-born son, and the main line of the family continued by the younger, or a younger, son. Thus instead of Ishmael, Abraham's first-born, his younger son, Isaac, inherited him; of Isaac's twin sons, the older, the actual first-born, Esau, lost out to Jacob; and now Jacob's first-born, Reuben, was deprived of the same right by his father.

In fact, Reuben, who must have known only too well the history of his family, might have feared exactly this. He might have felt that this family tradition almost obliged Jacob to make one of his other sons his chief successor, the leader among the brothers, and the heir to the family's greatest treasure, the assurance of divine blessing. What could I do, he must have pondered in many a sleepless night, sitting under the clear cool sky of the South Palestinian hill country, that sky studded with innumerable stars, symbols of the rich progeny promised by God to his father, what could I do to prevent what I foresee coming, the passing of my first-born right to Judah, that lion among men, or to Joseph, the son of Rachel, my father's beloved, but by now long dead, wife? There is only one way, he must have concluded after much and prolonged inner wrangling, and that is to invoke an old procedure—not practiced, it is true, in our own family, but nevertheless known not to fail in situations where desperate measures are called for—and thereby irrevocably establish my right of inheritance as the first-born of my father even during his lifetime: I shall go in unto my father's concubine, Bilhah, Rachel's handmaid. Thus all will know, not only that I claim, but that I actually have taken possession of, my father's heirship, and they will have no choice but to recognize me as the legitimate first-born heir and successor of Jacob's house.

Reuben was not the last one in Hebrew history to think thusly and to precipitate defeat thereby. In David's passion-torn family similar thoughts led to similar acts and to similar defeats. When David's son, Absalom, rebelled against his father and at one point succeeded in establishing his rule in Jerusalem—after David had fled from his capital city—he asked the advice of Ahithophel, the wisest counselor in the kingdom, as to what to do in order to establish manifestly the fact of his succession. Ahithophel's advice, immediately carried out by Absalom, was that he "go in unto" the ten concubines whom his father David had left behind when he had fled. The consummation of this state marriage was carried out with the greatest possible publicity: "they spread for Absalom the [wedding] tent on the roof, and Absalom went in unto the concubines of his father in the sight of all Israel" (2 Sam. 15:16; 16:20–22).

It is an interesting concluding note to this story that when David re-established his rule, he continued to maintain the ten concubines in the palace but "went not in unto them, and they were shut up unto the day of their death in widowhood, with their husband alive" (2 Sam. 20:3).

In Ahithophel's words, the motivation for his advice to Absalom was to make all Israel aware that Absalom has openly "made himself abhorred" by his father and thereby to create in his supporters an even greater determination to follow him, knowing that no reconciliation could be possible (2 Sam. 16:21). The true purport, however, of the act of publicly marrying the previous king's wives or concubines was to demonstrate definitely the fact of succession. This was well known and understood in Israel in David's time and no open disavowal could remove this connotation from a marriage between a man's possible heir and one of his wives or concubines. An incident that took place immediately following the death of David illustrates this clearly.

Toward the end of David's life open competition for the succession erupted between two of his sons: Adonijah, who was next in line after the death of his brother Absalom, and Solomon. Upon the initiative of Nathan the prophet, David had Solomon anointed king and recognized as his successor. Adonijah thereupon capitulated and Solomon pardoned him.

Now, following David's death, Adonijah came to Bath-sheba, Solomon's mother, and asked her to intercede with Solomon on his behalf and to ask the king to give him to wife Abishag, the beautiful Shunammite girl who was David's companion and source of warmth in his last days. Although David "knew her not," she was reckoned to be one of his concubines. From the Biblical narrative it is not at all clear what Adonijah had in mind with his request. He may have simply been in love with the girl; or he may have tried to reach his goal—the kingship— in this way, after he had failed in his earlier attempt. Whatever his motivation, Solomon's reaction was typical as to what such an act would have meant in the royal court: it would have been interpreted as a new bid for the succession. When his mother told him of Adonijah's request, Solomon therefore answered: "Why dost thou ask Abishag the Shunammite for Adonijah? Ask for him the kingdom also; for he is mine elder brother . . ." (1 Ki. 2:22). And he immediately had Adonijah killed, and, of his erstwhile supporters, he had Abiathar the priest exiled, and Joab, the captain of the hosts, killed in the very sanctuary.

Marriage with the widows or former concubines of rulers was contemplated or forcefully consummated by personages of high standing other than their sons, with a view to establishing their right of succession. An example of this is contained in the story of the aftermath of Saul's death. When Abner, Saul's general, had "showed himself strong in the house of Saul," (2 Sam. 3:6) he felt that he had good chances of becoming recognized as heir and successor to the king, and thereupon "went in unto" Rizpah, a concubine of Saul's. This act of Abner's evoked very great anger in Ish-bosheth, Saul's son and heir, and as a result of the ensuing quarrel between him and Abner, the latter severed relations with him and went over to David's side (2 Sam. 3:7ff.).

On the other hand, if a pretender succeeded in establishing himself on the throne as heir and successor of the former king, it was his good right to inherit, together with the royal power, also the wives of his predecessor. Thus, according to the words of Nathan the prophet, God gave David his master's (Saul's) house and his master's wives into his bosom (2 Sam. 12:8).

Unions between a man and his father's wives or concubines were still common in Jerusalem in the days of Ezekiel (sixth century B.C.), although by that time they were regarded as an abomination by the exponent of the prophetic morality (Ezek. 22:10) and as a mortal sin by Levitical legislation (Lev. 18:8; 20:11).

Marriage with the father's wives remained a feature of Middle Eastern family life in post-Biblical times for many centuries. The custom still existed in the days of Muhammad, who felt constrained to repeat the Biblical prohibition: "Marry not those women whom your fathers married, except what hath already happened (of that nature) in the past. Lo! it was ever lewdness and abomination, and an evil way" (Koran 4:22).

Chapter 6

THE REVENGE OF RAPE

Traditional custom, which has the force of a binding law, demands in practically all Middle Eastern rural and nomadic groups that the violator of a girl be put to death, while the girl herself is allowed to go unpunished. The Biblical law is less severe in its attitude to the rapist. Only if a man rapes a betrothed girl must he be put to death; if she is not betrothed, he must marry her and his only punishment is that he can never divorce her. The betrothed girl remains unpunished if she was raped "in the field" where she presumably cried for help but nobody heard her. She is put to death only if she was a married woman, or if she was betrothed and the rape took place in the city where she could have cried for help and did not (Deut. 22:22–29; cf. Ex. 22:15–16).

We have to go far back in Biblical history to patriarchal times to find the exact duplication of the outlook on rape characterizing the Middle Eastern peasantry and nomads of today. In this view the rapist (and his kinsmen, who share the responsibility for all his deeds) has to be put to death, wherever he found the girl, and whether she was a married woman, a betrothed girl, or a girl as yet not spoken for who lived in her father's house. In case of a rape the whole family rises as a man to avenge the girl, or rather to wipe off the blot from the face of the family. Even if the family thereby exposes itself to the danger of retaliation, revenge must be taken. Many a protracted blood feud, resulting in the deaths of a large number of people, has its origin in the violation of a single girl.

Charles Doughty, in his classic *Travels in Arabia Deserta*, describes such an incident. It is quoted here in the original inimitable style of Doughty, as he described it when it was told to him in Kheybar, less than a hundred miles north of Medina in Arabia, in the 1870s:

"Okilla, a slave of Marhab, the Emir of ancient Kheybar, had gathered a remnant of his villagers, and was become their sheykh. One year when the Annezy passed by with their cattle, they pitched by the (friendly) Kheybar valleys, as in a place of much water. A maiden of the Aarab entered Kheybar to see the daughters of the town: and there a young man was wounded with her love, who enticed the gazing damsel and forced her;— he was the sheykh Okilla's son! The poor young woman went home weeping;—and she was a sheykh's daughter. This felony was presently reported in the nomads' menzil! and 'It was not to be borne that a virgin should suffer violence!' said all the Beduw.

"The Annezy sheykhs sent to require satisfaction from the sheykh of Kheybar; who answered them shortly that the Annezy should no more water there. On the morrow the town sheykh, Okilla, rode to the nomads' menzil, with a few horsemen, and defied them. The Beduw set furiously upon them; and Okilla fell, and there were slain many of his people. The Beduw now overran all; they conquered the villages, and bound themselves by oath not to give their daughters to the Kheyabara for ever— 'Thenceforward the Kheyabara took bondwomen for wives; and at this day they are become a black people.' The Beduw left the villagers to husband the palm valleys, for the half fruits with them; and removed in the wilderness."

This incident closely parallels the Biblical story of the rape of Dinah and its revenge by her brothers as told in the Book of Genesis (chap. 34). Jacob and his family lay encamped in the vicinity of the city of Shechem in the central Palestinian hill country when prince Shechem, son of Hamor the Hivite, ruler of the land, violated Dinah, daughter of Jacob. The extreme brevity of the Biblical narrative does not allow us even to guess what transpired between Dinah and Shechem prior to the rape, but it states that after Shechem had his will on her, "his soul did cleave unto Dinah, and he loved the damsel and spoke comfortingly unto her," and that he asked his father the king to get him Dinah to wife. Hamor complied with his son's request, went to Jacob, asked for Dinah's hand in marriage for his son, and proposed a general alliance—expressed in terms of intermarriage—between his own people and Jacob's family. Shechem himself, amplifying his father's words, offered to give as much in bride price and gifts for Dinah to her father and brothers as the latter might wish to receive, and added in abject entreaty, "I will give according as ye shall say unto me, but give me the damsel to wife!"

Here was an offer which was more than reasonable, which was in fact extremely advantageous for Jacob's clan. They were newcomers in the land, having arrived only a few years prior to this event from Mesopotamia. They were still a relatively small, and therefore weak, group. An alliance, sealed with intermarriages on all levels, beginning with the highest, with an old-established city-state in the very heart of the country would at one stroke give them security and standing in the land, would enable them to fulfill to the full the divine commandment to become fruitful and multiply, and would give them even a chance to convert the people of an important city in Canaan to the new religion invented by their grandfather Abraham. Yet there were two considerations which made it utterly impossible for Jacob's sons to accept this peaceful solution.

One was of a general nature. Jacob's family was a nomadic group. We know from many reports describing the attitudes of the nomads in the Middle East today that they are in general contemptuous of the settled people, that they abhor the idea of becoming like them, and that they decry intermarriage with them. Earlier in this book it has been pointed out that the only proper marriage in the traditional Middle Eastern view is one between equals, if possible between close relatives, such as cousins. This view is especially strongly adhered to by the tradition-bound nomads, who regard themselves as the aristocracy of the land, and despise and shun the settlers. This consideration must have been the unspoken thought in the minds of Dinah's menfolk. It would have been a disgrace for them if their sister had been married to a "fellah," even though he be a ruler and prince of fellahin. Therefore the very proposal made by Shechem and Hamor was an insult, and a way had to be found to reject it without endangering the life of the whole family.

The second consideration was contingent upon the situation created by Shechem's impetuous act. He violated Dinah and defiled her; this was the gravest of all imaginable affronts to her whole family. Only several centuries later did the Biblical law adopt the point of view of the more tolerant settled society that in such a case marriage can wipe out the shame (Ex. 22:15–16; Deut. 22:28–29). In the uncompromising early nomadic-patriarchal days—as in the nomadic Middle Eastern society down to the present—the stigma of having left unavenged the rape of a daughter could not be erased by a subsequent marriage arranged between her family and that of her violator. According to their feeling and conviction, if they did not shed the blood of the offender they could never look into one another's faces, they could never again lift up their heads, they would be shamed, disgraced, and condemned forever. Attractive as the Shechemite offer was, Jacob's family therefore had no choice in the matter; their way of action was unavoidably prescribed from the very first moment by precept, precedent, and tradition. The only question was how to go about it, how to be able to take bloody revenge for the shameful deed that was committed on their sister, in the face of overwhelming odds represented by the male population of a walled-in sizable city. Evidently only a ruse could help in this desperate situation.

In the Biblical narrative Jacob's sons are represented at this point as speaking with a collective voice and answering

Shechem and Hamor "with guile." We can be sure that the deceitful suggestion put forward by them was not arrived at on the spur of the moment. As soon as the news of the terrible occurrence reached them, they must have gone into a huddle, withdrawn into the council tent, and discussed repeatedly and at length the alternative ways in which they could avenge their sister, who, during all that time, was kept hostage in Shechem's house. Whether Jacob himself participated in these deliberations we have no way of knowing; but modern Middle Eastern examples indicate that, knowing his peaceful disposition, his inclination to compromise and settlement, the sons must have held their meeting in secret, possibly out in the fields, leaving the supervision of their flocks to shepherds or to their own children, while old Jacob slumbered unsuspectingly in his tent to while away the hot midday hours.

Neither do we know whose advice prevailed in the sons' council. But again, modern Middle Eastern parallels of proceedings in the *majlis*, the tribal council, and the subsequent narrative in Genesis, give us a basis to assume that it must have been that of the older full brothers of Dinah, who emanated, not only from the loins of the same father, but emerged from the womb of the same mother, who therefore were closest to the girl and more responsible than the others for her safety and chastity, and whose voices began to assume weight with the passage of years. Their plan was simple but ingenious. It must have been adopted without opposition by the younger ones in the brotherly gathering.

They would state to Shechem and Hamor, it was resolved, that it was against the traditions of their tribe to intermarry with the uncircumcised. "It is not done in our family" has remained to this day the most powerful argument in traditional society against which there is no gainsaying. They could enter into a covenant of intermarriage with the city of Shechem only if its males underwent the operation. It was a minor thing, they must have explained convincingly, in fact not much more than the paring of a nail. It also would have the advantage for the Shechemites to imprint into their flesh the sign of the noble nomadic status and would thus elevate them above the other townsfolk of the country, the Canaanites and Perizzites.

The fact that the Shechemites fell for the ruse indicates that they must have shared with the modern Middle Eastern village folk the view which regards the nomads as of a higher and the settled agriculturists as of a lower social status. These considerations must have played an important part in the Shechemites' willingness to subject themselves to the circumcision, over and above the hope for economic gain, the acquisition of the no-mads' "cattle and substance and all their beasts" referred to in the Biblical narrative as the clinching argument. Nor could the operation itself have been abhorrent or entirely unknown to them—at least no word is wasted in the Biblical story on the manner in which the ceremony was performed or on who performed it.

Jacob's sons, however, knew something that the Shechemites, not having previously personally experienced circumcision, did not know. They knew that, on the third day following the op-eration, fever must set in; the mutilated member would swell up with a painful inflammation, and the patient would be tem-porarily incapacitated by the pain, the fever, and the weakness. This is what they counted on and this is exactly what came to pass. According to the Biblical narrative it took only Simeon and Levi, two of Dinah's elder full brothers, to come upon the city unawares and to slay all its ailing males, including Hamor and Shechem. In reality Simeon and Levi must have been ac-companied by their entourage in fulfilling the bloody duty of avenging their sister. When this was done, all the sons of Jacob joined in despoiling the city, captured its children and women, and enriched themselves at the cost of the enemy in true no-madic fashion.

When Jacob tried to remonstrate with his sons, and expressed his fear that in revenge the Canaanites and Perizzites would band together against him and destroy him, his sons countered with the clinching argument that is used to this day in the

Middle Eastern deserts and steppes: "Can we let our sister be dealt with as a harlot?"

When the rape of a woman is coupled with the violation of hospitality and with murder, passions can fly even higher, and one single such outrage can become a *cause célèbre* resulting in a total armed conflagration and the massacre of hundreds whose only crime is that they belong to the tribe of the original offender. The annals of both the villagers and the nomads in the Middle East contain numerous such occurrences still remembered and retold with great empathy around campfires, in village gatherings, and in urban cafés. Small causes have thus often resulted in such huge consequences, in such mass tragedies that in retrospect the narrator and his listeners are driven to the conclusion that the whole chain of events bears the evidence of the writing finger meting out preordained punishment to the guilty and their kinsmen in one sweeping, indiscriminate stroke.

It is against this background that we must view the Gibeah incident (Judg. 19–21) which resulted in the greatest tragedy in the early Biblical days of the Israelite judges, and as a consequence of which an entire tribe was almost totally wiped out from Israel. It all began with an insignificant incident of everyday occurrence: a Levite, who lived in the hill country of Ephraim, took a concubine from Bethlehem in Judah. His concubine, after a while, left him and returned to her father's house in Bethlehem. Four months later, the Levite went after her and succeeded in persuading her to return with him to his home. On the way back, the man, the woman, and the man's servant stopped over for the night in the Benjamite town of Gibeah near Jerusalem, in the house of a man who happened to be an Ephraimite.

Later in the evening, as the guests and the host were eating and drinking, "certain base fellows" began beating at the door and demanded that the host bring forth his guest "that we may know him"—ominous words, disguising only very thinly what they actually had in mind, namely to abuse the man for perverse homosexual pleasure. In keeping with the rules of hospitality, the host protested, first energetically, then desperately, and only when all this proved of no avail did he choose the lesser of the evil alternatives confronting him and delivered his guest's concubine up to the mob. The rabble, deprived of the special excitement it had anticipated, cruelly abused the woman throughout the night. In the morning she was found dead, hugging the threshold of the house.

The Levite carried the body of his woman back home. There he cut her up into twelve pieces and sent these through all the borders of Israel. The whole country was immediately shocked into action. An assembly was held at Mizpah, and messengers were dispatched to Gibeah demanding that the culprits be handed over for punishment. The people of Gibeah, however, felt that they must stand by their own kith and kin and refused to comply. Then, knowing what to expect next, they asked for and received the support of the entire tribe of Benjamin. After due religious ceremonies and oracular consultations in the course of which all Israel swore, saying: "There shall not any of us give his daughter unto Benjamin to wife," the fighting began. The first two days Benjamin prevailed and slew, according to the Biblical narrative, 40,000 men. The third day the tide of the battle turned, and Benjamin was practically exterminated: out of its 26,700 swordsmen only 1600 survived; or, according to another count, only 600, who escaped into the wilderness of Rimmon. As to the women and children of Benjamin—their fate is glossed over in silence in the narrative, but from the subsequent story it becomes clear that these too were massacred and that nothing but a few hundred young males remained from an entire tribe in Israel.

Not to participate in such a joint punitive expedition was in itself regarded as a crime to be punished by death. After the main fighting was over it was found that one city in Israel, Jabesh-gilead, had sent no contingent into the Israelite camp. Twelve thousand fighters were immediately dispatched to punish the city: every man and every woman "that hath lain by man" was put to the sword; 400 virgins found in Jabesh-gilead were captured alive and given to the surviving Benjamites so that "the tribe be not blotted out from Israel."

The numbers of the participants and of the slain in the above account are so large and round that one cannot help suspecting that some exaggeration—in itself typical of the Middle Eastern way of dealing with figures—must have crept into the narrative. Be that as it may, the proceedings recounted are precisely the same encountered in the Middle East down to the present time, when finally centralized governmental authority put an end in most places to fighting precipitated by private grievances and involving collective vengeance. Where a man suffers an injury and is not strong enough to take revenge with the help of his family alone, he applies to the larger community of which his family is a part. The kinsfolk of the offender, on the other hand, will feel that they are in duty bound to stand by their kinsman, right or wrong. Should they find that he and they are threatened by superior forces gathered in support of the offended party, they, too, will try to obtain help from their own larger kin group. Thus one village may become initially involved in a fight with another village, or one tribal sub-group with another one; in a short time both sides may be joined by related or allied groups, and the fighting may spread like a conflagration over an entire countryside.

DIVORCE

THE voluminous literature on divorce among the ancient Hebrews in comparison with other ancient Near Eastern peoples concentrates for the most part on legal aspects: the similarities and the differences between the Biblical, Egyptian, Babylonian, Hittite, etc., divorce laws and provisions are examined in some of these writings with meticulous care. We are therefore spared the trouble of re-examining the legal basis of Bib-

lical divorce, and can start our own observations on Biblical
and Middle Eastern divorce with a brief generalization:

In the legal systems of the ancient Near Eastern peoples,
including that of the Biblical Hebrews, the right to divorce is
accorded to the husband, as one would expect in patriarchal
societies. The home, the house, belongs to the husband. The
wife is under the husband's effective rule. When he, for any
reason, becomes dissatisfied with his wife, he can send her
away from his house, thereby dissolving the marital bond between her and himself. In practice, however, we find that a
wife, too, was (and still is) able to leave the home of her husband on her own initiative, and to return, in most cases, to the
home of her father or brothers. When such a situation developed, unless the husband was able to persuade her to return to
him, the marriage was dissolved. Also, instances are recorded
in the Bible in which marriage was dissolved upon the initiative
or the pressure of powerful outsiders.

In the older form of divorce—which, as we shall see anon,
has survived in the Middle East to this very day—a man could
divorce his wife by pronouncing orally a brief formula. An example of this is found in the Book of Hosea (2:4–5), where
the prophet addresses his children:

> "Take action against your mother
> Take action!
> Because she is not my wife
> And I am not her husband . . .
> Lest I have her stript bare
> And set out as the day she was born . . ."

The words "she is not my wife and I am not her husband" are
clearly a legal divorce formula. As to the prosecution of an
adulterous wife by her own children and her expulsion naked
from her husband's house, these, as C. H. Gordon pointed out,
are attested in earlier cuneiform tablets as well as in later Jewish Aramaic texts. Also Deutero-Isaiah (50:1), in a later generation, bases a prophetic utterance on the same domestic

situation: a husband addresses his children in reference to the divorce of their mother.

Sometime between Hosea and Jeremiah the requirement of a written bill of divorcement was introduced. In a vision Jeremiah hears God say: "And I saw, when, forasmuch as backsliding Israel had committed adultery, I had put her away and given her a bill of divorcement, that yet treacherous Judah, her sister, feared not, but she also went and played the harlot" (Jer. 3:8). Also Deutero-Isaiah, in the passage referred to above, speaks of the bill of divorcement given by God to Zion (Isa. 50:1). A written bill of divorcement is the central feature in the Deuteronomic (24:1-4) key passage regulating divorce procedure:

"When a man taketh a wife, and marrieth her, then it cometh to pass, if she find no favour in his eyes, because he hath found some unseemly thing in her, that he writeth her a bill of divorcement and giveth it in her hand, and sendeth her out of his house, and she departeth out of his house, and goeth and becometh another man's wife, and the latter husband hateth her, and writeth her a bill of divorcement, and giveth it in her hand, and sendeth her out of his house; or if the latter husband die, who took her to be his wife; her former husband, who sent her away, may not take her again to be his wife, after that she is defiled; for that is an abomination before the Lord; and thou shalt not cause the land to sin, which the Lord thy God giveth thee for an inheritance."

According to this law, divorce can be initiated only by the husband. The Biblical source material, however, clearly indicates that this was not always the case. In fact, in several cases of divorce recorded in the Bible the separation between man and wife (or concubine) came about as a result of outside influences. The first case is that of Abraham and Hagar. Hagar was Abraham's concubine, originally the handmaid of his wife Sarah. It was upon the instigation of Sarah that Abraham, against his better judgment, cast out Hagar and her son Ishmael (Gen. 21:8-14). Next, in the story of Samson and his

Philistine wife, it was his wife's father who actually terminated
the marriage of his daughter with Samson by giving her to
another man, although he excused himself by saying that he
had thought Samson had "utterly hated her" (Judg. 14:19-20;
15:2, 6). Still in the days of the judges, we hear of a case where
a concubine leaves her "husband" of her own free will, and
four months later the husband goes after her to her father's
house in an attempt to bring her back (Judg. 19:1-3).

One of David's wives was Michal, the daughter of Saul.
When David was forced to flee before Saul, he had to leave
Michal behind in his house (1 Sam. 19:12-17), and sometime
later Saul gave her to Palti the son of Laish (1 Sam. 25:44).
This example, as well as that of Samson's, clearly shows that
once husband and wife ceased to share the same roof, the wife's
father had the right to terminate his daughter's marriage by
simply marrying her off to another man. However, as soon as
David was in a position to do so, he demanded and received
Michal back (2 Sam. 3:13-16). Evidently the Deuteronomic
law that a man cannot remarry his former wife if she in the
meantime was married to another man (Deut. 24:1-4) was
not yet in force in David's time.

Several hundreds of years later, after the return from the
Babylonian exile, Ezra the scribe, in his capacity of temporal
and spiritual leader of the people, induced the men who had
married foreign women to divorce them (Ez. 10:3, 9, 17, 44).

The passage of hundreds of years, and even of millennia, has
not resulted in appreciable changes in the Middle East as to
the question of divorce. The Muslim law, the traditional-
religious *shari'a* which is based on the Koran and the Hadith
or oral legal tradition, as well as the *'urf* or local customary law
which still governs the lives of considerable segments of the
population in many Middle Eastern countries and which in
many instances goes back to ancient pre-Islamic traditions,
recognizes only the husband's right to divorce his wife. The
divorce procedure is as simple in the Muslim world today as
it was in Abraham's days: all that the husband has to do if he

wants to divorce his wife is to pronounce a short formula such as "thou art dismissed." This was the form of divorce among the Arabs in the pre-Islamic age, and, as indicated, it reflects a situation reminiscent of that of the Biblical-patriarchal period. The later Biblical development, where a man has to give his wife a written "bill of divorcement" (Deut. 24:1), is not paralleled in the Muslim world.

There is, moreover, one specific provision in the Biblical law of divorce which has its exact opposite in the Muslim law. According to the Bible, if a man divorces his wife, and she becomes the wife of another man who thereupon also divorces her, she cannot be remarried by her first husband. According to the Koranic law (Koran 2:230), if a man divorces his wife, using the triple formula which denotes final and definitive divorce, he can remarry her only if she first marries another man who consummates the marriage with her and then divorces her. It is surprising to find, in the midst of the general correspondences and similarities between Biblical and Muslim family laws, such a singular contrast.

As to the wife's right to initiate divorce, the situation has remained unchanged from the days of the concubine in Gibeah (Judg. 19:2) to the present. The wife can leave her husband and thereby effectively terminate her marriage. If a wife gets angry with her husband, or feels that she can no longer remain living with him, she can go back to her parents or her brothers and refuse to return to him. In such a case, all that the husband can do is to go after her, or send a trusted emissary to her parents' home, and try to persuade her to return. Such attempts at reconciliation are usually accompanied by promises of presents. If she refuses to return, he has to divorce her. Such cases of "desertion" are relatively frequent among the nomads and the fellahin.

Doughty describes how the wife of a petty sheik in the Arabian Desert leaves him several times and goes back to her own family. "The fugitive Beduin wife has good leave to run withersoever she would; she is free as the desert, there is none can retain her . . ." The husband tries to effect reconciliation, and on one occasion asks Doughty to intercede with her and her kinsmen on his behalf.

Among the fellahin of Egypt, if a man maltreats his wife she can go back to her father's house, and from its safety impose her own conditions before returning, such as the gift of a dress or a pair of earrings. Also among the Bedouins of the Sinai Peninsula, if a wife wishes divorce, she runs home to her father's or uncle's tent. The husband can then attempt reconciliation with the help of a judge specializing in law affecting women. In order to persuade her to return, the husband may have to give her some present, such as a ewe, a donkey, a cooking pan, a grindstone, or a sieve, or to erect her tent between two of her relatives' tents. If she refuses to return, he gives her the divorce, but in this case he does not have to pay her the part of the bride price which was retained by him at marriage and which has to be paid over to her if he divorces her upon his own initiative. In Upper Egypt either husband or wife can divorce by going to the cadi, the religious judge, and stating his or her wish.

The life of the nineteenth- and twentieth-century fellahin contains close parallels to the Biblical stories which show that marriages could still be terminated by the simple expedient of the wife being taken away from her husband by her own powerful relatives, as Saul did with his daughter Michal, the wife of David. One case, adduced by Miss Granqvist, is especially interesting, repeating as it does even the motivation of power rivalry that led Saul to take his daughter away from David. In the village of Artas in southern Palestine in the late nineteenth century, Sliman Khalil from the Shahin clan and Ethman Jibrin from the Rabay'a clan had married each other's sisters. A relative of Ethman, named Salem Ethman, was at the time the civil head of Artas, and when he arrogated too much power to himself, a party was formed against him, and it fell to the lot of the Shahin men, among them Sliman Khalil, to kill him. After the murder, the Rabay'a family at once took away their daughter from the murderer, and gave her in marriage to the son of the murdered man. Thereupon Ethman Jibrin was pressured and harassed until he, too, was finally forced to divorce his wife, whom he dearly loved but whom he had received in exchange for his now divorced sister.

The marital history of the village of Artas contains several examples in which it is the wife's father or her brother(s) who demand and eventually obtain her divorce.

Many interesting details have remained unmentioned in this brief comparison of Biblical and Middle Eastern divorce. There is, for instance, the question of grounds which motivate husbands to divorce their wives, and which impel wives to leave their husbands. The Bible in general is silent concerning these, and the law of divorce (Deut. 24:1) contains only the very vague statement that if the wife find no favor in the husband's eyes "because he hath found some unseemly thing in her," he can give her a bill of divorcement and send her away from his house. This general rule stands in curious apparent contradiction to the case treated in Deuteronomy 22:13–19. This passage prescribes the procedure to be followed if a husband hates his wife and accuses her of premarital infidelity: "I took this woman and when I came nigh to her I found not in her the tokens of virginity" (v. 14). If the father of the woman can produce the bloodstained garment (also called "tokens of virginity") and thereby prove the charge false before the elders of the city, the man is to be chastised—beaten, according to Josephus Flavius, the first century A.D. Jewish historian, and the Talmud—he has to pay damages to the woman's father in the amount of a hundred shekels (equaling twice the amount of the bride price of a virgin) and is never allowed to divorce his wife (Deut. 22:18–19). On the other hand, if the accusation proves to be true, the woman is to be put to death by stoning (vv. 20–21).

David R. Mace, in discussing this passage, asks the question, why need the husband go to the trouble and take the risk of lodging such an accusation against his wife when he could divorce her at will without giving any reason? He finds the answer in assuming that in Biblical law certain financial arrangements must have accompanied divorce similar to those found in the Code of Hammurabi. According to that code—several hundreds of years older than the Biblical law in question—when a man divorces his wife he must compensate her financially. Although the Biblical law contains no such provision, the Mishnah—codified some hundreds of years after the canonization of the Biblical scripture—states clearly that in the marriage contract the bridegroom must pledge himself to assign a certain amount of money to the bride in the event of his death or of his divorcing her. Therefore, argues Mace, a husband, if sufficiently unscrupulous, could attempt to get rid of his wife by "an accusation of prenuptial unchastity . . . without cost . . ."

Modern Middle Eastern parallels entirely support this theory. In discussing the bride price (above, p. 58), it was pointed out that the general rule in all those sectors of Middle Eastern society among whom the payment of the bride price is still practiced is that the husband pays out to the bride's father only two thirds of the stipulated bride price at the time of the wedding, while the remaining third becomes payable only in case he divorces his wife, or in the case of the husband's death. This undertaking in itself closely parallels the Mishnaic and Talmudic *ketubba,* or marriage contract. Now, not infrequently, cases are reported of husbands wishing to divorce their wives, yet reluctant or unable to pay the remainder of the *mahr* (bride price) which thereupon would become due. In such cases some husbands resort to trying purposely to make the lives of their wives miserable, for instance by beating them, in order to induce them to run away. If a wife leaves her husband's house and returns to her own consanguineal family, and thereupon the husband agrees to divorce her, he does not have to pay her the remainder of the bride price.

Another ground for divorce was, in Biblical times, and has remained down to the present, the unchastity of the wife. Although the prescribed punishment for a married or betrothed woman who committed adultery was death (Lev. 20:10; cf. Gen. 38:24), there must have been husbands in all periods who, like Joseph in St. Matthew's gospel (1:19), were not willing to make a public example of their wives but were content with divorcing them instead. This is what Hosea did to his adulterous wife (Hos. 2:4ff.), and this is the social background of the prophetic similes of Isaiah (50:1) and of Jeremiah (3:8), who speak of Israel as the adulterous wife who was given a bill of divorcement by her husband, the Lord. In fact, in Jesus' bold reinterpretation of the Deuteronomic law of divorce, he eliminates all other grounds for divorce and says plainly: "And I say unto you, Whosoever shall put away his wife, except it be for fornication, and shall marry another, committeth adultery . . ." (Matt. 19:9).

Barrenness, one of the most frequent, if not *the* most frequent of the grounds for divorce in the modern Middle East, is not mentioned at all in the Bible. Yet there can be no doubt that in a patriarchal society with its enormous emphasis on the procreation of children, a childless woman would be regarded as being useless for her husband and be dismissed. The stories of the patriarchs contain sufficient indications as to the insecurity of the childless woman's position in the household of her husband. Leah's words, pronounced by her in explanation of the name she chose for her third son, Levi, sum up the situation: "Now this time will my husband be joined unto me because I have borne him three sons . . ." (Gen. 29:34). A wife who gave three sons to her husband can be secure in her husband's house and family; she is safely on her way to becoming a matriarch, and can count also on the increasing support of her growing sons. And after Leah has borne six sons to Jacob, she exclaims even more triumphantly, "Now will my husband dwell with me because I have borne him six sons" (Gen. 30:20). This contrasts sharply with the insecurity of the childless woman (Gen. 30:1), who remains her husband's wife only as long as he loves her and wants her.

In fact, the continuation of the marital status with a barren woman was regarded as undesirable and even immoral. Philo of Alexandria, the Hellenistic Jewish philosopher of the first century A.D., regarded marriage with barren women as immoral, and the Mishnah, about a hundred years later, recommended the dissolution of such marriages. The same mentality is expressed in proverbs current to this day in all parts of the Middle East, such as, "A tree without fruit—to cut her down is lawful." A proverb current in the Hejaz recommends even the divorce of a woman who has borne children, once she reaches her menopause: "A woman is like a bag of dates; when full, she is useful in more ways than one, when empty she is of no further use and can be thrown away."

Chapter 7

FAMILY DYNAMICS:
COLLECTIVE RESPONSIBILITY

SEVERAL features of the Biblical and Middle Eastern family can conveniently be discussed under the heading of family dynamics. The most important of these in all probability is the position and function of the family head in relation to the members of his family.

As a consequence of the organic unity within a family, not only is the family head an almost absolute ruler over his household, but he is believed to be intrinsically responsible for the well-being of the entire family. The members of the family must, of course, obey him; but neither is he free to act or do as he wants. His acts and deeds must redound to the benefit of the family and must therefore closely follow and conform to age-old traditional patterns. He may, if the occasion demands, sacrifice a member of his family for the welfare of the entire group, but never can he contemplate doing something which, in the view of the family and of the larger society of which the family forms a part, would be detrimental to his family as a whole.

Great therefore is the responsibility which rests on the shoulders of the patriarch. Not only is he the one who keeps the family together, who makes all the decisions—after due consultation with the mature members of his entourage. Not only must he constantly bear in mind in every act and every word and in his entire deportment that the prestige and honor of his family depend on him. In addition to all this, since he and his family are one body, his moral posture has great and fateful bearing on the family's welfare. If the head man, as a result of proper behavior, finds favor in the eyes of God, his entire family will be blessed. If he sins, his entire family is punished.

When viewed in this perspective, a basic Hebrew legal-religious concept which otherwise may appear strange, and indeed repugnant, to us, becomes intelligible, and we recognize that it represents an inevitable logical necessity. This concept is that of collective responsibility. Upon first reading in the Ten Commandments that God "visits the iniquity of the fathers upon the children unto the third and fourth generation" (Ex. 20:5; 34:7), our individualistic sense of justice is offended. We can only go along with the later Deuteronomic repudiation of this ancient idea: "Fathers shall not be put to death for children, and children shall not be put to death for fathers, but every man shall be put to death for his own sin" (Deut. 24:16; 2 Ki. 14:6). This is the principle to which we subscribe and which is operative in all modern law codes.

But the older view of collective responsibility was a direct outgrowth of living conditions in a patriarchal society. The individual in that society did not exist—vis-à-vis the outside world —as a separate person; he was merely a member of his family. If a family head sinned against God or man, his punishment therefore included the entire body of his family. When Korah and his followers rose up against Moses, God punished them with death, them "and their households": the earth opened her mouth and swallowed them all, including their wives, their sons, and their little ones (Num. 16:27, 32, 33).

According to the ancient Hebrew concept of God, God regarded the entire people of Israel as one large family in this respect: if any leader, king or priest, sinned, God punished the whole nation indiscriminately. When King David held a census of the people, which was regarded by God as a sin, God slew 70,000 innocent persons by pestilence because of the sin of their king (2 Sam. 24:1–15). This incident strikes us as the more cruel, since in the first place it was God's command to David that he should "go, number Israel and Judah" (v. 1). In fact, the later author of the Book of Chronicles took offense at this old tradition to the extent that he boldly substituted Satan for God: according to him it was not God, but Satan, who "moved David to number Israel" (1 Chron. 21:1ff.).

In a somewhat earlier instance, a famine which devastated the land for three years was attributed to the fact that the slaying of the Gibeonites by Saul had remained unavenged (2 Sam. 21:1ff.). Again the nation as a whole was punished for the king's sin.

In the Hebrew view also other nations were merely enlarged families, with the kings at their head. Therefore, when Abimelech, king of Gerar, and Pharaoh, king of Egypt, sinned, God smote their entire house or land (Gen. 12:17; 20:9; 26:10).

Justice attributed to the divine will is duplicated in the human courts of the early days. When Achan was found guilty of a sin, he, "and his sons, and his daughters, and his oxen, and his asses, and his sheep" were put to death (Josh. 7:24–25). For Saul's crime against the Gibeonites, two of his sons and five of his grandsons were delivered up to the Gibeonites to be hanged by them (2 Sam. 21:8–9).

Collective responsibility of the family for the sins or crimes committed by its members has its complementary feature in the collective hurt or damage suffered by the whole family if one of its members is injured. This is exemplified in the Bible in the function of the nearest male relative of a murdered man: he is the victim's "avenger of blood" whose duty it is to seek out the murderer and kill him (Num. 35:19, 21; Deut. 19:6, 12; Josh. 20:5, 9). This avenger is, typically, a brother of the victim. After Zebah and Zalmunna, the kings of Midian, killed Gideon's uterine half-brothers, it was his duty to kill the two kings personally; he could, however, delegate the actual slaying of the two to his first-born son, a nephew of the murdered men (Judg. 8:19–21).

The same socio-legal concepts prevail to this day in Middle Eastern folk society. The nearest relatives of a man, those who comprise his *khamseh*, or five group, are bound to mutual protection, both aggressive and defensive. A murder is an injury suffered by the entire *khamseh*, which comprises all the patrilateral relatives of a man within five degrees; in other words, a man's father and sons; his paternal grandfather and grandsons; his brothers, paternal uncles; his grandfather's brothers; his father's brothers' sons; and his grandfather's sons' sons. All the members of this group are in duty bound to revenge the murder of their kinsman. On the other hand, all the men in a *khamseh* are likely to be killed if one of their kinsmen commits a murder; they all share the responsibility for his deed. A murder therefore is not a matter between the murderer and the state as it is in our society; it is a conflict between two families, and in tradition-bound circles it constitutes very often the beginnings of a blood feud between the two.

Another consequence of the organic unity within the Biblical and Middle Eastern family is the specific position of dependence in which the individual members of a family find themselves in relation to the head of the family and the family as a whole.

In English usage, when we speak of a "member" of a family or of any other group of persons, we no longer feel that the original meaning of the word "member" is a limb, a part, or organ of the body. There is no corresponding term in Biblical Hebrew. But in the actual situation it becomes apparent that the members are dependent on the family as a whole and on its head in the most organic manner. Just as a limb, such as a leg or an arm, has value only in relation to the body as a whole, is useful only as long as it is attached to the body and serves its needs, so a member of the family is valuable and useful only as long as he subordinates his own interests to those of the family, as long as he faithfully serves the family and obeys its commands as expressed by its head. And just as a limb becomes useless when it is cut off from the body, a family member, too, loses his value once he severs the ties between himself and his family.

Conversely, the individual member, under ordinary circumstances, is scarcely able to survive outside the protective framework of the family. Therefore, the gravest of all punishments that could be meted out to a family member who became guilty of a serious crime was to cast him out, to deprive him of his "membership" in the family, to cut him off like a gangrenous limb: it was, at least under primitive conditions, the equivalent of capital punishment without actually shedding the offender's blood which was abhorrent when done within a family.

When Cain killed his brother Abel, God cursed him with a double curse: that the earth yield not her strength to him, and that he become a fugitive and a wanderer. Cain's reaction is typical: he does not waste a word on the first part of the divine curse; but he cries out desperately and repeatedly about the second part: "My punishment is greater than I can bear. Behold, Thou hast driven me out this day from the face of the land; and from Thy face shall I be hid; and I shall be a fugitive and a wanderer in the earth; and it will come to pass that whosoever findeth me will slay me" (Gen. 4:11–14).

The man cast out from his family immediately envisages total destruction and death which, in all probability, are due to overtake him shortly. This is why it was such an extraordinary manifestation of unquestioning obedience and trust in God when Abraham, following the divine call, left, not only his country, but also his kindred and his father's house and went to the land of Canaan (Gen. 12:1). This is why it was such a cruel act for Sarah to cast out Hagar, who had no family on which to fall back (Gen. 16:6; 21:10). To be cast out in the deserts of the Negeb actually meant almost certain death; only a miraculous intervention could save a person there (Gen. 21:14–21). This is why Abraham had to love Isaac exceedingly in order to "send away," not only his first-born, Ishmael, but also all his younger sons, born to him by Keturah, whom he had married after the death of Sarah, and by his concubines (Gen. 25:1–2, 6).

To be cast out from one's family and tribe has remained to this day the most cruel fate that can befall an individual in the traditional sectors of Middle Eastern societies. To cast out a son or a brother from the family means, first of all, to disinherit him, as it meant in Biblical times (Gen. 21:10; 25:5–6; Judg. 11:1–3). But more than that: it means to deprive him of the status which was his due to his belonging to the family. It means to degrade him socially. And it means to deprive him of the only protection a person has in that specific cultural setup against the superior physical power of others: the threat of retaliation. An outcast has no family, nor *khamseh*, no kingroup which would retaliate an injury done to him. He can therefore be molested, humiliated, robbed, and even killed without fear.

THE POWERS OF THE PATRIARCH

PATRIARCHAL power is the next subject that offers itself for discussion in connection with family dynamics. At its extreme, patriarchal power means the father's unlimited power over life and death of his dependents, including his sons and their wives, his unmarried daughters, and his slaves. Examples from the Bible and the life of the nineteenth- and twentieth-century Middle East can be culled at will to illustrate this.

During Jacob's lifetime, we read in the Book of Genesis, a severe famine overtook the land, and Jacob was forced to send his sons to Egypt to buy corn. Brought before Joseph, whom they did not recognize but who knew them instantly, the brothers were given the corn but were required to leave behind one of their number, Simeon, as a hostage. Upon arriving back home, Reuben, Jacob's eldest son, reported the happenings of the journey to his father, including the imprisonment of Simeon and the further demand of the Egyptian viceroy that they return with their youngest brother as well if they wished to effect the release of Simeon at all. "Then shall I know that ye are no spies but that ye are upright men," the viceroy had said, "so will I deliver you your brother and ye shall traffic in the land" (Gen. 42:34).

The apparent unreasonableness of the viceroy's demand makes Jacob cry out in anguish: "Me have ye bereaved of my children: Joseph is not and Simeon is not, and ye will take Benjamin away!" (Gen. 42:36).

Then Reuben uses the sole argument calculated to sway his father: "Thou shalt slay my two sons, if I bring him not back to thee" (Gen. 42:37). The desperate offer is in accordance with the principle of retaliation: if, in consequence of Reuben's action, Jacob loses one or two sons, let him deprive Reuben of his two sons: an eye for an eye, a life for a life, the rights of one father against the rights of another. The notion that Reuben's two sons would have died without any blame or guilt of their own does not at all enter. They are merely pawns in the larger game whose goal is to secure the survival of the family as a whole.

In the subsequent narrative, when the prolonged famine and the acute starvation of the family finally force Jacob to let Benjamin go with his brothers, we find yet another example of the absolute power of the father over his sons' lives. The long hesitancy of Jacob makes it clear that he regarded the sending off of Benjamin to Egypt as a highly hazardous venture. At the end he even says resignedly: "And as for me, if I be bereaved of my children, I am bereaved" (Gen. 43:14). Benjamin at the time must have been a young adult, certainly capable of having a mind of his own with reference to the trip; yet not a word is said about what he wanted or did not want to do. The whole matter was his father's decision; he himself had nothing to say in an issue that concerned his own life or death.

The absolute power of the father over the life and the death of his children is taken so completely for granted in the earliest narrative portions of the Bible that never is there any thought given to the fears, the desperation, or other feelings a son (or a daughter) may have when he learns that he has to die because of a decision of his father. When an external force, such as a famine, or a divine command perceived in a vision, induces a father to jeopardize or actually to sacrifice the life of a child, the decision is the father's, and his alone; the involvement of the son is incidental, he has no independent existence at all of his own, his life which is about to be extinguished is merely a part or an annex of the larger life of the father. The entire matter is handled by the narrator exactly as if he would tell a story in which a man, for reasons of his own, decides to cut off his left hand. Why waste a word on what the hand feels? The classical example that comes to mind is, of course, the story of Abraham's willingness to sacrifice his son Isaac.

When God commanded Abraham to sacrifice his son as a burnt offering on Mount Moriah, he obeyed unquestioningly. The tenor of the narrative (Gen. 22) is to point up the faith of Abraham, his obedience, his willingness to sacrifice his beloved son. The question of Isaac's role in this story, of his feelings, of his—to use a modern phrase—individual problem never arises, is never for a moment considered. There is an exclusive concentration on Abraham's feelings and actions, on his great merit in having obeyed his Lord and in having been ready to overcome his love for his son. But as to the right of the father to do away with his son in order to gain merits and rewards for himself—this is never questioned. The son's life is completely at the disposal of his father to do with it as he likes. The same attitude—the unquestioning assumption of the father's absolute right to put to death a son—underlies also the sacrifice of children practiced by the ancient Semites, the Moabites, Ammonites, Aramaeans, Phoenicians, Canaanites, and Greeks. When the Hebrew prophets bitterly denounced the heathenish Israelite practice of child sacrifice, they therefore opposed a religious custom which was in strict accordance with the deeply ingrained social tenets of all the powerful and ancient civilizations surrounding the lands of Israel and Judah.

The same right—that of disposal over life and death—was the prerogative of the father also with reference to his daughters, as attested in several Biblical stories. The earliest of these is the story of Lot and the two angels who came to warn him of the impending doom of Sodom. After Lot invited the two angels, who appeared in the guise of ordinary mortals, to spend the night in his home, the Sodomite mob assembled in front of his house and demanded that he bring the two men out to them that they may "know them" (Gen. 19:5), that is to say, use them for their homosexual practices. Lot, by honor bound to protect guests to whom he extended his hospitality, tries to dissuade the Sodomites from doing this evil (v. 7), and offers them his two daughters instead: "Behold now, I have two daughters that have not known man; let me, I pray you, bring them out unto you, and do ye to them as is good in your eyes . . ." (v. 8). Apart from the obvious observation that according to this patriarchal concept of honor it was a lesser evil to have one's virgin daughters violated by a mob than to allow a breach of hospitality, one can find here an indication that the father had the unquestioned right to dispose of the fate of his daughters.

That the fate of a woman who was in this manner delivered into the hands of a mob could be expected to be, not only rape and cruel abuse, but also actual death, we know from the story of the Levite in the Book of Judges (chap. 19), already quoted above in another connection, which closely parallels that of Lot and his daughters. The heroes of this story are a Levite and his host for a night. The Levite's concubine had left him and returned to her father's house. The man went after her to bring her back, and was hospitably received by his father-in-law. After several days he departed with his rewon concubine and his servant. On the way, near the town of Gibeah, inhabited by Benjamites, he was invited to stay overnight in the house of an Ephraimite. As the night drew on, "certain base fellows" from Gibeah, who were no better than the Sodomites a few generations earlier, "beset the house round about, beating at the door" and saying, "Bring forth the man that came into thy house, that we may know him" (v. 22)—the very words used by the Sodomites. The answer the man gives is also identical with the one given by Lot before him: "Nay, my brethren, I pray you, do not do so wickedly . . . Behold, here is my daughter a virgin, and his concubine; I will bring them out now, and humble [literally torture] ye them, and do with them what seemeth good unto you . . ." (v. 24). As the result of the abuse to which she was thereupon subjected all night, the concubine died at dawn (vv. 25–28). Again we see that the father holds the life of his daughter in his hands.

The story of Jephthah and his daughter (Judg. 11:29–40) shows the same patriarchal right. Jephthah vowed that if victorious over the Ammonites he would offer up as a burnt offering to the Lord "whatsoever cometh forth of the doors of my house to meet me" (v. 31). When it came to pass that it was his virgin daughter who came forth from his house to welcome him, he nevertheless felt bound by his vow and sacrificed her.

The Hebrew father also had the right to sell a daughter into slavery (Ex. 21:7); and to approve, or disapprove and thereby nullify, a vow made by her (Num. 30:4–6). While a father thus could dispose of the fate of a child of his at will, because of considerations that had nothing to do with the guilt or innocence of the child itself, it was both his right and his *duty* to put to death a son or a daughter who committed a crime or sin which required capital punishment according to the local customary law, or which he himself regarded as deserving such a punishment. When Jacob fled from Laban's house, Rachel took along the teraphim, the household gods of Laban, without Jacob's knowledge. When Laban overtook Jacob and his family in Gilead, he reproached him: "But wherefore hast thou stolen my gods?" (Gen. 31:30). Jacob thereupon denied the charge with righteous indignation, and added: "With whomsoever thou findest thy gods, he shall not live" (v. 32). These were no empty words: it would indeed have been in the power of Jacob to put to death any member of his household for any transgression which he deemed punishable by death.

The most sensitive area in the patriarchal power-and-honor complex was (and is to this day) the sexual morality of the womenfolk. A transgression in this field was punishable by death—meted out by the father, in case of an unmarried daughter; or by the husband, in case of a married woman; or by her father-in-law, in case of a widow. It is the last mentioned case of which an example is found in the story of Judah and Tamar in the Book of Genesis (chap. 38). When the patriarch Judah was told that his son's widow, Tamar, committed adultery and became, as a consequence, pregnant, he decreed summarily, "Bring her forth and let her be burnt" (Gen. 38:24). Judah had jurisdiction over Tamar because she was his son's widow and, having no children, she was supposed to wait to be married to another son of Judah or to another next of kin of her deceased husband in order to obtain a son through him.

The fate which would have overtaken Tamar had she been found guilty of adultery still threatened girls of the nomadic tribes in the Arabian and Syrian deserts in the twentieth century. Alois Musil observed in the course of his intensive study of one of the largest and most powerful tribes, the Rwala, that ". . . many a Rwala girl becomes pregnant before the wedding. As soon as this is noticed by her relatives they try to help her by various means, even if injurious to her health. Should the girl die from an abortion, nobody will ever hear of it, as the women keep silent and the men as a rule pay no attention to matters concerning women. If the girl cannot rid herself of the fetus, she presses her lover to marry her at once, but in case he refuses, or is absent, she often commits suicide. For should her father or brother find that his daughter or sister is with child, he would coax her on some pretext outside the camp, kill her, cut her body in ten pieces, and then bury them. Nobody will take the girl's part, nobody asks the reason, they simply talk of her as if she had died a natural death. The pregnant girl can run away, seek refuge in the settled territory or in a town, etc.

"The girls therefore put a saber between themselves and their lovers at their night meetings, saying: 'I am a maiden! Fear Allah!'

"Only when a girl has been raped will her relatives spare her, but in this case they kill both the violator and the child, and then demand from the murdered man's kin the blood price for the child. The child cannot be left alive for it would have no kin (the father has not acknowledged it as his own), and compensation is asked because it had weakened the girl, a member of their kin."

Also in Transjordan, "If a girl allows herself to be seduced, she is stabbed to death by her father or other close relative. The sister of Talal, shaykh of the Beni Sakhr, failed in her duty with a Druze who was a guest in her father's tent. The Druze, profiting from the darkness of the night, succeeded in escaping; but the guilty girl was stabbed to death the following morning. Among the Jahalīn, a girl or a woman who fails in her duty is conducted into the middle of the camp and one of her near male relatives cuts off her head with a blow of the saber."

Similarly in Oman, in southeastern Arabia, an unmarried girl or a married woman who engages in an illicit relationship and becomes pregnant is killed by her father, or brother, or paternal cousin, but not by her husband. In the neighboring Qara mountains, the woman's life would be spared, but she would be cast out of the tribe and would have to go to the coast to fend for herself. Also among the Egyptian fellahin, if as much as a suspicion is cast on the morals of a married woman she will be killed, not by her husband, but by her father or brother in order to wipe off the shame she brought on her father's house. In Upper Egypt, if a girl misconducts herself before marriage and is discovered at marriage to be unchaste, she will be killed by her own parents in the desert. This is, however, only a theoretical issue, because, as another authority flatly states concerning an Upper Egyptian village, there are no premarital pregnancies. The very early marriage of girls is, of course, the main preventive measure against any premarital misconduct.

Among some noble tribes of the Syrian Desert the sensitivity with regard to a girl's moral conduct has developed to such extremes that even the slightest inclination of a girl toward a young man who, because of his lower status, is unsuited to be her husband, is regarded by her father as sufficient reason to kill her. Fulanain tells the tragic story of such a girl who is killed by her father because he finds out that she fell in love with a young man from an inferior tribe, although the young man has asked for the girl in honorable marriage and has never even met her face to face but saw her only from a distance.

In the patriarchal social order the emphasis on the supremacy of the father is so great that even a slight threat to it becomes punishable by death. This is how we must understand the Biblical law which decrees death to a son who hits or curses his father and, by extension of the same principle, his mother: "He that smiteth his father or his mother shall surely be put to death. . . . He that curseth his father or his mother shall surely be put to death" (Ex. 21:15, 17; cf. Lev. 20:9; Matt. 15:4). Three thousand years have wrought no change in the inviolableness of paternal authority expressed in this law. Père Antonin Jaussen observed among the twentieth-century Transjordanian Arabs that if a son, in his insubordination to his father, forgets himself to the extent of insulting him or hitting him insolently, the father can use his right over life and death without having to render account for his acts.

In fact, the Biblical law went even farther than this in its endeavor to protect the authority of the parents. No such direct affront as hitting or cursing a parent was needed in order to have a son be put to death. If a son was generally intractable, his parents could "lay hold on him, and bring him unto the elders of his city and unto the gate of his place, and say unto the elders of his city: 'This our son is stubborn and rebellious, he doth not hearken to our voice, he is a glutton and a drunkard.' And all the men of his city shall stone him with stones, that he die. So shalt thou put away the evil from the midst of thee, and all Israel shall hear and fear" (Deut. 21:18–21). To our morality it seems outrageous to have a juvenile put to death because of disobedience, gluttony, and drunkenness; in the patriarchal social order, where the authority of the father was the sole basis of law and order backed by no external enforcement agency, where inner cohesion within the family was an indispensable prerequisite for its survival in competition with other families, the putting to death of a rebellious son could have been regarded as the father's duty: the diseased limb has to be cut off in order to save the body as a whole.

These conditions still prevailed in the Middle East in the nineteenth century when Lane observed in Egypt that "disobedience to parents is considered by the Muslims as one of the greatest sins, and classed, in point of heinousness, with six other sins, which are idolatry, murder, falsely accusing modest women of adultery, wasting the property of orphans, taking usury, and desertion in an expedition against infidels. An undutiful child is very seldom heard of among the Egyptians or the Arabs in general."

In fact, the patriarch's absolute power over life and death of the members of his family included the right to decide at the time a child was born to him whether to let it live or to condemn it to die. We know from historical documents relating to the Arab world from pre-Islamic times down to the nineteenth century that often a father decided to put to death a daughter either immediately upon her birth or at a later date. The usual method of putting a newborn daughter to death was to bury her alive in the sand of the desert. Muhammad himself militated against this custom: "When if one of them receiveth tidings of the birth of a female, his face remaineth darkened, and he is wroth inwardly. He hideth himself from the folk because of the evil of that whereof he hath had tidings, [asking himself]: Shall he keep it in contempt, or bury it beneath the dust. Verily, evil is their judgment" (Koran 16:58–59).

In spite of this outspoken condemnation, the old pre-Islamic custom of burying daughters alive in the sand has survived in several places in the Middle East, down to the twentieth century, e.g., among the Beni Sakhr, in Iraq, in the Sinai Peninsula, etc., as well as in some other isolated localities. In keeping with this custom, but in contradiction to the spirit of the Koranic statement quoted above, is an early Muslim tradition, according to which daughters buried alive enter paradise.

Illegitimate children of either sex used to be killed among certain Arab tribes down to recent times. Among some tribes of southern Transjordan, as late as the beginning of the twentieth century, the navel cord was not bound upon an illegitimate child, and it was buried alive in the sand. Among the Rwala, who also maintained the same practice, the motivation was that the child born to a girl who had been raped and whose father was killed in revenge could not be left alive because he would have no kin.

That female infanticide was the father's prerogative also among the Hebrews and the other peoples of Canaan in Biblical times seems to be indicated by a famous allegory of Ezekiel (chap. 16). The prophet compares Jerusalem to a girl child who at the time of her birth was condemned to die—and the only one who could have the right to do so was her father: " . . . in the day thou wast born thy navel was not cut, neither wast thou washed in water for cleansing; thou wast not salted at all, nor swaddled at all . . . thou wast cast out in the open field . . ." (Ezek. 16:4–5).

The same attitude—that of regarding a child merely as an adjunct or satellite of his father and not as an individual in his own right—is attributed in certain early Biblical narratives to God. In keeping with this idea, when David sins with Bathsheba, wife of Uriah the Hittite, God punishes him by causing the child which was born out of their adulterous union to die (2 Sam. 12:14–18).

And again, as in many other cases, divine justice is paralleled by human. When the Israelite tribes found that the men of

Jabesh-gilead were guilty of a crime which deserved capital punishment, they sent 12,000 men to "smite the inhabitants of Jabesh-gilead with the edge of the sword, with the women and the little ones" (Judg. 21:10). This was an example of the *herem*, of the complete annihilation of a guilty or enemy community which would not have been possible without the conviction that women and children are in some mysterious way involved in the crimes or sins committed by their husbands and fathers respectively. Thus was Midian annihilated by the Israelite tribes: only "female children that have not known men by lying with them" (Num. 31:18) were spared. Thus were Sihon's and Og's Transjordanian kingdoms utterly destroyed by them, "the men and the women and the little ones," (Deut. 2:34; 3:3–6) as well as other enemies.

On the other hand, in the patriarchal family setup, the killing of a man by an outsider becomes a crime against the victim's father: it is his seed that is wiped out, it is his line that is cut off, his name that is faced with oblivion. This is the explanation of the statement with which the narrator concludes the story of Abimelech, who murdered his seventy brothers: "Thus God requited the wickedness of Abimelech which he did unto his father, in slaying his seventy brethren . . ." (Judg. 9:56). Over and above the crime of the bloody deed itself, Abimelech committed a sin against his father by wiping out his progeny.

This is the view which underlies both the Biblical and the modern Middle Eastern law of revenge. The bloody deed of murder is a crime against the father of the victim who loses a son; against his brothers who lose one of their ranks; against his other kinsfolk who lose a kinsman. It is they, therefore, who have to take revenge, thereby restoring the balance of power between the family of the murderer and their own family and wiping away the shame and disgrace implicit in the fact of suffering a murder.

SEXUAL HOSPITALITY

IN THE foregoing we have seen a number of examples of the great emphasis put on hospitality in the patriarchal mores. The observance of the rules of hospitality, the protection of the guest against any attack or molestation are supreme duties. Their fulfillment redounds to the honor of the patriarch, their neglect would be an insupportable shame. The patriarchal honor which is here at stake outweighs by far all other considerations which, in other circumstances, would count heavily, such as the chastity or inviolability of the female dependents of the household. The duty of hospitality is, in fact, so much more important than the preservation of the womenfolk even from sexual abuse that in the narratives about Lot and the Gibeah incident we can discover no traces of the conflict which may have preceded the decision to sacrifice the daughters, rather than the guests, to the lust of the mob.

In some places in the Middle East the emphasis on hospitality has been so great that it has entailed the practice of supplying a guest, not only with shelter, food, and protection, but also with a female companion for the night. This custom, which has been reported from various Arabian tribes, throws additional light on the mores and the relative evaluation of hospitality *versus* female chastity which constitute the background of the Lot and the Gibeah incidents.

To begin with medieval documents, Yaqut, the famous fourteenth-century Arab geographer, makes the statement about the people of the town of Mirbat who belonged to the Mahra tribes of southern Arabia that "their customs are those of the ancient Arabs. They are good people but have rough and repulsive manners . . . they have little jealousy which is a result of the customs of the country. Every night their women go outside the town and entertain the men who are not forbidden to them [i.e., would not be forbidden to marry them] and they play with them and they sit with them until most of the night passes; and the man passes by his wife or sister or mother or paternal aunt, and if she plays with another he lets her, and goes to another woman and sits with her as one does with one's own wife . . ."

While the custom described in this passage smacks more of general moral laxity than of specific sexual hospitality, since the men with whom the women "sat as one does with one's own wife" were not guests or strangers but inhabitants of the same town, it provides the background against which sexual hospitality no longer appears as a surprising deviation from the strict rules of sexual morality. Similar conditions prevailed in those days in neighboring Oman to the east, where, in the main town, Nazwa, according to Ibn Battuta, most famous of medieval Arab travelers, "The women are very bad in their mores without the men becoming jealous because of it, or disapproving their behavior." Then he goes on to state that all women, standing under the protection of the prince, give themselves up to immorality, and their closest relatives, even their own fathers, cannot prevent their doing so.

Sexual hospitality proper is also attested from the same period in southern Arabia. Ibn el-Mojawir (who lived in the fourteenth century), in speaking about the el-Hali of the Asir coast, makes the following statement:

"In the east of these countries there is a people called the Bahimiyya [literally: "the beastly ones"] and they come from the Āl 'Amīr who derive their origin from the Sinḥān. When a guest comes to them, the master of the house says to him: What do you want for supper? And he says: this and this. And what do you want for breakfast? and he will give him only what he asked for and desired. And when he ate supper, the man says to his wife: Go and honor the guest! And the woman goes and sleeps between the arms of the guest until the morning, without fear and without worry. And they get up in the morning, and everyone goes to his work."

According to Ibn el-Mojawir, a similar but more restricted

custom was practiced also by the neighbors of the Bahimiyya, the inhabitants of Dhahban, only four miles away, who belonged mostly to the Beni Asad, Beni Rih, Beni Ma'asim and Beni Rufayda tribes. In this locality, "when a guest arrives, they say to him: 'Kiss and rub and bite and embrace [the mistress of the house] but do not enter her, because if you enter her I shall enter you with this sword.'"

There can be little doubt that these customs date back to pre-Islamic times. In fact, at least two independent statements seem to support this assumption. A passage in the *Kitab al-Aghani*, that huge storehouse of ancient Arab lore, was interpreted by no less an authority than Julius Wellhausen to the effect that sometimes the guest of the house was not left during the night without a woman; and el-Mubarrad states that the Hodeylites, when they became Muslims, asked Muhammad that he allow them fornication.

As to the forms of sexual hospitality in recent times, information covering southern Arabia is more ample.

John Lewis Burckhardt, who traveled in Arabia in the beginning of the nineteenth century, reports that "the el-Merekede, a branch of the great Asyr tribe, indulged in an ancient custom of their forefathers by assigning to the stranger who alighted at their tents or houses some female of the family to be his companion during the night, most commonly the host's own wife; but to this barbarous system of hospitality young virgins were never sacrificed. If the stranger rendered himself agreeable to his fair partner, he was treated next morning with the utmost attention by his host, and furnished, on parting, with provisions sufficient for the remainder of his journey: but if, unfortunately, he did not please the lady, his cloak was found next day to want a piece, cut off by her as a signal of contempt. This circumstance being known, the unlucky traveler was driven away with disgrace by all the women and children of the village or encampment. It was not without difficulty that the Wahábys forced them to renounce this custom, and as there was a scarcity of rain for two years after, the Merekede regarded this misfortune as a punishment for having abandoned the laudable rites of hospitality practiced during so many centuries by their ancestors.

"That this extraordinary custom prevailed in the Merekede tribe I had often heard during my travels among the Syrian Bedouins, but could not readily believe a report so inconsistent with our established notions of the respect in which female honor is held by the Arabs; but I can no longer entertain a doubt on the subject having received, both at Mekka and Tayf, from various persons who had actually witnessed the fact, most unequivocal evidence in confirmation of the statement."

In his subsequently published book, *Notes on the Bedouins and Wahábys*, Burckhardt adds a few additional details. He states that the Merekede live on the frontiers of Yemen, and that among them "custom requires that the stranger should pass the night with his host's wife, whatever may be her age or condition." When, in consequence of the abandonment of the custom a two-year drought ensued, they "applied to the Waháby chief (Abd el Azyz) for permission to honour their guests as before, which he accordingly granted."

Information regarding the same or similar customs from other South Arabian tribes (as well as from Middle Eastern population groups in the Sahara and in Afghanistan, cf. below), render the sexual hospitality practiced by the Merekede less unique than it was regarded by Burckhardt.

Count Carlo Landberg collected information on this custom as practiced by several South Arabian tribes of the Datina coast. Concerning two of the mountain tribes, the Ahl Arwal and the Ahl al-Milḥ, he states that the morality of these tribes is lax, and "they do not attach the same importance to the virginity of girls as in Islam. However, a girl must not give herself up to love before the age of fifteen. If, after that time, she sacrifices to the goddess, that is her private affair. The child which she brings into the world, referred to as 'child of fornication' (*walad zanu*) remains with her, if the man whom she declares to be the father does not marry her. Among these

tribes all the men are procurers. The brother leads the stranger
to his sister, the brother-in-law to his sister-in-law. The married woman is exempted—if the husband is in the camp and
if the secret cannot be guarded. For the others—everything
takes place almost in public. The technical term for this ma-
neuver is 'I shall lead you to a woman.' People offer themselves
voluntarily to strangers for this service. This custom is also
practiced by other tribes, like the Say'ar, the Karab, the Dhub-
yan and the Marad to the east of Yemen, and by the Ba Kazim
of the Lower Aulaqi. This supreme sentiment of the duty of
hospitality must have existed in the whole of South Arabia.
I was told that the inhabitants of Asir put a woman of the
house at the disposal of the guest. The same in Central Arabia,
the female slave who serves the voyager must also submit to
his desires of sensuality . . ."

In support of this general statement the following experience
is quoted by Landberg in another volume: ". . . we came to
Bedouins from the Ahl Arwal tribe whose name was Beyt Ahl
el-Sureymi, who are among the heads of the tribe. And they
made us sit down in the meeting place and one of them said
to me: 'Let me lead you tonight to a girl.' And I said: 'Fine.'
And we ate supper, and the Arwali said: 'Let us go.' And I
said: 'Let us go.' And we went, I and he together, and we entered a tent in which there was a girl, than the shape of whose
face and figure from the belly to the heels nothing was more
beautiful. She welcomed us and got up to prepare us something
to eat and she prepared us coffee and rubbed us [i.e., our feet]
with butter and brought us the coffee. When we finished the
coffee the one who led went away and the one who was led
remained. And I had intercourse with her, and I slept with her
until the morning. And I gave her nothing, and if one would
want to give her anything she would refuse. And if she becomes
pregnant she names the one who slept with her, and he must
marry her, or else give her family damages as ruled by the 'Aqil
according to the custom of the country." Landberg remarks
that this South Arabian mountaineers' custom may be the sur-

vival of an ancient lascivious rite in which religious sentiment played a role which, however, was lost by the time he observed the custom. The fact that the Asir tribes referred to above regarded the drought as a heavenly punishment for having given up the custom of sexual hospitality indicates that they must have attributed a religious or magical significance to the custom.

Elsewhere Landberg reaffirms that "that which is known of the Arwal is also known of the inhabitants of Wadi Marran, the Mayasir and the Hasaneh . . . Several hundreds of Datinese confirmed it to me . . . Whenever they ascend the mountains of the Arwal they always profit by their very great hospitality . . . All the Bedouin tribes of the high mountains between Yemen and the Hadhramaut practice the same custom . . . It has to be observed that it is not the husband who acts as a procurer for his wife, but the *muwarrid* (the one who leads the guest to a girl) can be one parent of the husband; there is no shame in it."

In another part of the Upper Aulaqi state, in the present-day Aden Protectorate, a similar custom prevails. "The al-Marāzīq at Jebah, between Hanak and Yeshbum, a tribe of the Mahājir confederation in the country of the Upper 'Awaliq, have a practice which ought to be unique in the world and which has as its purpose the increase of the population. They call it *al-faḥl talaq*, the stallion is free. Everybody may take the girls and use them in any way he wishes. It is first of all the present shaykh, Ṣāliḥ b. Jāz' who encourages this love in every fashion. He has well assured the increase of the tribe which had 200 men and today counts 900. But also, he has almost only bastards, *zinwān*. This facility of love has as its consequence that men marry very late, when they have almost become impotent and when they need the care of a housewife. The girls are very pretty and give themselves to this service of Mylitta with the most perfect grace in the world. The man brings her a small pot of butter and she rubs with it his feet and the legs, which is a general Bedouin custom. Towards midnight, when everybody sleeps or seems to sleep, one proceeds with the act without fanfare. One finds this the most natural thing . . ." Also the al-Ja'ādinah, the Quseyl, the Ba Kazim, the Morqosh, the Ahwari, the Hanashi, the Qeynashi, the Mashari, the Mahtuti, all of whom are nomads, are known to be *muwarridin,* procurers, and also have the practice of "the free stallion." They have a proverb in this connection: "The grazing cattle is free to the wolf."

Also a later traveler, Wyman Bury (Abdullah Mansur), gathered, in the course of his explorations of the Aden Protectorate, that the Rabiz, a vassal tribe of the Upper Aulaqi sultanate, practiced sexual hospitality, and that the Fathani, to the southeast of the Upper Aulaqi border, "owing to decimation by smallpox suspended the marriage laws in favour of all guests of fighting stock and also among their own community."

Southern Arabia is by no means the only part of the Middle East where sexual hospitality was practiced. In neighboring Egypt, Lane observed the same custom among the Bisharin tribe who inhabit the desert between the Nile and the Red Sea: "I ascertained that there are many persons in this great tribe who offer their unmarried daughters to their guests, merely from motives of hospitality, and not for hire." The same type of sexual hospitality is found also among the tribes of North Africa, such as the Ketama, the Amer, several groups of the Kabilia, the Tuaregs of Hoggar; and, at the eastern end of the Middle East, among the lesser and obscurer tribes of Baluchistan. Also on the southern outskirts of the Middle East, among the Shilluk and the Bahima in the southern Sudan, similar customs prevail.

Chapter 8

HARLOTRY

As in other societies with double sexual morality, also in the Middle East prostitutes have always been accepted constituents of the social stratification, in rural as well as in urban life. The Judah-Tamar story (Gen. 38) gives us a picture of the countryside in which a lone traveling harlot plies her trade on the roadside and expects the wealthy nomads to be her customers. In the towns, the prostitutes had their own houses in which they received their visitors. Rahab the harlot had her house at the city wall of Jericho; she could receive there city people as well as foreigners, and was able to continue her trade following the conquest of the city by the Hebrews (Josh. 2:1ff.; 6:25). The most interesting thing, however, in the story of Rahab is that she was able to engage in prostitution, publicly and openly, in spite of the fact that her father was alive, and that she had brothers (Josh. 2:12–13). Evidently her father and brothers—the natural guardians of female morality in the Middle East—could not prevent her from becoming a prostitute. She may have been a widow who chose this way of life rather than to return to her father's house. She lived alone but maintained friendly relations with her family, and saved them from death by gathering them into her house just before the Hebrew tribes attacked and took the city (vv. 13, 18; 6:22–25).

No moral judgment of any kind is passed by the Biblical narrative on either the *ad hoc* harlotry engaged in by Tamar, or on the professional prostitution of Rahab. Similarly, no

moral reprobation accompanies the statement that Jephthah
was the son of Gilead and a harlot (Judg. 11:1). Even when
Gilead's other sons, born to him by his legitimate wife, drive
Jephthah away, they do not castigate him, as one would expect
in a society in which harlotry is regarded as shameful, by referring to his mother the harlot; they merely say: "Thou shalt
not inherit in our father's house for thou art the son of another woman" (Judg. 11:2). Also Samson's visit to the harlot
in Gaza (Judg. 16:1) is referred to without any reproach, even
though Samson himself was a Nazirite, a man dedicated to
God from the womb. The story of the two harlots who quarrel
over the surviving child, and who come to Solomon for judgment (1 Ki. 3:16–27), contains a number of significant details concerning the social position of prostitutes in the days of
the Hebrew monarchy. Two, and possibly more, prostitutes
could occasionally share a house. They wanted children as
much as married women wanted them. They had access to the
king's audience chamber just like all his other subjects.

Further light is shed on the position of the prostitute by the
Levitical legislation which prohibits the priests, the descendants of Aaron, from marrying harlots or divorced women (Lev.
21:7), and which prescribes the death penalty, burning with
fire, for the daughter of a priest who becomes a harlot (v. 9).
It is evident that other, that is, non-priestly, Israelites were not
prevented from marrying prostitutes, and that the daughters of
other Israelites, although warned not to become prostitutes
(Lev. 19:29), were not killed if they nevertheless chose that
ancient trade.

This leniency in the law seems to reflect the actual situation
which prevailed in the latter days of the Hebrew monarchy.
Harlots were an accepted part of the urban society. They
could be seen everywhere, washing themselves in the public
pools (1 Ki. 22:38); passing along city streets, singing and
playing the harp (Isa. 23:16); sitting at the intersections of
streets (Ezek. 16:24–25; Prov. 7:12); or at the doorsteps of
their own houses (Prov. 9:14); calling out to the passers-by

(Prov. 9:15); or parading their provocative attires (Prov. 7:10). The harlot's house, first encountered by the Hebrew tribes in Jericho, became a permanent feature of ancient Israelite city life (Prov. 5:8), where "troops" of men assembled lustfully (Jer. 5:7). Brazenness and arrogance, riotous and rebellious behavior, smooth words ("her lips drop honey, her mouth is smoother than oil"), and seductive glances figure in the harlot's arsenal (Jer. 3:3; Prov. 2:16; 5:3; 6:24–25; 7:5, 11; Ecclus. 9:3–9; 19:2; 26:9).

The later Hebrew attitude to prostitution is expressed in several chapters of the Book of Proverbs and of Ecclesiasticus (Prov. 2:16–19; 5:3–11; 7:25–27; Ecclus. 9:6; 19:2; 26:9). The interesting thing is, as has been noted by David R. Mace, that no essentially moral judgment is passed on prostitution and prostitutes. Barely the faintest traces are found of "the idea that association with prostitutes is morally wrong. Rather the attitude is that of an older and more experienced man, warning another to beware of whoredom (Tob. 4:12), much as he might today advise him to avoid speculation and invest his money instead in gilt-edged securities."

No decisive change occurred in the status, position, and regard of the prostitute in the Middle East from Biblical to Muslim times. In pre-Islamic days there was public prostitution among the Arabs, and traffic with whores seems not to have been considered as shameful even for men of good repute. Just as Rahab's house was identified by a scarlet thread to be recognized by the invading Hebrews (Josh. 2:18), so the houses of prostitutes were marked by a special flag in pre-Islamic Arabia.

Islam introduced a stricter attitude to prostitution. In contrast to the ancient Hebrews, who called Jephthah "son of another woman" when in fact he was the son of a whore (Judg. 11:1–2), in early Islamic times several men were referred to contemptuously as "son of a whore." Yet in spite of the stronger disapproval indicated by such phrases, prostitution has never been abolished under Islam. Prostitutes continued to live in their own houses, as did Rahab; were found at markets and fairs; and frequented the busy streets and bazaars of the cities. Down to most recent times, prostitutes have been found in practically every Middle Eastern country.

SACRED PROSTITUTION

No CLEAR-CUT distinction can be found in the Bible between common or profane prostitution, on the one hand, and temple prostitution or sacred prostitution, on the other. Although the use of two different terms, zōnāh for the profane, and q'dēshāh for the sacred, prostitute, would indicate that in popular consciousness—at least as reflected in linguistic usage—the two were viewed as fulfilling two different functions, it can be demonstrated that the dividing line between them was fluid, and that each one of the two partook to a considerable extent of the characteristics of the other. And this is exactly as one would expect it to be in a culture in which the entire sexual aspect of life was surrounded—as we have seen—by an aura of sanctity. When the sexual powers are regarded as God-given; when the sexual act itself is a divine commandment; when its intended result, the procreation of progeny, is the expression of divine blessing—it is impossible to expect a complete divorcement between religious rite and sexual gratification, even the one purchased for an occasion.

In fact, the satisfaction of physical, bodily needs in a traditionally sanctioned manner and the performance thereby, at one and the same time, of a sacred ritual act, were typical of the religion of the Hebrews in the patriarchal period, as it was of all the ancient Near Eastern religions, and as it has remained to this day in the folk societies of the Middle East, whatever their particular formal religious affiliation. In this view, eating meat is at the same time a sacrifice; tilling the fields, a godly act; building a house, a religious deed; begetting children, a religious duty; and even consorting with a prostitute, something of a sacred act.

A lack of distinction between profane and sacred prostitution is reflected in the oft-quoted Judah-Tamar episode. When Judah sees a veiled woman he believes her to be a *zōnāh*, a profane prostitute. In the agreement as to her payment, in the whole tenor of the narrative, one feels that a definitely profane, businesslike encounter is taking place between a whore and her client of the hour. Yet when Hirah, Judah's Adullamite friend, goes to look for Tamar in order to pay her, he inquires, "Where is the *q'dēshāh* [the sacred prostitute] that was at Enaim by the wayside?" and the local people reply, "There hath been no *q'dēshāh* here" (Gen. 38:15, 21–22).

It would seem that in the early days of the Hebrew tribes, after they had conquered Canaan, and undoubtedly under the influence of indigenous Canaanite practices, prostitutes were attached to local sanctuaries, serving the visitors and pilgrims. Both men and women served in this capacity as adjuncts of the shrines. The words of Eli, chief priest of the Shiloh sanctuary, when he reproaches his two sons for "lying with the women that congregated at the door of the Tent of Meeting" (1 Sam. 2:22–24) clearly reflect the advanced religious sentiment which condemned these practices, not necessarily as immoral, but certainly as idolatrous.

To perform the sexual act in honor of a deity was a religious practice of the indigenous Canaanites and of the neighboring peoples to which the Hebrew tribes inevitably and repeatedly succumbed. One such incident took place in Shittim while the Hebrews skirted the territory of Moab to the east of the Jordan. In the fragmentary and confused account of this occurrence, harlotry with the daughters of Moab, sacrifice to their gods, and "joining up to Baal-peor," are mentioned in one breath (Num. 25:1–3). The punishment, meted out by Moses according to the narrative, was death by hanging (v. 4).

The mentality reflected in this narrative governs also the Deuteronomic legislation in the matter: "There shall be no fe-

male sacred prostitute (*q'dēshāh*) of the daughters of Israel,
and there shall be no male sacred prostitute (*qādēsh*) of the
sons of Israel. Thou shalt not bring the hire of a female profane prostitute (*zōnāh*) and the price of a male profane prostitute (*keleb*, literally, dog) into the house of the Lord thy God
for any vow; for even both these are an abomination unto the
Lord thy God" (Deut. 23:18–19).

It is difficult to fix the date when this negative view on male
and female sacred prostitution was adopted by the prophets
and other spiritual spokesmen of the Hebrews. Throughout the
Book of Kings—which carries the history of Israel and Judah
down to the end of the monarchy in the sixth century B.C.—
we find two facts: the actual existence of the practice and its
complete condemnation as an idolatrous abomination by the
narrator.

Thus we find that, under King Rehoboam, the son of Solomon, many idolatrous practices were maintained, among them
"there were also male sacred prostitutes (*qādēsh*) in the land"
(1 Ki. 14:24). King Asa, Rehoboam's grandson, "put away the
male sacred prostitutes from the land" (1 Ki. 15:12). He was,
however, unsuccessful in trying completely to eradicate the
practice, and thus his son, King Jehoshaphat, had to put away
"the remnant of the male sacred prostitutes out of the land"
(1 Ki. 22:47). That this royal decree, too, was either ineffec-
tive, or became soon inoperative, we learn from a passage in
Hosea, who somewhat later complains that the men of Israel
"consort with female profane prostitutes and sacrifice with female sacred prostitutes" (Hos. 4:14), and from a still later historical passage which states that King Josiah (638–608 B.C.),
in the course of his sweeping religious reform, "broke down
the houses of the male sacred prostitutes that were in the House
of the Lord, where the women wove coverings (literally,
houses) for the Asherah" (2 Ki. 23:7). While the reference in
the last part of the verse is unclear, there can thus be no doubt
that down to the sixth century B.C. male sacred prostitutes
still lived in the Jerusalem Temple, where their services were

available to visiting women. But even after this reform, male sacred prostitution did not completely disappear from Hebrew life, as we learn from a somewhat obscure passage in the Book of Job (36:14).

Thus both male and female sacred prostitution seem to have remained a part of Hebrew religious worship in Jerusalem and elsewhere, down to the Babylonian Exile (586 B.C.).

While sacred prostitution disappeared from Judaism presumably in the fifth century B.C., it remained a part of other ancient Near Eastern religions, and traces of it can be found even in Islam. The hallmark of the sacred prostitute has remained her close association with a shrine or sanctuary, and the availability of her services to pilgrims who visit the holy site was a religious observance. Such a sacred prostitute of the period immediately preceding the days of Muhammad was the famous Kharqā of the Banū 'Āmir tribe, who kept herself for pilgrims and considered herself as "one of the pilgrimage rites." She would unveil herself only before strangers and kept her face covered in the presence of any man she knew. Some of the Banū 'Āmir women used to perform the *tawāf*, the circumambulation of the Ka'ba, the sacred Black Stone, in Mecca, in a naked state, reciting in the meantime obscene verses.

According to nineteenth-century travelers, traces of sacred prostitution were still present at the time in a Bedouin tribe in Syria, while in a village near Aleppo and in a sect near Alexandretta, some kind of Venus service was observed in the eighteenth century.

Down to the nineteenth century in Egypt, prostitutes used to attend "all the great religious and other festivals of which they are, to many persons, the chief attractions." They used to dance or to sit around in the streets leading to the mosques and literally grab the men who were on their way to the religious function. At the festivities connected with the circumcision of boys in Upper Egypt, prostitute dancing girls are still being invited to entertain all those present with their dances and the young men with their other accomplishments.

Just as in ancient Israel respectable men could marry prostitutes, also in Egypt, down to the nineteenth century, sometimes a *ghāziyeh* (prostitute) would make a vow of repentance and then marry a respectable man. The man marrying such a reformed prostitute was not generally considered as disgraced by such a connection.

SEX RULES AND TERMS

THE Biblical and later Middle Eastern rules governing sexual intercourse are based on the idea that all sexual functions result in a ritual uncleanness. According to the Bible, a man and a woman who have had sexual intercourse must bathe themselves in water and they are unclean until the evening (Lev. 15:18). This law has its parallels in Middle Eastern folk custom today. For instance, among the nomads of the Syrian Desert, "both man and woman must have a complete bath after sexual intercourse. This is a precept of religion, and the wildest Badawin must conform to this rule. Even though only a small bowl of water may be available, the whole body must be washed all over." Similarly among the fellahin of Egypt, "after sexual intercourse, husband and wife are enjoined to take a bath in a prescribed way, otherwise they are unclean."

Menstrual blood is regarded by many folk societies all over the world as either unclean, or dangerous, or both. Consequently it is enjoined upon both the woman and her husband not to have sexual intercourse during her menstrual period, and even for some time after its cessation. Occasionally one finds that the fear of menstrual blood is so strong that the husband (or any other person) is not allowed even to touch a woman in her menses, or to touch anything she has touched, or that she must remove herself from the house and retire to a special hut erected for the purpose well outside the inhabited locality.

The Levitical law of menstrual impurity is one of the most severe ones: "And if a woman have an issue, and her issue in her flesh be blood, she shall be in her impurity seven days; and whosoever toucheth her shall be unclean until the even. And every thing that she lieth upon in her impurity shall be unclean; every thing also that she sitteth upon shall be unclean. And whosoever toucheth her bed shall wash his clothes, and bathe himself in water, and be unclean until the even. And whosoever toucheth any thing that she sitteth upon shall wash his clothes, and bathe himself in water, and be unclean until the even. And if he be on the bed, or on any thing whereon she sitteth, when he toucheth it, he shall be unclean until the even. And if any man lie with her and her impurity be upon him, he shall be unclean seven days; and every bed whereon he lieth shall be unclean" (Lev. 15:19–24).

It is interesting to note that the prohibition of intercourse with a menstruating woman had a moral connotation. This emerges from the words of Ezekiel, who lists among the observances of a "just man" that he does not "come near to a woman in her impurity" (Ezek. 18:6).

Similar laws determine the conduct of any woman who has an "issue of blood many days not in the time of her impurity" and of any man who has an "issue out of his flesh." They are unclean for the duration of the issue and for seven days following its cessation, and similarly defile everybody and everything they touch (Lev. 15:2–15, 25–30).

In contrast to the above-mentioned law which merely pronounces a man who lies with a menstruating woman unclean for seven days thereafter (Lev. 15:24; cf. Lev. 18:19), a subsequent Levitical law imposes capital punishment on both the man and the woman who commit this sin: "If a man shall lie with a woman having her sickness, and shall uncover her nakedness—he hath made naked her fountain and she hath uncovered the fountain of her blood—both of them shall be cut off from among their people" (Lev. 20:18).

While no such severity characterizes the Koranic law, it, too,

prohibits intercourse with menstruating women: "They question thee (O Muhammad) concerning menstruation. Say: It is
an illness, so let women alone at such times and go not in unto
them till they are cleansed. And when they have purified themselves, then go in unto them as Allah hath enjoined upon you.
Truly Allah loveth those who turn unto Him, and loveth those
who have a care for cleanness" (Koran 2:222). The same rule
remained a part of the later Muslim tradition.

In actual practice, the Arab woman is forbidden to have intercourse with her husband for a full seven days during the
monthly periods, after which she still remains unclean until she
washes all over. This ritual washing is called "the washing of
the head." Among the Rwala a man must not touch his wife
for three to five days during her monthly period.

It was not unusual in Biblical times for wealthy and pam-
pered women to feel incapacitated by menstruation to a degree
where it was difficult for them to stand up on their feet. When
Laban entered the tent of his daughter Rachel in search of the
teraphim, the household gods she had stolen from him, Rachel,
sitting upon the camel saddle in which she had hid the teraphim, said to him: "Let not my lord be angry that I cannot
rise up before thee; for the manner of women is upon me"
(Gen. 31:35). The excuse was accepted by Laban as a matter
of course.

In addition to the monthly period, a woman is regarded as
unclean, and consequently must not have sexual intercourse,
after the birth of a child. According to the Biblical law which,
as we shall see anon, has its exact parallels in modern Middle
Eastern folk custom, the young mother who gave birth to a
boy is unclean for seven days thereafter, followed by a period
of purification lasting for another thirty-three days. On the
fortieth day she has to bring an offering which results in her
cleansing "from the fountain of her blood." If the child born
to her is a daughter, the period of uncleanness lasts fourteen
days, and the period of purification sixty-six days, so that the
offering up of a sacrifice and the subsequent purification of the

mother takes place on the eightieth day (Lev. 12:1–8). Although the law does not specify it, it is nevertheless clear that during the period of forty, respectively eighty, days, intercourse between the young mother and her husband is prohibited.

Similar rules regulate sexual intercourse subsequent to childbirth in the Middle East today. Among the Palestinian Arab villagers, both the Muslims and the Christians, as well as among the Palestinian Armenians, the mother is unclean for forty days after the birth of a son and for eighty days after the birth of a daughter.

Among the Arabs of Kuwait, as soon as the child is born the mother becomes unclean and her husband must not touch her for forty days. Also among the Rwala of the Syrian Desert and the Bedouins of the Arabian Peninsula proper, the mother is unclean for forty days after childbirth and is taboo for her husband. The fellahin of Palestine explain this prohibition by saying that for forty days the woman's "grave is open." After forty days "her grave is shut again. The bones are together again and her strength returned." Then her husband can again come to her. The expression, "her grave is open," is used in the same sense also in Morocco, where the forty-day period of uncleanness and abstinence is likewise observed.

The phrase, "her grave is open," refers to the woman's body, and to the uterus in particular. According to an early Muslim tradition, Muhammad made the following statement to Ali: "A woman, when she gives birth, goes apart with the child. Her shame is open thus, and then goes together again when the child has come forth. And then the angel Gabriel waves his wings over her and it closes." This takes forty days. This ancient tradition underpins the Muslim law according to which the husband must not have intercourse with his wife forty days after childbirth.

The expression "grave" for the uterus occurs in the Mishna and the Talmud. When the child is being born, the "grave opens," that is to say, the womb of the mother opens. The "grave" begins to open when the woman is placed on the birth stool, or when blood begins to issue from her body, and remains open, according to varying opinions, three, seven, or thirty days, respectively.

Menstruation and childbirth are phenomena of the sexual life cycle of women which incapacitate them temporarily and make sexual intercourse with them illicit and sinful. Other considerations which interfere temporarily with sexual life are based on the belief that the state of impurity engendered by sexual intercourse is incompatible with the performance of certain religious acts or duties which by their very nature require a state of ritual purity.

When the children of Israel were encamped around Mount Sinai and were about to witness the revelation of the law, they were warned by Moses: "Be ready against the third day; come not near a woman" (Ex. 19:15). Only persons who "had kept themselves from women" were allowed to eat "holy bread" (1 Sam. 21:5–6). Men engaged in a battle also had to keep themselves in a state of sexual purity by abstaining from intercourse (2 Sam. 11:11–13). The rules of fasting (on the tenth day of the seventh month: Lev. 16:31; 23:29; Num. 29:7), referred to in the Biblical text only in general terms ("afflict your souls" is the phrase used on several occasions), included, according to Paul (1 Cor. 7:5) and the Mishna (Yoma 8:1), the prohibition of sexual intercourse. In Muslim law, sexual intercourse is prohibited during the annual thirty-day fast of Ramadhan during the day but not during the night, when also all the other prohibitions of the fast become inoperative.

Sexual intercourse, the physical union of man and woman, results in their becoming "one flesh" (Gen. 2:24). The sexual union establishes a tie between the man and woman similar to the one that exists between first-degree blood relatives. Therefore a man is forbidden by Levitical law to have sexual intercourse, not only with his sister, mother, daughter, etc. (Lev. 18:6, etc.; 20:17), but also with the wife of his father (other than his own mother), the wife of his father's brother, the wife of his son, the wife of his brother as well as with a woman and her daughter or a woman and her sister (Lev. 18:8, 14–18; 20:11–12, 14, 20–21).

As David Mace has aptly put it, "the sex relationship has established a mystical bond between the two which makes her a kinswoman without ties of blood."

It is an interesting sidelight on the attitude toward sex among the Biblical Hebrews that, notwithstanding all the importance attached to this aspect of life, practically no sexual terminology proper is found in the Bible. Reference to sexual activities and sexual organs is always couched in euphemistic terms. Thus no word for penis is found in the Bible, but the organ is instead referred to as "flesh" (*bāsār*; Lev. 15:2–3); the same euphemistic term is used also for the female genitals (Lev. 15:19). When the reference is to the genitals of either a male or a female with whom sexual intercourse is forbidden, the term used is "nakedness" (*'erwāh*), which has the definite connotation of shameful nakedness (Lev. 18:6ff.; cf. Ex. 28:42). The same term, "[shameful] nakedness of a thing," or, as usually translated, an "unseemly thing" (*'erwat dābhār*), is used in the Deuteronomic divorce law as a sufficient ground for a man to divorce his wife (Deut. 24:1). Incestuous sexual intercourse is referred to as an "uncovering of the [shameful] nakedness" (Lev. 18:6ff.).

Both the male and female genitals are also referred to as "feet" (Deut. 28:57; Judg. 3:24; 1 Sam. 24:4; Isa. 7:20). Other euphemistic terms for the penis are *shofkhāh*, literally, "outflow" (Deut. 23:2), and *m'bhushim*, literally, "shames" (Deut. 25:11).

When especially great refinement of language is required, none of these terms is used, but instead the name of the general region of the body is mentioned in which the genitals are located. Thus, when Abraham wants Eliezer to render an important oath, instead of saying "Touch my penis," he says "Put your hand under my loin" (or "thigh") (Gen. 24:2).

In fact, only two actual terms denoting parts of the male genitals exist in Biblical language. The testicle, *eshekh*, is mentioned once as an anatomical term in connection with a list of physical disabilities which automatically exclude a priest from the temple service (Lev. 21:20). The foreskin, 'orlāh, is mentioned repeatedly (Gen. 17:11, etc.), since the cutting away of the foreskin, i.e., circumcision, was a very important religious ceremony.

No term proper is found in the Bible for the female genitals. However, because of the religious-ritual significance of menstruation, a term was coined (niddāh) and used repeatedly to denote this state of monthly impurity of a woman (Lev. 12:2; 15:19ff., etc.).

To have sexual intercourse is expressed through the verb "to approach" (Lev. 18:14, 19) or "to lie with" (Lev. 18:22); or to "lie the lying of seed" (Lev. 15:18); or "to go in unto" (Gen. 29:23, 30, etc.) or "to know" (Gen. 4:1). To practice coitus interruptus is called "to spoil [namely one's seed] on the ground" (Gen. 38:9).

The sex act itself is called "lying" (Lev. 18:23); or "lying of a woman" (Lev. 18:22); or "lying of seed" (Lev. 15:18).

The sex act performed by quadrupeds is also referred to only by the euphemistic term of "crouching on all fours" (Lev. 18:23; 19:19).

SEX: SANCTITY AND MORALITY

It is a characteristic of all folk cultures, and especially of folk cultures as conservative and tradition directed as those of the Middle East, that the permitted, the expected, and the duty bound are narrowly circumscribed in all walks of life, and that the disapproved and the forbidden are equally closely delimited. When a man does something in a certain way, he laudably fulfills a sacred duty; if he does it differently, he commits an abominable crime. Perhaps no other field of human life is as heavily surcharged with such rules, both positive and negative, as the sexual one.

We have emphasized above that sex, sexual powers, and the sexual act have at all times been so highly valued in the Middle East that a veritable sanctity has been attached to them. The reverse side of the coin is the equally emphatic horror of all illicit sexual activity.

Licit sexual activity is a sacred duty. It is the greatest joy. The procreation of progeny is the ultimate crowning achievement, the continuation in this world of a man's name and life. Illicit sex, on the other hand, is the archsin, the gravest crime, a transgression which carries in itself its horrible punishment. Not satisfied, however, even with the firmly assumed automatic retribution of sexual transgression, Middle Eastern cultures have developed detailed codes of sexual rules and established capital punishment for their violation.

It can be observed that the greater the sexual freedom enjoyed by a society the smaller the attention paid to sex laws and to their violation by its legal codes and courts. Conversely, the presence of detailed sexual legislation—whether in codified written or in customary oral form—indicates that sex is a vexing problem, that it is a focal concern. Judging from the great preoccupation of Middle Eastern cultures with sex, in both its positive and negative aspects, one is driven to the conclusion that the Middle East has always been a world area of high and intense sexuality, one in which all the cruelty of folk law could not prevent sexual transgressions by those unable to find licit sexual outlets or by those dissatisfied with them.

One of the characteristics of Middle Eastern sexual life, and one which has not only survived in the area itself from the earliest times to the present but which has greatly influenced the modern Western world as well, is the double standard of sexual morality. In Middle Eastern cultures this was an inevitable corollary of the institution of polygyny and concubinage. Where a man could have several wives and concubines while a woman could belong to only one husband at a time, this situation in itself implied a much greater sexual freedom for men than for women. From polygyny and concubinage to irregular or occasional sexual connections between a man and women neither married to him nor owned by him, there is only one step. Therefore, in ancient Near Eastern legal systems, including the Bible, as well as in modern Middle Eastern codified or customary law, no restraints are imposed on either married or unmarried men in the sphere of extramarital or premarital sexual intercourse. Such an act of a man becomes punishable only if the woman involved is married or is an unmarried girl responsible for her conduct to her father or brothers or other next of kin. In such a case the man who has relations with her commits a crime against the husband or the consanguineal next of kin of the woman and is punished by death, either by the legally constituted authorities that be, or by the next of kin, who act as avengers under the traditionally sanctioned customary law. This being the case, the only licit sexual outlet countenanced by popular outlook is for a man to go to a prostitute. If he is fortunate enough to have the means to do this, even if his peccadillos become known, he can still remain a respected member of the family and social group to which he belongs. This was the early patriarchal attitude with regard to men visiting prostitutes, as is clearly illustrated in the story of Judah and Tamar (Gen. 38:15–23).

However, very few of the men who have ever lived or live today in the Middle East have the means to pay a "harlot's hire" (Deut. 23:19). The others, the overwhelming majority, have always had to find sexual gratification in one of the forbidden areas of adultery with married women, fornication with unmarried girls, homosexuality, or bestiality.

Faced with the intensity of his own sexual drive, ancient Hebrew man asked himself the usual etiological questions: Why does this desire drive man to woman and woman to man? Whence did it originate? The answers given are clad, like many another authoritative tradition-sanctioned answer to the riddles of existence, in the guise of historical narrative: Something fateful and decisive occurred in the primordial days of Creation which determined from then on forever the course of human life, its joys and sufferings, its hopes and fears.

God created Woman out of the rib of Man—thus the story goes—she is bone of his bone and flesh of his flesh (Gen. 2:23), she is similar to him and yet different, she is his helpmeet (cf. v. 20), and "therefore a man leaveth his father and his mother and cleaveth unto his wife and they become one flesh (Gen. 2:24).

For the man, the lord and master over his house, his wives, his children, this explanation is sufficient. His desire for the woman does not place him in a position subordinate or subservient to her; to possess her, to quench his sexual thirst in her fountain (cf. S. of Sol. 4:12, 15), to intoxicate himself with her wine (S. of Sol. 5:1) is for him a blessing, a miraculous experience. For the woman the situation is different. She has to pay dearly for the sexual gratification she finds in the attentions of her husband. She has to suffer the pangs of childbirth, she has to bow to the rule of her master. Why is it that, in spite of all this, she is desirous of man, she is willing and even eager to marry, to become a lifelong servant for the short and far-in-between pleasures of sex? Can it be that she does this out of her own free will? Certainly not. Not even a woman, foolish as she is in comparison with man (cf. Prov. 11:22; Eccl. 7:28), could be as foolish as that. It must rather be that she suffers under an ancient curse placed by God upon all womankind when Eve, the first woman, sinned. What was that primeval, but still effective, curse? "I will greatly multiply thy pain and thy travail," God had said to Eve, "in pain shalt thou bring forth children; and thy desire shall be to thy husband, and he shall rule over thee" (Gen. 3:16). Thus did God curse in Eve all the women of all ages.

Be this as it may, man and woman as each other's objects of sexual desire continued to people the pages of the Bible. In some instances, such as that of Jacob and Rachel (Gen. 29:20) sexual desire and romantic love were intrinsically interwoven.

In others, like in the case of David and Bath-sheba, sexual desire flared up at first sight but later matured into love (2 Sam. 11:2ff.; 12:24). In yet other cases, a man's sexual desire, while not yet gratified, was so overwhelming that it broke through all barriers of decency and of honorable custom, yet after it achieved satisfaction it turned into a hateful contempt of the woman whom he had brutally violated—as it happened between Amnon and Tamar (2 Sam. 13:1–17).

Sexual desire and the drive for its gratification have remained primary motivating forces in the life of Middle Eastern peoples to this day. Many a European traveler or resident, who had an opportunity to gain an insight into this side of Middle Eastern life, has commented on the extremely powerful sex drive of the peoples inhabiting the area. Depending on their own upbringing and ingrained attitudes, these observers either condemn what they saw and found, or describe it factually, or else even display a certain appreciation of it.

Edward William Lane, for instance, who studied Egypt in the first half of the nineteenth century, talks with barely disguised disapproval of the sensuality of the Egyptians, as well as of other natives of hot climates, expressed in their indulgence in libidinous passions. Both he and Miss Winifred Blackman, a late representative of Victorian morality, decry the obscene talk which is conducted in Egypt by both men and women, including the most genteel among them, and which, in other countries, "would only be fit for a low brothel." Of the same subject, but in a very different vein, H. R. P. Dickson states that "sexual intercourse is loved by the ordinary Arab above all pleasures in the world. It is the one great pleasure common to rich and poor alike, and the one moment of forgetfulness in his daily round of troubles and hardships that Badawin or townsman can enjoy. Men and women equally love the act, which is said to keep man young, 'Just like riding a mare.' The Arab seems to possess strength above the average for sexual purposes. . . ." And he quotes King Ibn Saud as having expressed himself to the effect that "the most wonderful experience of his life and that above all things worth living for had always been 'to put his lips to the woman's lips, his body on her body, and his feet on her feet.' "

This indulgence in sex to the fullest is part of the cultural pattern. As a psychologically oriented sociologist put it, among the fellahin of Upper Egypt, "a part of the married male ethos is not to regulate his sex desires, but to give them full play whenever the need arises . . . To have sexual intercourse with his wife is a good religious deed. One should not counteract sexual desires but rather stimulate them, and hence the various devices such as special food and aphrodisiacs like hasheesh and opium are resorted to for sexual potency." This sexuality is already emphasized during childhood, e.g., in connection with games which are suffused with sexuality either in the use of obscene language or in the phallic symbols. With the onset of adolescence, however, a very high degree of repression of sexuality sets in as a part of the maturation process, and this is maintained, in theory at least, until marriage, in which full play is given to the accumulated and pent-up sexuality of the preceding years.

These observations made on a twentieth-century Egyptian village scene have a wide validity, and help us to a better understanding of sexuality in the Bible. The attitude of the ancient Hebrews toward sex was the same as that of the Egyptian villagers: a people endowed with a very strong sexuality, they closely circumscribed the forbidden and the allowed in the realm of sexual activity. To keep the people from indulging in the forbidden, sinful sex was surrounded by a heavy battery of religio-legal sanctions: death was the penalty for any breach of the approved sexual morality. Yet, even so, transgressions were frequent, as they are in the Egyptian village whose folk mores still maintain the same sanctions. Without these, given the prevailing strength of sexual desires, the entire social organization would be disrupted and chaos would ensue. Orgies of a sexual nature were the consequence whenever the children of Israel threw off, for a short while, the yoke of the Law, as witness the incidents of the Golden Calf (Ex. 32:6, 19) and of the whoring with the Moabite women in honor of Baal-peor (Num. 25:1ff.). Even in the very Temple in Jerusalem, licentious and orgiastic rites were celebrated at least once a year down to relatively late times. Sexual orgies and similar license were integral parts of many other religious cults in the ancient Near East, and orgiastic celebrations succeeded in surviving in several parts of the modern Middle East in spite of hundreds of years of official Muslim repression. For a religio-ethical outlook, such as that of all Middle Eastern religions, it was therefore of primary, nay, vital, importance to hold sexual passion in check and to regulate rigidly the channels through which it could be allowed legitimate outlet.

The emphatically positive outlook on the value of legitimate sexual enjoyment is the other side of the same coin. The strong sexuality of the Middle Eastern populations, both ancient and modern, is expressed in the positive, affirmative attitude toward sex within marriage, its only legally and morally approved context. Man and woman are not only allowed, they are commanded, to marry. They are not only permitted, they are supposed, to enjoy the sexual act in each other's legally sanctioned embrace. They are, by religious law as well as by social expectation, bound to procreate many children. In brief, what the Middle Eastern mores say to the individual is not only, "You are forbidden, under the penalty of death, to indulge in sex in these and these ways!" but also, "You are commanded to engage in frequent and intensive sexual activity in this approved way!"

This emphatic condemnation of illicit sex and the equally emphatic commendation of legally and morally sanctioned sex in marriage bring with them a similar dichotomy in the judgment of all those female enticements whose purpose is to awaken the sexual appetite of man. If these are displayed by bad women, who wish to entice virtuous, but potentially always fallible, men to illicit enjoyment of sex, they are evil in themselves. If, on the other hand, the same attractions and

charms are exhibited by one's own wife or bride, they are good
and praiseworthy from a moral point of view.

The evil daughters of Zion, who behave like harlots, "walk
with stretched-forth necks and wanton eyes, walking and minc-
ing as they go and making a tinkling with their feet" (Isa.
3:16), cries out Isaiah in deep moral indignation. Yet the same
wicked enticements become blessed charms when observed in
the beloved bride during the wedding celebrations: "Thy
cheeks are comely with circlets, thy neck with beads" (S. of
Sol. 1:10); "Thine eyes are as doves'" (v. 15); "Thy neck is
like the tower of David builded with turrets, whereon there
hang a thousand shields" (S. of Sol. 4:4); "How beautiful are
thy steps in sandals, O prince's daughter!" (S. of Sol. 7:2).

When the adulterous woman perfumes her bed with myrrh,
aloes, and cinnamon and invites a youth to take upon it his
fill of love until morning (Prov. 7:17–18), this is of course
the epitome of abomination for the Hebrew moralist. Yet the
very same enticements are highly commendable and the subject of enthusiastic love poetry when they serve the enhance-
ment of legitimate love between bride and groom: "Spikenard
and saffron, calamus and cinnamon, with all trees of frankincense, myrrh and aloes, with all the chief spices . . . let my
beloved come into his garden . . . I am come into my garden,
my sister, my bride; I have gathered my myrrh with my spice
. . ." (S. of Sol. 4:14–5:1; cf. 5:5–6).

Female beauty, made to arouse the sexual desire in the male,
has remained of the same coinage from Biblical times to the
present in the Middle East. The female beauty ideal among
the ancient Hebrews can be synthetized from scattered passages in the Song of Songs: white skin; eyes like doves'; the
hair black or dyed purple with henna; even teeth; scarlet lips;
prominent nose; rosy temples; long straight neck; firm breasts;
round full thighs; round belly; a figure erect as a palm tree;
and beautiful steps. The ancient Hebrew beauty used plenty
of perfume, wore much dangling and tinkling jewelry, and
looked coquettishly through a transparent veil.

Similarly the ancient Arabian female beauty ideal consisted of a woman who had firm breasts like swelling pomegranates, wide hips, a narrow waist, legs like marble columns, white skin, a gait like a hen or dove, a figure like a palm tree; she was perfumed with myrrh and wore many tinkling pieces of jewelry. In very similar terms, closely resembling those of both the Song of Songs and pre-Islamic Arabic poetry, is the beauty of the bride described in numerous wedding songs, and the beauty of the beloved in innumerable love songs which still constitute an important part of the folklore of every Middle Eastern people.

Rwala love poems, for instance, describe the beloved as having long, thick, plaited tresses; eyes like a pure pool or a gazelle's, black, with long curved lashes; teeth like grains of rice, or like snow, or like pearls; sweet-tasting spittle; smooth cheeks; a neck like that of a glass vessel or a gazelle; breasts rounded like eggs or apples, or a china coffee cup used by emirs; a slender waist; hips—Allah be thanked!—shapely and full; a belly soft and smooth; calves round and plump like the rollers over which the well ropes pass; her whole body is white as ivory and fragrant as costly spice; she has a gait like a young mare or a gazelle; in her nose she wears a ring; and on her legs many tinkling anklets.

While the sex drive—when properly channeled into legitimate outlets—was regarded by the ancient Hebrews as a good in itself, traditional morality unquestioningly subordinated it to a greater and higher good—that of the procreation of children. The sexual powers, implanted by God into man, subserve the great divine purpose of maintaining the seed of Abraham, of bringing the divine blessing of a progeny as numerous as the stars in the sky and the sand on the seashore closer to fulfillment. Therefore it is only fitting that man should wear the mark of the covenant of Abraham stamped onto his organ of procreation. For a man to be a member of the community of Israel he had therefore to be circumcised. But, more than that, he also had to be in the full possession of undamaged sexual organs: "He that is crushed or maimed in his privy parts shall not enter into the assembly of the Lord" (Deut. 23:2).

The male sexual organs are inviolate. According to a Biblical injunction, if two men fight and the wife of one of them tries to help her husband by inflicting damage to the genitals of his opponent, her punishment is that her hand be cut off, "thine eye shall have no pity on her" (Deut. 25:11–12).

The sacredness of the male genitals as the seat of reproductive power is invoked in swearing a particularly solemn oath, both in the Bible and the modern Middle East. When Abraham entrusted his servant Eliezer with the important mission of choosing a wife for Isaac in a faraway land, he said to him: "Put, I pray thee, thy hand under my loin, and I make thee swear by the Lord, the God of heaven and the God of the earth, that thou shalt not take a wife for my son of the daughters of the Canaanites among whom I dwell, but thou shalt go unto my country and to my kindred and take a wife for my son, for Isaac" (Gen. 24:2–4). Whereupon Eliezer "put his hand under the loin of Abraham his master and swore to him concerning this matter" (v. 9). In precisely the same manner Jacob made his son Joseph swear that he would bury him, not in Egypt, but in the cave of Machpelah (Gen. 47:29).

The Hebrew word for "loin" used in these passages (yārēkh) is a general term for sexual organs. The offspring of a man is often called in Biblical language "those who came out of his loins" (Gen. 46:26; Ex. 1:5; Judg. 8:30). The person who is called upon to swear touches the sexual organ of the man to whom he renders the oath while speaking the solemn words; this makes the oath especially powerful.

A similar procedure is followed among the Rwala Bedouins in the Syrian Desert to this day. When a man must be compelled to speak the truth, "the chief springs suddenly at [him] . . . lays his right hand on his belly under the belt so as to touch his sexual organ, and exclaims: 'I adjure thee by thy belt, by thy sexual organ, and by that which lies down to sleep be-

fore thee in the evening to give me a report such as will please
God.' The belt signifies the wife, for it is laid aside when the
man desires to have intercourse with her; the sexual organ
means children; and that which lies down to sleep before the
tent at night signifies herds."

HOMOSEXUALITY

IN DEALING with homosexuality in the Middle East, careful
distinction must be made between the legal position and folk
mores. The law of the Bible treats homosexuality summarily:
it is an "abomination" (Lev. 18:22). "A man who lies with
a male as with a woman, both have committed abomination;
they shall surely be put to death; their blood shall be upon
them" (Lev. 20:13). It is remarkable that while both men and
women are warned against the practice of bestiality, no reference at all is made to female homosexuality in the Levitical
law, nor anywhere else in the Bible. Although female homosexuality must have existed among the ancient Hebrews just
as it did in Greece and as it still does in the Middle East today,
it seems that either it was regarded as a matter of no consequence, or—being an affair of women among themselves—little
notice of it was taken by men. "The men as a rule pay no
attention to matters concerning women"—this observation
made by Musil among the Rwala of the twentieth century
seems to hold good for the Biblical society as well. Similarly,
in the very voluminous nineteenth- and twentieth-century literature on the manners and customs of the Middle East which
contains ample material on male homosexuality, scarcely ever
is there any mention made of the female counterpart of the
practice.

One of the exceptions is Colonel H. R. P. Dickson's account
of Arab life in the Kuwait area. He observed that among the
widows and the sexually starved women there is found a "very
uncommon form of vice" referred to by the Arabs as having

"a negress woman for a husband." Some Negro women, reports Dickson, manage to "get hold of an Arab girl and satisfy her desires by cohabiting and acting the part of the man in intercourse. The method is safe, the woman is satisfied, and no questions are asked. Results for the Arab girl, however, are said to be deplorable in the extreme. She develops a depraved and absorbing affection for the negress, who becomes an overbearing, jealous tyrant and gets her protégée completely into her power."

According to other authorities, female homosexuality seems to be a vice occurring in urban society, e.g., in Mecca and in Syrian towns.

As opposed to the law, in actual practice male homosexuality was rampant in Biblical times and has so remained in the Middle East down to the present day. It may not have been as general as it was in ancient Greece, but the folk mores certainly did not regard it with any measure of disapproval.

The mob in Sodom and in Gibeah was addicted to homosexual practices (Gen. 19:4–8; Judg. 19:22–26), and there is no reason to suppose that the mores of these two localities were greatly different from those of the other Canaanite and Israelite towns and villages. Even the authors of the passages describing the incidents in Sodom and Gibeah, who lived in later days when individuals with a stricter morality may have regarded the practice with abhorrence, have not a word of condemnation for homosexuality per se. What they condemn and execrate is the intended violation by the Sodomite and Gibeahite mobs of the visiting strangers. This would have been rape and, as such, just as sinful as the rape of a woman, and, in fact, worse, because it would have been also a flagrant violation of the sacred institution of hospitality. Incidentally, both the Sodom and the Gibeah incidents clearly indicate that the men involved in the brutalities were bisexual rather than exclusively homosexual in their carnal appetites.

The Koranic reaffirmation of the official Biblical-legal attitude against homosexual practice (Koran 26:165–66)—made in the context of retelling the story of Lot in Sodom—has had as little effect on the actual conduct of the folk as the older Biblical law itself.

The only Biblical story which possibly could be interpreted as a Hebrew counterpart of the Greek *paiderastia* (pederasty), the voluntary love-relationship between two male individuals, is the one told of David and Jonathan. The love between the two young men is described in exactly the same terms and phrases which are used in connection with the love of man and woman: "The soul of Jonathan was knit with the soul of David, and Jonathan loved him as his own soul . . ." (1 Sam. 18:1). "Jonathan Saul's son delighted much in David" (1 Sam. 19:1). As to David's feelings toward Jonathan, these are described in his beautiful lament over his friend after Jonathan's death: "I am distressed for thee, my brother Jonathan; very pleasant hast thou been unto me. Wonderful was thy love to me, passing the love of women!" (2 Sam. 1:26). The reference here could be to homosexual love. The high praise accorded in this Davidic lament to love between two men as against heterosexual love, reminds us, of course, of the spirit that pervades Plato's *Symposium*.

The love story between Jonathan the son of King Saul, and David the beautiful young hero, must have been duplicated many times in royal courts in all parts of the Middle East and in all periods. One example is reported by Mas'udi (VIII:299) from eighth-century Baghdad: Amin, the son of the Caliph Harun al-Rashid, fell deeply in love with a page boy named Kautar. Thereupon Amin's mother, Zobaida (who, incidentally, was Harun al-Rashid's cousin), in order to divert him from this passion, had her most beautiful slave girl dressed in the garb of a page boy, with a turban and a short tunic held together with a belt. Her stratagem was successful, and the female page proved very attractive for Amin. Thereafter, it became the fashion for the rich to keep slave girls dressed in page boys' clothing in their palaces. In fact, this practice has survived in some parts of the Middle East down to the twentieth century. Jewett, the American engineer who lived in Afghanistan in the 1920s, reports that he was once called upon to carry out some repairs in the Amir's harem, on which occasion he was shown around by a young girl who was dressed in European men's clothes of the latest fashion, with her hair cut short. Jewett's inquiries disclosed the fact that there were two such young women in the harem who acted as go-betweens for the harem and the outside world and were allowed to be seen by male outsiders and to talk to them.

This leads us into the realm of actual or simulated transvestitism. The wearing of the clothes of the opposite sex by individuals either actually attracted to members of their own sex or willing to lend themselves to homosexual practices is a phenomenon well attested from the Middle East. Again, as with the actual practice of homosexual love, the evidence is ample as far as males are concerned, and meager and for long periods entirely absent for women.

To begin again with the Bible, there is the Deuteronomic prohibition, "A woman shall not wear that which pertaineth to a man, and a man shall not put on a woman's garment, for whosoever doeth these things is an abomination unto the Lord thy God" (Deut. 22:5). It seems more than probable that the very strong emphasis the Biblical law puts on the prohibition of this practice has something to do with the custom of homosexuals of wearing the garb of the opposite sex.

Bukhari, the famous ninth-century Koran commentator, has an entire section (VII:159) on "men who wish to resemble women, and women who wish to resemble men." These men were called *mukhannathūn*, while the name of these women was *mutarajjulāt*. Not much additional information is available on the women, but we know that the effeminate *mukhannathūn* were in many instances male singers who imitated women in their clothing and external appearance, painted their hands with henna, wore loose, brightly colored women's clothes, and had their hair combed and braided. They were performers-entertainers, who sang accompanied by drums and

probably by castanets as well, and may have had a guild of
their own.

Another name by which these early Islamic entertainers
were known and by which they were still called in Egypt in
the nineteenth century, is *khawal*, dancers. The inimitable
Lane describes these dancers, mostly young men, as follows:
"They are Muslims and natives of Egypt. As they personate
women, their dances are exactly of the same description as
those of the *Ghawazi*; and are, in like manner, accompanied
by sounds of castanets: but, as if to prevent their being thought
to be really females, their dress is suited to their unnatural
profession; being partly male and partly female: it chiefly consists of a tight vest, a girdle, and a kind of petticoat. Their
general appearance, however, is more feminine than mascu-
line: they suffer the hair of the head to grow long, and generally braid it, in the manner of the women; the hair on the
face, when it begins to grow, they pluck out; and they imitate
the women also in applying kohl and henna to their eyes and
hands. In the streets, when not engaged in dancing, they often
veil their faces; not from shame, but merely to affect the manners of women. They are often employed in preference to the
Ghawazi, to dance before a house or in its court, on the occasion of a marriage-fete, or the birth of a child, or a circumcision; and frequently perform at public festivals.

"There is in Cairo, another class of male dancers, young men
and boys, whose performances, dress, and general appearance
are almost exactly similar to those of the *khawals*; but who
are distinguished by a different appellation, which is '*Gink*'; a
term that is Turkish, and has a vulgar signification which aptly
expresses their character. They are generally Jews, Armenians,
Greeks, and Turks."

The *ghawazi*, referred to in this passage, are dancing girls,
professed prostitutes, who, again according to Lane, "are not
infrequently introduced into the harems of the wealthy, not
merely to entertain the ladies with their dances, but to teach
them their voluptuous arts; and even indecent puppets are

sometimes brought into such harems for the amusement of the inmates." Moreover, the women of the harems were also allowed to view, from behind their windows of wooden latticework, the voluptuous dances of the effeminate *khawals*.

Another profession which called for the donning of female attire by men was that of acting in the popular and vulgar plays. These players were called *mohabbazīn* and they performed, either in public places in Cairo or in the houses of the wealthy, at the festivals preceding weddings and circumcisions. The actors were only men and boys, the boys performing the parts of women.

Boys in female garb formed a part of the rich men's harems in Afghanistan down to the nineteenth century and in Bukhara even in the twentieth. We have it on the authority of Sir Richard Burton that "the Afghans are commercial travellers on a large scale and each caravan is accompanied by a number of boys and lads almost in women's attire, with kohl'd eyes and rouged cheeks, long tresses and hennaed fingers and toes, riding luxuriously in *Kajawas* or camel-panniers: they are called *Kuch-i safari*, or travelling wives, and the husbands trudge patiently by their sides." When the Khan of Bukhara had to flee his country in 1920, he had to leave his immense riches behind, but it is on record that he succeeded in taking with him both his female and boy harems.

One has to distinguish between these cases of merely external assumption of female attire and cosmetics on the one hand and the psychologically conditioned acquisition of a female character which reportedly has occasionally occurred among Palestinian dervishes. Baldensperger states that a dervish may become a female saint, *waliyeh*, and "then sits among the women as he is for the moment changed into a woman." He goes on to explain that saintliness and femininity are regarded as being somewhat akin: "the woman is considered in many instances holy, as being the mother of mankind, carrying no arms, and often suffering beating, baking the bread, entering the oven" which in itself is regarded a *wali* or saint.

To return once more to the subject of homosexuality without the concomitant of female attire, the general statement can be made that neither in the Middle Ages nor in modern times has the practice been opposed by popular opinion. This can be clearly established from the stories contained in the great medieval collection of Arabic folklore known as the *Arabian Nights*, in which homosexual love between men is spoken of in the same matter-of-fact tone in which heterosexual love is described, and from the tales still current among the simple folk in many Middle Eastern countries. One of the latter, for instance, heard among the Muntafiq tribes of the Lower Euphrates region in Iraq in the 1940s by C. G. Campbell, tells about the son of the Amir who was wont to spend his days in the desert in a happy twosome with the son of the Wazir, "in the pleasures of friendship and companionship," and whose escort, "six Circassian slaves, youths of great beauty," became so jealous of their master that they plotted the destruction of the son of the Wazir. At the same time the story makes it clear that both boys desired and enjoyed the love of women as well, and this appears to be the general situation in all those Middle Eastern societies in which homosexual love is practiced. Strictly speaking, therefore, these societies or individuals are bisexual rather than homosexual, as were the men of Sodom and Gibeah.

One of the places in which local traditions surviving from antiquity have strongly favored these bisexual practices is the oasis of Siwah in the Western Desert of Egypt, close to the Libyan frontier. In antiquity, this oasis was the site of a Roman sanctuary dedicated to Jupiter Amon, and it has preserved many archaic features in its culture down to the present day. As recently as a few decades ago, marriages used to be celebrated here between men and boys as well as between men and women. "The feast of marrying a boy was celebrated with great pomp, and the money paid for a boy sometimes amounted to fifteen pounds, while the money paid for a woman was little over one pound, besides the clothes which do not exceed two or three pounds for this abnormal marriage." Marriage to a boy has become subsequently outlawed, but the practice of pederasty has nevertheless continued as an accepted and overt feature of the local culture. In fact, all the reports on Siwah— and we happen to have quite a number of them dating from the twentieth century—agree on one point, and this is that the passion of men for boys in Siwah is greater than their passion for women, and that consequently jealousies over boys flare much more violently than jealousies over women. "They will kill each other for a boy; never for a woman," says Maugham. As to the women's reaction to this situation, Count Khun de Prorok, who visited Siwah in the 1920s, tells us that "the women were frantic by the neglect shown to them. Homosexuality was not only rampant, it was raging, and the usurping boys went in danger of their lives from the women."

The anthropologist, Walter Cline, who studied Siwah in 1926–27 in the course of a field trip, found that "all normal Siwan men and boys practice sodomy . . . Among themselves the natives are not ashamed of this; they talk about it as openly as they talk about love of women, and many, if not most of their fights arise from homosexual competition . . . Men rent boys for five or ten piastres a night . . . Prominent men lend their sons to each other. All Siwans know the matings which have taken place among their sheikhs and their sheihks' sons . . . Most of the boys used in sodomy are between twelve and eighteen years of age . . . In many but not in most cases the boy is the active rather than the passive agent."

Both Maugham and Prorok described in colorful details the public orgies held in honor of local saints in Siwah. At the climax, "gorged and inflamed, brains and bodies fired, men and women, and men and men, with bodies interlaced thrust and retreated, fell to the ground, or grappled and fought in a frenzied hold . . ." In this connection it must be stated that these orgiastic rites are definitely Siwan and African, and not Middle Eastern. The traditional Middle Eastern folk mores countenance homosexual love, as long as it is practiced in secret

with no witnesses present, but they would never condone public orgies, whether of a homosexual or a heterosexual character.
Public orgies, it is true, were a part of ancient Near Eastern
cultures and religious cults, but they were first opposed by the
Hebrew prophets and legislators, and a thousand years later
practically eliminated by the religious zeal of the early con-
verts to Islam. Only in a few outlying and marginally located
places, like Siwah and other oases in the Sahara, have such
age-old religious rites as public orgies survived, reinforced as
they were by African influences from the south. In other parts
of the Middle East, all that can be observed in public and taken
as an indication of homosexual practices is the frequently seen
picture of two men walking side by side in the streets with
their little fingers intertwined.

BESTIALITY

G. ROBINSON LEES, a keen observer of Palestinian Arab folk
life in the beginning of the twentieth century, states: "The
nomad offence of lying with the cattle (Lev. 20:15) and the
lewd conversation of the men employed in looking after them
(Gen. 37:2) depict the ordinary features of pastoral life."
The same was reported by Doughty of the Arabian nomads:
". . . lying with cattle . . . in Arabia . . . is but a villainous
mock, and which the elder sort acknowledge with groans and
cursing." Also among the Egyptian villagers "jokes about sexual pleasure from animals are not uncommon amongst the
adolescents and young men."

Bestiality occurs rarely among the Rwala Bedouins, occasionally in Central Arabia, and quite frequently among the
semi-Bedouins of Northern Palestine and in Mecca. In Morocco, intercourse with she-asses is practiced by young boys in
order to make the penis grow. In the case of grown-up men
bestiality is despised or ridiculed, although a man can do it
with impunity with his own animals.

The practice of bestiality is as old in the area as Middle Eastern culture itself. It was repeatedly prohibited by legislation
but continued nevertheless to constitute an "ordinary feature"
of life, especially among the pastoral nomadic tribes for whom
it has always been very difficult to obtain normal heterosexual
outlets.

The Hittite law, which antedates the Bible by several centuries, prescribes the death penalty for sexual intercourse with
an animal, but allows the king to pardon the offender. Uncon-
ditional death is prescribed for it by the Bible: "Whosoever
lieth with a beast shall surely be put to death" (Ex. 22:18).
"Thou shalt not lie with any beast to defile thyself therewith;
neither shall any woman stand before a beast to lie down
thereto; it is a perversion" (Lev. 18:23). "If a man lie with
a beast, he shall surely be put to death; and ye shall slay the
beast. And if a woman approach unto any beast and lie down
thereto, thou shalt kill the woman and the beast; they shall
surely be put to death, their blood shall be upon them" (Lev.
20:15–16).

Two of the passages cited above are followed by the general comment that the nations which God cast out before the
Israelites from Canaan were guilty of these abominations (Lev.
18:24–25; 20:23). One of the main intents of the law, therefore, appears to be to prevent the children of Israel from following the customs of the heathen Canaanites.

However, what the law denies, the lore confirms. Legend and
story know that when no women are available men will try to
quench their sexual thirst with animals even though these be
but unsatisfactory substitutes. They know that in the life of
many a nomad lad sexual experience starts with animals from
which he graduates only later to normal sex relations with a
wife. This is what happened, ancient stories and epics tell us,
to early man.

Ugaritic mythology (fifteenth century B.C.) tells of the god
Baal copulating with a heifer. According to the Babylonian
Gilgamesh epic, the hero Enkidu had in the beginning sexual

relations with animals until he was enticed away from his animal companions by intercourse with a sacred female prostitute, the Babylonian equivalent of the Biblical *q'dēshāh*.

In exactly the same sense does Rabbi Eleazar, a Talmudic sage, interpret the Biblical story of the creation of Eve. After God had created Adam, we read in the Book of Genesis, he said, "It is not good that the man should be alone: I will make him a helpmeet for him." Thereupon God formed out of the ground "every beast of the field and every fowl of the air, and brought them unto the man to see what he would call them . . ." Evidently the ancient Hebrew narrator presupposes here that one of the animals could have proved satisfactory for Adam to become his helpmeet. However, among all the animals "for Adam there was not found a helpmeet for him." The first series of experiments proved unsuccessful. Thereupon God caused a deep sleep to fall upon Adam and of one of his ribs made a woman and presented her to Adam. "This time," Adam immediately exclaimed, "this is bone of my bones and flesh of my flesh . . ." (Gen. 2:23). It is to this last verse that Rabbi Eleazar appends his comment: "This teaches us," he says, "that Adam had intercourse with all the animals and all the beasts, but he was satisfied only when he had intercourse with Eve."

To the foregoing can be added that, according to Ugaritic mythology, the sacred marriage between Baal and a cow, which resulted in the birth of a child named Mes or Mos, had a definitely ritual character. This detail contributes to our understanding of the vehemence of the Biblical prohibition of bestiality: if the practice is condemned on moral grounds alone, it is doubly condemned when it is associated with a heathen cult.

Chapter 9

PRENATAL FORMATION AND INFLUENCES

AMONG many peoples the belief in prenatal influences on the child is still strong. What the mother does, sees, experiences, eats, drinks, etc., is believed to have a direct effect on the child's form, size, shape, color, character, abilities. In the Middle East, these beliefs are present in all social classes, and in a pronounced form among the tradition-bound sectors. To mention only two examples, the Palestinian Arab villagers believe that if the woman is not pure at the time she has sexual intercourse with her husband, the child she conceives will be leprous or syphilitic or will have a bad smell all his life. If a pregnant woman craves something and does not get it, and at that moment touches her own body, her child will have a mark on the same spot.

We have no direct evidence as to the existence of this belief among the Biblical Hebrews. But indirect indications make it more than probable that such beliefs must have formed part of their outlook. We find in the story of Samson that when the angel announced to his mother that she would conceive and give birth to a son who would become a Nazirite unto the Lord, he also commanded her to observe during her pregnancy some of those rules of abstinence which a Nazirite was supposed to follow: "Now therefore beware and drink no wine nor strong drink, and eat not any unclean thing" (Judg. 13:4, 14). Clearly, the implication here is that the child in the mother's womb is influenced by the mother's behavior: if he is supposed to be a "Nazirite unto God from the womb" (Judg. 13:5), the mother must behave as if she herself were a Nazirite.

Similarly John the Baptist is said to have been "filled with the Holy Ghost even from his mother's womb" (Luke 1:15).

The Talmud contains a rich array of source material attesting to the continuation of the same belief. To quote only a few instances, Jews in Talmudic times (first to fifth centuries A.D.) believed that if a pregnant woman ate mustard, her child would be a big eater; if she ate earth, her child would be ugly; if she ate meat and drank wine, her child would be strong; if she ate eggs, her child would have big eyes.

Yet with all the well-known and well-defined prenatal influences to which the child was believed to be exposed in its mother's womb, the weeks and months during which the child's body developed within that of his mother remained a period of deep mystery. When the author of Ecclesiastes wants to illustrate the inscrutability of the work of God, he says: "As thou knowest not what is in the way of the wind, nor how the bones do grow in the womb of her that is with child, even so thou knowest not the work of God who doeth all things" (Eccl. 11:5).

It is, of course, God, the opener of the womb, who also fashions the form of the embryo.

> For Thou hast made my kidneys
> Thou hast knit me together in my mother's womb. . . .
> My frame was not hidden from Thee,
> When I was made in secret,
> Wrought in the lowest parts of the earth
> (Ps. 139:13, 15)

The mythical-mystical folk idea that God fashions every child in the womb of the earth and yet at the same time also in the womb of his mother is referred to also by Job:

> Thy hands have framed me and fashioned me. . . .
> Remember, that Thou hast fashioned me as clay,

And wilt Thou bring me into dust again?
Hast Thou not poured me out as milk,
And curdled me like cheese?
Thou hast clothed me with skin and flesh,
And knit me together with bones and sinews.
Thou hast granted me life . . .

(Job 10:8–12)

Two parallel creative processes are envisaged in these passages as leading to the formation of a child and its birth: the one takes place in the bowels of the earth where God fashions the clod, the *golem* (Ps. 139:16). The other, also the work of God, takes place in the mother's womb: it begins with a fluid state—perhaps a reference to the seminal fluid—then comes a process of coagulation, of jelling, the bones and sinews are formed and finally are clothed into flesh and skin. When all is ready, God grants life, and the great moment of delivery arrives:

For Thou art He that took me out of the womb
Thou madest me trust when I was upon my mother's breasts,
Upon Thee I have been cast from my birth
Thou art my God from my mother's womb.

(Ps. 22:10–11)

The belief in the simultaneous double process of prenatal formation, in the earth and in the womb, is, of course, completely beyond our understanding, confined as our thinking is by logical boundaries. But it presented no difficulties to the ancient Hebrew mind which never allowed itself to become aware of such insignificant details as a logical contradiction. Especially when a thought or a feeling is expressed in the winged words of poetical language, logical discrepancies are overlooked. Thus Job, after having silently suffered all the blows visited upon him by Satan contending with God, finally opens his mouth to express his submission to God in all his trials and pronounces the memorable words:

> "Naked came I out of my mother's womb,
> And naked shall I return thither."
>
> (Job 1:21)

Or, as the same idea is expressed by Ecclesiastes:

"As he came forth of his mother's womb, naked shall he go back as he came . . ."

(Eccl. 5:14)

Now, certainly, a man does not return to his mother's womb when he dies. But he is dust and returns to dust (Gen. 3:19); and while mentioning only the mother's womb, Job in his tortured mind and Ecclesiastes in his utter resignation may have thought of that other great womb, in the bowels of Mother Earth, where the clod of every man is formed and whither every man returns.

The idea that every man is formed out of clay was current also among the friends of Job. Elihu the Buzite says to Job: "I also am formed out of the clay" (Job 33:6).

Thus man is clay and dust, not only in the historical sense, having descended from Adam whose body was fashioned by God from dust, but also in the more immediate sense of being made, individually and actually, of dust. "We are dust," says the Psalmist (103:14) in pious resignation. God fashions each human being of clay, as the potter fashions his pots (Isa. 29:16; 45:9). "We are the clay and Thou our potter, and we all are the work of Thy hand" (Isa. 64:7). The image of God as the potter and man as the clay in His hands recurs in the New Testament as well (Rom. 9:21).

At the same time, however, God also fashions man in the womb: ". . . the Lord that made thee and formed thee from the womb" (Isa. 44:21; cf. v. 24), says Isaiah to the people of Israel. "Before I formed thee in the belly I knew thee, and before thou camest forth out of the womb I sanctified thee . . ." are the fateful words Jeremiah hears God address to him (Jer. 1:5). God fashions in the womb the master and the slave, the rich and the poor alike (Job 31:15; 34:19).

The same idea, that every person is created from earth and returns to the very earth from which his clod was taken still reverberates in the folk thought of tradition-bound Middle Eastern societies. In an attempt to reconcile the two simultaneous but different and separate processes of prenatal formation, the women of the Palestinian Arab village of Artas told Miss Granqvist that the angel Gabriel takes a little earth, kneads it together, and gives it to the woman, or places it in her womb, the night when her husband comes to her. The shape of the child born depends on the quality of the earth from which his body was formed. If a person is ugly, it is because the clay or the earth or the dust from which he was made was too much, or was trodden upon, or was frozen and lumpy.

The mystical component of the idea aside, it is clear from the passages quoted above that in the Biblical view the mother's body was regarded as merely a vessel in which the embryo is formed by God out of the seed of the father. This view, so typical of a patrilineal society, is also found to this day in the Middle East. The Arabic proverb, already quoted above, states: "In descent people rely on the father; the mother is like a vessel that is emptied." The same idea is expressed in another proverb current among the Egyptian fellahin: "The man is a river, the woman an embankment."

BIRTH

DELIVERY is the great moment in the Middle Eastern woman's life. From the time of her own early childhood she was being impressed with the imperative of fruitfulness, with the need for becoming a mother. From the day of her marriage she hopes to be blessed with conception, and during the months of her pregnancy she looks forward to the birth of her child.

Only occasionally, and probably due to exceptional circumstances, did the birth of a child take place in the open air in

Biblical times (S. of Sol. 8:5), or does it in the twentieth-century Middle East.

Under normal and usual conditions, the Hebrew women gave birth in their homes, in their tents (Gen. 35:16, 21) or houses, with the help of midwives (Gen. 35:17; Ex. 1:16). The birthstool used by them in Egypt and later in Palestine was in its original form nothing but two stones upon which the parturient woman crouched and between which the midwife received the emerging child. This crouching or kneeling was the typical position of childbirth. The same verb (*kara'*) is used in the Bible for both the human and the quadruped female when assuming the position of parturition (1 Sam. 4:19; Job 39:3). The woman kneels or crouches, either on the two stones, or on the ground.

Among the Egyptian fellahin to this day the woman is seated on three stones for the delivery, with one woman holding her back, two her legs, and two her arms. Parturition takes place in a very similar position among the Palestinian Arab villagers. One or two stones are placed on the floor, the midwife stands before the woman, her mother and sister behind her. Also among other Middle Eastern peoples the same position is assumed by the parturient woman.

The space between the ground and the body of the woman, bounded by the two stones on both sides, is called in Arabic the "pit." This reminds us of the prophetic utterance of Isaiah who refers to Sarah, mother of all Hebrews, as "the hole of the pit whence ye were digged" (Isa. 51:1–2).

Only women were supposed to be present in the house during the hours of labor (1 Sam. 4:20). The father had to remove himself to a distance and await there the arrival of a messenger who announced to him whether a son or a daughter was born unto him (Jer. 20:15). Similarly among the fellahin of Palestine and Egypt, only women are supposed to be present during the childbirth.

From the statement attributed to the Hebrew midwives in Egypt, "The Hebrew women are not as the Egyptian women;

for they are lively and are delivered ere the midwife come unto them," (Ex. 1:19) it would appear as if delivery had been generally easy and quick. However, this statement was merely a white lie made by the Hebrew midwives to Pharaoh in an attempt to excuse themselves for not having obeyed his command to kill all the sons born to the Hebrew women. In fact, childbirth was regarded as very painful, as the greatest trial in the life of a woman. The true experience of mothers of all generations is echoed in the old mythological tradition which attributes the pangs of childbirth to God's curse. Following Adam's and Eve's disobedience in the Garden of Eden, God punished Adam: "In the sweat of thy face shalt thou eat bread" (Gen. 3:19), while to Eve he said, "In pain shalt thou bring forth children" (Gen. 3:16).

The pangs of childbirth were a recurrent theme in Biblical imagery and are still regarded by the Middle Eastern folk as the inescapable nemesis of womankind. Several prophets, when speaking of fear, desperation and suffering, compare these to the "pains of a woman in travail" (Isa. 13:8; 21:3; 26:17; 42:14; Jer. 4:31; 13:21; 22:23; 30:6; 48:41; 49:24; 50:43; Hos. 13:13; Mic. 4:9–10; 5:2; Rev. 12:2).

The travailing woman is in pain (Isa. 13:8); pangs take hold of her (Isa. 21:3; Mic. 4:9); she cries out in her pangs (Isa. 26:17); she gasps and pants (Isa. 42:14; Jer. 4:31); she puts her hands on her loins and her face turns pale (Jer. 30:6); her heart weakens (Jer. 48:41); she trembles in anguish (Jer. 49:24). Two cases of women dying in childbirth are recorded in the Bible: Rachel (Gen. 35:16–19) and the wife of Phinehas the son of Eli (1 Sam. 4:19–20).

To this day, some Middle Eastern peasant women experience great pains and difficulty in childbirth. Some of them come very close to death during delivery. For Bedouin women, on the other hand, childbirth is, as a rule, easier. They have no specialized midwives. When their hour is near, they leave the camp and go out into the desert, accompanied by a few female neighbors who help them. A few hours later, the young mother walks back into the camp. Occasionally a woman gives birth to her child without any assistance.

Once the child was born, the navel cord was cut and tied and the child washed, rubbed with salt, and swaddled (Ezek. 16:4; cf. Luke 2:12). Each of these four operations is still performed for the newborn child in the Middle East. All are more than mere practical or hygienic measures—they are ceremonies of ritual significance.

The cutting and tying of the navel cord signifies the formal acceptance of the child into the family. If, for any reason, the child is not admitted but condemned to die, its navel cord is not cut and tied. A daughter unwanted by her father would thus be thrown into the field in Biblical times (Ezek. 16:4), or, among the Bedouins of the Syrian Desert, buried in the sand with the navel cord untied. If, on the other hand, the child is allowed to live, as would, of course, be the case nowadays almost invariably, the navel cord is cut ceremoniously. In Egypt, while the cutting is being done, short verses are sung which express the expectation of the family with regard to the child. In the case of a boy, the relatives sing:

> "Who supports his father,
> Except him who descends from his loins.
> May your legs be fit for the stirrup,
> And your mouth for an answer."

For a girl they sing:

> "She will make her father enter into the shade,
> And she will visit him every day."

"Entering the shade" means sitting in a cool, and hence comfortable, place.

Among the Palestinian villagers and even townspeople it used to happen that the ceremony of cutting a girl's navel cord assumed a specially important aspect: "her navel cord was cut for So-and-so," that is, the girl was betrothed to somebody. Such a bride was called "the gift of the navel cord."

The cutting of the navel cord used to take place about twelve hours or more after the birth, and it was regarded as a very propitious moment when "the heavens stand open" and wishes expressed by the women gathered for the occasion are fulfilled. In some nomadic tribes, the child is given a present when his navel cord is cut: a camel, or a goat, or a sheep.

The washing of the child is also a rite rather than a mere hygienic performance in many Middle Eastern folk societies. In many cases the child is not washed immediately but only on the third, the seventh, or even the fortieth day of his life. The washing has a definitely ceremonious character and it is accompanied by a feast for the women. In the Palestinian Arab village of Artas, for instance, the child is washed on the seventh day, called "the day of the bathing," when the neighbors are invited to a snack. On the fifteenth day, and again on the fortieth day, the child is washed again. While washing the child, the women sing a bath song, whose final lines clearly point to the prophylactic character of the bath:

". . . the water on thee—mayest thou be protected and tended!
In the name of God, the Beneficent, the Merciful!
He who is distant may not come to us,
And those who are near may not harm us."

The reference in the last two lines is to the evil spirits, whom the washing must keep away from the child.

The rubbing of the child's body with salt is practiced to this day and is regarded to be of great importance for the safety and satisfactory development of the child. One variant or another of this custom can be found in many places scattered all over the surface of the globe. The Samaritans, the Syrians, the Yemenites, and many other Middle Eastern peoples rub the newborn child's body with salt water.

Among the Arabs of Palestine they also rub him with salt and oil mixed together. The salt strengthens the child, or makes him clever or modest, or gives him a strong character, protects him against the jinn or against the Evil Eye—these are some of the beliefs that motivate this act, which has been faithfully carried out from Biblical times down to the present. In fact, it was regarded as being so essential for the well being of the child that Talmudic legislation permitted its performance even on the Sabbath.

Immediately upon its birth the child is swaddled quite tightly—this is the general rule all over the Middle East to this day.

In Artas, they swaddle him for forty days; among the Arabs of Jerusalem for three or four months, in the winter even for six months. The ritual character of swaddling becomes evident from the fact that no "unclean" woman is allowed to touch the swaddling clothes; this would harm the child. The child is wrapped tightly in the swaddling clothes so that it almost looks like a mummy. Old, washed, or even dirty clothes are used. Also the head of the child used to be tied tightly until the fortieth day, in order to give it proper shape.

NAMING

THE custom prevalent all over the Middle East today is to name a child after an ancestor, and in the first place after his paternal grandfather. Thus if a man named Ahmed has a son named Hassan, then Hassan's first-born son will be named Ahmed. This custom is a very old one in the area, and is, of course, found in other parts of the world as well.

In the days of the Biblical patriarchs, however, it was not yet customary to name a child after his grandfather or other ancestor. In fact, in the entire Old Testament there are very few examples indicating conformity with this custom which in later times became the general rule both among the Jews and the Arabs. Saul's captain was called Abner; his father's name was Ner (2 Sam. 2:8, 12). Since the name Abner means "father of Ner," we can assume that Abner had a son whose name was Ner. To this day it is the custom among the Arabs to call a man, not by his own name, but by the name of his son with the prefix "abu"—"father of." Thus a man whose own name is Ibrahim, and who has a son named Yaqub, is called Abu Yaqub—Father of Jacob. Since also Abner's father was called Ner, it follows, therefore, that Abner's son was named after his paternal grandfather, the custom still in vogue in the Middle East. Another Biblical example of this custom is that Absalom's mother was called Maacah and so was his daughter (2 Sam. 3:3; 2 Chron. 11:20).

By the time of Jesus the custom of naming a child after an ancestor assumed the character of an almost obligatory rule. When John the Baptist was born, the neighbors and cousins "named him Zacharias, after the name of his father." When his mother insisted that he should be called John—as the angel of the Lord had instructed Zacharias (Luke 1:13), the neighbors and cousins "said unto her: There is none of thy kindred that is called by this name" (Luke 1:59ff.).

Much attention has been paid by Biblical scholars to the question of who gives the name to the child. Some thought that the parent who names the child must have, or have had, a dominant position in the family; and since in many cases in the Bible it was the mother who named the child, they regarded this as evidence for a matriarchal order in the ancient Hebrew family. This argument, however, seems to be tenuous. Even if it was the prerogative of the mother to name the child, this can be more readily explained as a function falling within the realm of the woman's traditional activities: she gives birth to the child, she suckles it, she takes care of it exclusively during the first six or seven years of its life—that is to say a child organically belongs to the mother in this period, and therefore it is she who chooses a name for him.

In the story of the first human couple it was the mother, Eve, who named her sons, Cain (Gen. 4:1) and Seth (Gen. 4:25). According to a parallel source, however, Seth was named by his father Adam (Gen. 5:3). On the other hand, the sons of Seth (Gen. 4:26) and of Lamech (Gen. 5:29) were named by their fathers. Abraham named his son Isaac, following divine instruction (Gen. 17:19; 21:3). However, in the family of Abraham and of his descendants, the custom was for the mother to name the children. Hagar did this, following the instruction of the angel (Gen. 16:11). Again a second version attributes the naming of Ishmael to Abraham (Gen. 16:15). All the sons of Jacob were named by his wives. Leah named her own six sons: Reuben, Simeon, Levi, Judah, Issachar, and Zebulun; her daughter, Dinah; as well as the sons of her handmaid, Gad and Asher (Gen. 29:32–35; 30:10–13, 18–21). Rachel named her own two sons, Joseph and Benjamin, and the sons of her handmaid, Dan and Naphtali (Gen. 30:5–8, 24; 35:18). However, Jacob changed the name Rachel originally gave to Benjamin, so that it should not mean "son of my sorrow," but "son of the right hand" (Gen. 35:18). Judah named his first son, Er, but his wife named her next two sons, Onan and Shelah (Gen. 38:3–5). Joseph's sons, on the other hand, were named by their father, possibly because his Egyptian wife could not have chosen proper Hebrew names for them, like Ephraim and Manasseh (Gen. 41:51–52). Also Moses' sons were named, not by his Midianite wife, but by himself, Gershom (Ex. 2:22), and Eliezer (Ex. 18:3–4), possibly for the same reason.

Samson was named by his mother (Judg. 13:24), and so was Samuel (1 Sam. 1:20). Also the wife of Phinehas, the son of Eli, named her son, Ichabod (1 Sam. 4:21). David's wife Bath-sheba named their son Solomon (2 Sam. 12:24).

A concubine, it seems, did not have the right to name her child. The son born to Gideon by his Shechemite concubine was named by him Abimelech (Judg. 8:31).

Also according to the prophecy of Isaiah, it is the mother who names her child Immanuel (Isa. 7:14). Jabez and Peresh were named by their mothers (1 Chron. 4:9; 7:16). Beriah was named by his father (1 Chron. 7:23).

To sum up: in the great majority of cases it was the mother who chose her children's names.

This motherly prerogative remains in force in many, but by no means all, Middle Eastern societies to this day. Among the Rwala Bedouins, for instance, only the mother names the child. In the South Palestinian (now Jordanian) Arab village of Artas, in general, the mother names the daughters, the father the sons.

In Biblical times the name was given immediately following the child's birth, and this is the custom to this day.

In Biblical times the name chosen often reflected the circumstances of the birth. The usual formula is that the mother gives a name to the child and then goes on explaining in a few words why she chose that particular name, giving as a rule the popular etymological derivation of the name. Eve named her first son Cain and said, "*I have gotten* a man with the help of the Lord" (Gen. 4:1), the Hebrew verb form *qānītī*, I have gotten, being used as an explanation of the name Qayin (Cain). The name Seth is similarly explained by Eve: "For God hath appointed (*shēth*) me another seed instead of Abel" (Gen. 4:25). Noah was given this name, because "this shall comfort us in our work and in the toil of our hands which cometh from the ground which the Lord hath cursed" (Gen. 5:29). However, the key word in this explanation (*naḥēm*—to comfort) is not at all identical with the verb *nūaḥ*, to rest, which is the root of the name Noah.

In a very similar manner are the names of children chosen to this day in the Middle East; that is, once the ancestral names have been taken care of. Usually the first boy is called after the father's father and the first girl after her father's mother, if these grandparents are dead. Thereafter, the name may reflect a situation at the birth of the child. When the wife of the Rwala Amir Nuri gave birth to her son, the tribe was encamped near a castle called al-Khafaji; she therefore named the boy Khafaji. Another Rwala woman who gave birth to a child during a heavy rain, called her son Matar, rain. Like Rachel, when a woman gave birth to a child after a very painful delivery, she

called him Asir, born in pain. These examples could be mul-
tiplied at will.

LACTATION

IN BIBLICAL times a mother used to breast feed her child for
a very long period, probably for three or even four years. This
is attested by a number of Biblical references. When Hannah,
after a long period of miserable barrenness, gave birth to her
son Samuel, she no longer went up with her husband Elkanah
to the sanctuary to offer up the yearly sacrifices, but stayed
behind at home, for she said, "Until the child be weaned,
when I will bring him, that he may appear before the Lord and
there abide for ever. . . . So the woman tarried and gave her
son suck, until she weaned him. And when she had weaned
him, she took him up with her . . . and brought him unto the
house of the Lord in Shiloh; and the child was young. And
. . . the child was brought to Eli" (1 Sam. 1:22–24). After
she had offered up sacrifices, Hannah and her husband returned
home, and the child was left in Shiloh and "ministered unto
the Lord before Eli the priest" (1 Sam. 2:11).

There can be no doubt that this narrative envisages Samuel
as at least a three- to four-year-old boy at the time he began to
serve in the sanctuary. This, therefore, was the age when he
was weaned.

When Isaiah speaks of a "sucking child" who, in the mes-
sianic days, will "play on the hole of the asp" (Isa. 11:8), he
must have in mind a three- to four-year-old boy who already
accompanies his father to the field where he could chance upon
an asp's hole in the ground.

In another passage, Isaiah says:

> "Whom shall one teach knowledge?
> And whom shall one make to understand the message?
> Them that are weaned from the milk,
> Them that are drawn from the breasts."
>
> (Isa. 28:9)

It is clear that here, too, the prophet speaks of a child who at the time of his weaning is old enough to be taught the Lord's message.

Similarly, the Psalmist's praise of God, "Out of the mouth of babes and sucklings hast thou founded strength" (Ps. 8:3, cf. Matt. 21:16) presupposes that children were still sucklings at a time when they were already quite well able to speak and to praise God. According to the Book of the Maccabees, the suckling period lasted three years (2 Macc. 7:27).

These periods appear to us, of course, as exceedingly long. We might even be inclined to dismiss them as exaggerated. However, a glimpse into the present-day life of the traditional sectors of Middle Eastern peoples will readily show us that this is not the case.

According to the Koran (2:233), "Mothers shall suckle their children for two whole years, [that is] for those who wish to complete the suckling." In Palestine and Jordan the Arab women still breast feed their children for such long periods. Especially boys are being nursed up to three or four years, or even longer. Cases are known where a child was suckled until his tenth year. Girls are nursed, as a rule, for a shorter time, up to two years. Similar conditions prevail in other Middle Eastern countries.

Wet nurses were used in Biblical times only in exceptional cases. When the daughter of Pharaoh found the child Moses in the bulrushes, she hired a wet nurse who, in fact, was Moses' mother (Ex. 2:6–9). A wet nurse occasionally remained with the child she had suckled for several years after the termination of the lactation period; sometimes to the end of her life. When Rebekah went from her father's house in Mesopotamia to Canaan to become Isaac's wife, her wet nurse, Deborah, went with her (Gen. 24:59), and remained in Rebekah's household until her death (Gen. 35:8). The wet nurse of young Prince Joash, the future king of Judea, remained hidden with the boy in the house of the Lord for six years (2 Ki. 11:2–3; 2 Chron. 22:11–12). No wonder that such a nurse, on whom the child was completely dependent, in turn conceived great affection for him (1 Thess. 2:7).

Also in the modern Middle East wet nurses are employed only when there are special reasons for it. If a young mother dies, or is sick, or has no milk, a female relative will take over the task of suckling her child. Only if no such female relative is available will those who can afford it employ the services of a paid wet nurse. Others will give the child goat's milk or, among the nomads, camel's milk mixed with water.

When a woman suckles a boy and a girl who are not siblings, they become milk brother and milk sister, and, when they grow up, they are not allowed to marry each other. This is the Koranic law (Koran 4:23). Since the preferred marriage partners are the children of two brothers (cf. above, p. 28), a woman is not supposed to suckle the child of her husband's brother, in order not to create such an impediment to an otherwise preferred marriage.

Since such foster siblings are not allowed to marry, they are not subject to those rules of avoidance which govern the behavior of non-related men and women in Middle Eastern society. Such a boy "throughout his life can look upon the face of the girl so nursed with him." He can often visit the girl in her home and remain on the friendliest terms with her. A similar rule must have existed in Biblical times as well and must have formed the background of an otherwise obscure passage in the Song of Songs. In an outburst of love and desire, the girl says to her lover:

"O that thou wert as my brother,
That sucked the breasts of my mother!
When I should find thee without, I would kiss thee;
Yea, and none would despise me.
I would lead thee and bring thee into my mother's house
That thou mightest instruct me . . ."
(S. of Sol. 8:1–2)

The wish expressed here by the maiden is not that her lover

be her actual uterine brother; that would make a love relationship between them incestuous and unthinkable. Her wishful thinking takes on another form: if her lover would be her milk brother, "as" her brother, she could meet him anywhere, invite him into her mother's house, kiss him, enjoy his company, and nobody could utter a word of reproach against her.

The weaning of a child was, in Biblical times, the occasion for a festive celebration. When Isaac "grew and was weaned, Abraham made a great feast on the day that Isaac was weaned" (Gen. 21:8). Such celebrations are still held in the Middle East, or, at least, an animal is slaughtered and eaten by a group of invited friends in honor of the occasion.

CIRCUMCISION

CIRCUMCISION is a religious-ethnic rite practiced by many peoples in different parts of the earth. It usually consists of the cutting away of the prepuce or foreskin of the penis. Less frequent, but still sufficiently widespread, is the circumcision of females.

In the ancient Near East, male circumcision was practiced by the Egyptians, and the custom may have spread from them to the other peoples of the area.

It is not at all improbable that also the origin of Hebrew circumcision lay in Egyptian influence. Early in his life, Abraham and his wife had, on account of a famine in Canaan, to go to Egypt where they sojourned for a considerable period of time. In Egypt Abraham acquired menservants and maidservants, as well as herds and flocks, silver and gold (Gen. 12:10–13:2). Abraham's concubine, who became the mother of his first-born son, was an Egyptian woman, Hagar (Gen. 16:1). All this certainly resulted in some Egyptian influence on Abraham and his household. He must have become familiar with the old Egyptian rite of male circumcision, which, in turn, may have formed the cultural basis of Abraham's vision in which he received the divine command: every male in Abraham's seed, including slaves, must be circumcised when eight days old. The non-fulfillment of this commandment became punishable by death (Gen. 17:10–14). Abraham was ninety-nine years old, and Ishmael thirteen, when they, and all the men of Abraham's house, were circumcised (Gen. 17:24–27). Isaac was born about a year later (Gen. 17:21) and was circumcised when eight days old (Gen. 21:4).

Three generations later circumcision was firmly established among the descendants of Abraham as a mandatory rite. When Jacob's daughter Dinah was violated by Shechem and thereafter was asked in marriage by Shechem and his father Hamor the Hivite prince, Jacob's sons answered with guile: "We cannot do this thing, to give our sister to one that is uncircumcised, for that were a shameful thing for us" (Gen. 34:13–14). The fact that the stipulation was accepted unquestioningly by Shechem indicates that he and the people of his city were well aware of the great emphasis Jacob's nomadic family put on circumcision. The guile lay not in this part of the statement, which simply reminded Shechem and Hamor of a known fact, but in the subsequent action which they planned: to make use of the inevitable "pain," fever, and weakening, which would ensue on the third day after the operation, for attacking the city and killing all the males therein. Shechem and Hamor and the men of their city regarded the circumcision required of them by Jacob's sons as an unpleasant but not unknown or unheard-of religious ceremony preliminary to the contracted and agreed-upon mass intermarriage between themselves and Jacob's family. Additional indications of an integral connection between circumcision and marriage, as we shall see anon, are found both in the Scripture and in Middle Eastern folk custom.

During their sojourn in Egypt, the descendants of Jacob and his sons continued to practice the rite of circumcision (Josh. 5:5). In this respect, therefore, they did not differ from their Egyptian overlords. However, children born to the Israelites outside their Egyptian settlements, whether before or after the exodus, were not circumcised. Why the custom lapsed, we do not know. According to a tradition connected with the explanation of a place name, when the children of Israel reached a locality called Gibeath-ha-araloth, or the Hill of the Foreskins, God commanded Joshua to circumcise all the males born in the desert after the exodus (Josh. 5:2ff.).

Another fragmentary and obscure story, one of the very few in the Bible in which a dark, demoniac character is attributed to God, reveals that the son of Moses, born to him by his Midianite wife, Zipporah, was not circumcised in childhood. Because of this, in the dead of the night, God attacks the family, father, mother, and son, sojourning in a lodging place on their way from Midian to Egypt. God "met him and sought to kill him" is the enigmatic statement in the text. Kill whom? Moses, who, although he himself was circumcised, omitted to have the rite performed on his son? Or the uncircumcised son, who, not carrying in his flesh the sign of the covenant, forfeited his life? We do not know. Whoever it was whose life was threatened by the demoniac power, Zipporah with her quick womanly instinct knew instantly what to do to save a beloved life. She "took a flint and cut off the foreskin of her son and touched it to his feet" (Ex. 4:24–25). Again we do not know whose feet she touched with the cut-off prepuce: Moses'? Her son's? Or possibly those of the attacking mysterious being? And when saying "feet," does the narrator really mean feet, or does he, in his reticence to talk bluntly of the events of the mysterious encounter, use the word "feet" as a euphemistic expression for genitals?

The veiled, indistinct language used in reporting a frightful, nocturnal clash between a chosen man and a hostile divinity who must, so to speak, be tamed, is not new for those who have attentively followed up to this point the history of the Abrahamic family. Jacob had a similar experience, also at nighttime, when a being attacked him and he had to wrestle with him, a being who is once called a man and then again God, who starts with trying to kill Jacob but ends up with blessing him instead. Also in recounting that earlier nocturnal encounter the style is terse and obscure. There, too, full use is made of the peculiarity of Hebrew syntax which allows the narrator to refer in one sentence to two or more persons, clearly if he wishes, but confusingly and doubtfully if he so prefers. There, too, a "touching" figures: one of the two wrestlers touches the hollow of the other's thigh—the text purposely leaves us in doubt as to who does this to whom. Only in a later stylistic reworking of the passage did a shyer editor try to indicate that it was Jacob's thigh which was strained, and that as a consequence he retained a limp to the end of his life (Gen. 32:25–33). And, again, there, too, the question arises whether the word "thigh" is not merely a refined substitute expression for genitals, as it is in many another passage in the Bible.

Be this as it may, Jacob's fight with a demon god, and Moses' encounter with an inimical deity, have very much in common both in style and in frightening numinous atmosphere. Both reflect a human view of God much more ancient and much more primitive than that of the context into which they are placed. The obscurity of the style may, therefore, partly, at least, be accounted for by the attempt to tone down what to later ages, from their higher moral plane, seemed offensive, and to retain, at the same time, as much as possible of the original, tradition-hallowed versions of the myths.

Zipporah's words—winged words must always accompany action in the realm of ancient Hebrew experience with God— also bear the hallmark of great age. At a period when in actual practice circumcision was a rite to be performed on infants, and had been for many generations, she, in an enigmatical exclamation, harks back to an earlier age when it was part of the marriage ritual. "Surely, a bridegroom of blood art thou to me!" (Ex. 4:25) she cries out into the dark. To whom her words are addressed, we do not know. Neither do we know what the exact meaning of the brief sentence is which closes the episode and which possibly can be interpreted as a statement as to how the foregoing story explains the phrase "bride-groom of blood" applied to newly circumcised boys (Ex. 4:26). Middle Eastern material, to be adduced anon, can help to clear the matter up to some extent.

First, however, let us conclude our review of the information contained in the Bible with reference to circumcision.

At an early time, circumcision became the ceremony through which a stranger was admitted into the community of the children of Israel. Only a man who was circumcised was allowed to participate in the great national family feast of the Passover: "When a stranger shall sojourn with thee and will keep the Passover of the Lord, let all his males be circumcised and then let him come near and keep it, and he shall be as one that is born in the land; but no uncircumcised person shall eat thereof" (Ex. 12:48).

Circumcision thus became a kind of religious-national body mark of the Israelites, the mark of God's "covenant in the flesh" (Gen. 17:13), imprinted into the genitals of male children on the eighth day of their life (Gen. 17:12; 21:4; Lev. 12:3; Luke 1:59; 2:21; Phil. 3:3, 5). Correspondingly, the absence of circumcision became a symbol of foreign, and hence contemptible, identity. Whenever a person or a people was called "uncircumcised," it was done with a derisive connotation. The "uncircumcised Philistines" (Judg. 14:3; 1 Sam. 31:4), the "daughters of the uncircumcised" (2 Sam. 1:20), and similar expressions are succinctly scornful. In several other passages "uncircumcised" appears as an abusive word (1 Sam. 17:36; 1 Chron. 10:4). "Father of the foreskin" is to this day an insulting appellation for an uncircumcised person among the Arabs.

It was not until the great historical encounter between the Jews and the Greeks, following the conquest of Palestine by Alexander the Great, that the Jews met a people who regarded circumcision as a barbarous custom and circumcised males with contempt. This resulted among some Jews in allowing their sons to go uncircumcised, and occasionally even in sub-

jecting themselves to a painful operation whose purpose was to
restore an uncircumcised appearance to their genitals (1 Macc.
1:15; Jos. Ant. 12:5:1; Jer. Peah i, 16b; 1 Cor. 7:18ff.). When
Antiochus Epiphanes attempted to destroy Judaism, he prohibited circumcision (1 Macc. 1:48) under the threat of death
which, nevertheless, was risked by many a pious mother
(1 Macc. 1:60). As soon as conditions allowed, many hurried
to fulfill the neglected commandment (1 Macc. 2:46). On the
other hand, when Judean rulers were in a position to do so,
they, in turn, imposed circumcision on neighboring peoples
whom they succeeded to subjugate. Thus Hyrcanus forced circumcision on the Idumaeans, and Aristobulus on the Ituraeans
(Jos. Ant. 13:9:1 and 13:11:3).

The attitude of early Christianity to circumcision was fore-
shadowed by that of the Hebrew prophets. The term "circumcision" gradually assumed the meaning of excellence, purity,
and goodness, with an element of humbleness in it. In this
sense phrases like "uncircumcised lips" (Ex. 6:30), "uncircumcised ear" (Jer. 6:10), "uncircumcised in the heart" (Jer.
9:25), "uncircumcised in heart and ears" (Acts 7:51) appear
in various Biblical books. The phrase, "circumcise the foreskin
of your heart" is used repeatedly in the sense of "purify your
hearts" (Deut. 10:16; 30:6; Jer. 4:4). Ezekiel goes so far as to
reinterpret the Mosaic command and say, "no alien, uncircumcised in heart and uncircumcised in flesh, shall enter into my
sanctuary . . ." (Ezek. 44:9, cf. v. 7). The final step was
taken by Paul, who, in his Epistle to the Romans, explains to
the gentiles that the fulfillment of the law is more important
than circumcision, "For he is not a Jew which is one outwardly;
neither is that circumcision which is outward in the flesh. But
he is a Jew which is one inwardly, and circumcision is that of
the heart, in the spirit, and not in the letter . . ." (Rom. 2:28–
29; cf. Gal. 6:15; Col. 2:11).

While Christianity thus discarded circumcision at an early
date in its attempt to win over the gentiles, Islam retained it,
although it is not mentioned in the Koran. Zipporah's expres-

sion, "*ḥatan dāmīm*" (bridegroom of blood), re-echoes in the Arabic term for circumcision, *Khatn* or *khitān*, derived from the same Semitic root verb which in its Hebrew form means to perform marriage, while in its Arabic form it denotes to perform circumcision. More than that, in several localities in the Middle East, folk custom retained the older, more primitive, form of circumcision in which it was a part or a preliminary of the marriage ceremony.

Among the fellahin of Palestine it happens that "a young man at the circumcision ceremony gets a bride whom he marries almost at once." Among the semi-Bedouins of northern Palestine circumcision in some cases was deferred until one month before marriage. In Mecca circumcision occasionally takes place in front of the man's bride at marriage. In Upper Egypt, although the ceremony is performed when the boy is three to six years old, he is called "the bridegroom," and there is a close connection between circumcision and marriage; the former is a preparation for the latter, and the similarities between the public celebration of the two events are striking. Among the 'Abābda of the Eastern Desert of Egypt circumcision may be combined with a marriage. Both festivals are called '*irs*, the common Arabic name for wedding. A hut is pitched for the circumcision ceremony, and later the bride and groom will inhabit it. In northern Arabia, the circumcision ceremony, carried out on three-year-old boys, is the occasion for a get-together of girls and young men in dancing and merrymaking and for choosing wives. In the Mahra tribe of southern Arabia circumcision used to be carried out the night before the wedding, but in recent years an interval is allowed to pass between the two ceremonies.

In some parts of the Arabian Peninsula circumcision has the character of a test of personal courage and endurance, much in the fashion of initiation ceremonies known from many primitive peoples. The bride, or bride-to-be, of the young man is always present, and if he fails in the test, she refuses to marry him. This is the general rule, for instance, among the tribes of the Tihama district in Asir, south of Mecca. They celebrate circumcision with great pomp and ceremony, and the operation among them is of a particularly severe and barbarous nature. It consists in the cutting of the skin across the stomach below the navel and thence down to the thighs, after which it is peeled off, leaving the stomach, the pelvis, the penis, the scrotum, and the inner legs uncovered and flayed. Many young men are said to have succumbed to the ordeal which in recent years has been prohibited by the Saudi Arabian government as a relic of ancient paganism inconsistent with Islam. However, the custom is still being followed and it will probably take some time to eradicate such an age-old tribal tradition. The brides-elect of these twentieth-century "bridegrooms of blood" are present at the ceremony, and they have the right to reject a man if he so much as flinches under the ordeal. The same type of circumcision, with precisely the same details, is practiced also by the Beni Da'd and Beni Fahm divisions of the Quraysh tribe between Mecca and et-Tayif, as well as by the Kabakab and Talaha.

In other parts of the Arabian Peninsula, the circumcision itself is less cruel, but the boys have on the same day to undergo other tests of bravery. In the Qara Mountains, for instance, the boy, about fifteen years of age, sits on a rock in the midst of a large number of men and women, holding a sword in his hand which has been blunted for the occasion. He throws the sword into the air and then catches it again in its descent, his palm clasping the naked blade. Before him sits the circumciser, usually a sheik or an old man of good family, and behind him stands a virgin, usually a cousin or a sister, also sword in hand. "She raises and lowers her sword vertically and at the bottom of the stroke strikes it quiveringly with the palm of her left hand . . . The boy sits, his left hand outstretched palm upwards, in suppliant manner, waiting for the actual operation. This done, he has promptly to rise bleeding and run round the assembly raising and lowering his sword as if oblivious of pain, and by his performance his manliness will be judged. The rite is attended by brave songs and drumming and the firing of rifles, the women opening their upper garments as a gesture of baring their breasts . . ."

The performance of circumcision between puberty and marriage is an old Arab custom which is attested from the pre-Islamic centuries. Among the ancient Arabs, as well as among the Egyptians before them, thirteen years seems to have been the age of circumcision.

A few special features of circumcision remain to be discussed, albeit briefly. According to the early Biblical references to circumcision, it was carried out with flint, or stone knives (Ex. 4:25; Josh. 5:2–3). The use of a stone cutting implement at a time when the use of metal was well established testifies to the antiquity and sacred-archaic character of the rite. Sharp stone knives remained in use for circumcision among the Arabs of Palestine down to the present time.

Another point is the group character of the ceremony. Although the religious commandment makes it clear that every male child must be circumcised on the eighth day of his life, which rules out group circumcision, several examples in the Bible show that occasions for group circumcision were nothing uncommon. Abraham and his family underwent group circumcision, so did the people of Shechem, so did the Hebrew tribes in the desert after the exodus, and so did the Idumaeans and the Ituraeans in the second century B.C. Group circumcision has remained the general rule for Muslim boys in many parts of the Middle East. In Palestine and Transjordan most of the boys are circumcised at the Nebi Musa feast at Eastertime. Also the sanctuaries of Jerusalem and Hebron are favorite places of circumcision for the Muslims who live nearby. It seems possible that the ancient Hebrew sanctuary at Gilgal was also such a place for group circumcision, and that the story about the Hebrew males having been circumcised there prior to their entrance into Canaan (Josh. 5) is a myth which was told in explanation of the preference for the place for group circumcision.

Female circumcision, not mentioned in the Bible or in the Koran, is practiced in many societies in the Middle East. In some places, e.g., in Oman, all that is being done is an incision in the top of the clitoris. In others, e.g., the Qara Mountains and Upper Egypt, clitoridectomy, or cutting away of the clitoris, is practiced. In contrast to the circumcision of boys, which is everywhere a great public ceremony and feast, the circumcision of girls is carried out either in complete secrecy and privacy, or in the presence of a few invited women only. The men, even the father of the girl, are not supposed to show any interest in it.

The purpose of female circumcision is, according to the view of the Egyptian fellahin, to ensure premarital chastity in girls by removing the clitoris, which is regarded as the center of sexual excitability in women.

In societies where female circumcision is practiced, it is regarded as shameful for a woman to remain uncircumcised. A favorite curse in Oman is, "Oh, you misbegotten of an uncircumcised mother!"

EDUCATION

As AMONG the tradition-directed nomadic tribes of the Middle East today, in Biblical times, too, the education and socialization of children was a task left entirely to the parents of the children. In the first few years of its life the child was exclusively in the hands of his mother, who nursed him and took care of all his needs. As long as the child was suckled he was in frequent and close bodily contact with his mother, and it was in this period that the close emotional attachment between the two developed. "Can a woman forget her suckling child, that she should have no compassion on the son of her womb?" (Isa. 49:15) asks Isaiah in an impassioned prophetic parable. Also Hosea harks back to the same image: "When Israel was a child, then I loved him . . . And I, I taught Ephraim to walk, taking them by their arms . . . I drew them with cords of a man, with bands of love . . ." (Hos. 11:1–4).

Only in wealthy houses was the education and rearing of children given over to male or female nurses. Jonathan, the son of King Saul, had a lame son who was taken care of by a nurse (2 Sam. 4:4). Ruth's son Obed was nursed by her mother-in-law, Naomi (Ruth 4:16; cf. also Isa. 49:23).

One of the duties of the mother, and occasionally of the father, was to carry around the child too young to walk. The nursing father used to carry around the sucking child in his bosom, that is to say, to hold him in his arms in front of him (Num. 11:12). Another method was to carry the child sitting on the shoulder (Isa. 49:22) or on the side of the parent's body (Isa. 60:4; 66:12).

Each of these methods of carrying small children is still in use in the Middle East. Among the Palestinian Arab villagers, the mother carries the very young child either in its hammock or in her arms; when the child gets a little older, she lets it "ride on one shoulder or on the neck with the legs hanging over its mother's breast. In order that it shall not fall, the mother sometimes holds one leg or hand, or the baby holds its mother's head." The same methods of carrying the child are found in Transjordan, in Egypt, and elsewhere. For short distances, the Egyptian mother lets the child ride sideways on her hip.

The first words the Hebrew child was able to pronounce were "my father" (*abhi*) and "my mother" (*immi*; Isa. 8:4). Thus to this day the Arab child's first words are "father" (*bābā, yāba*) and "mother" (*māmā, yamma*).

In the villages and towns of Biblical Palestine it was an everyday sight to find small children, boys and girls, playing in the dust of the streets (Jer. 6:11) and of the "broad places" (Zech. 8:5). The same can be observed to this day in Middle Eastern villages and towns everywhere.

Among the games played by children in the markets and other open places special favorites were imitative games in which they mimicked the behavior and activities of adults, such as marriages or burials (Matt. 11:16–17). To this day, the games of Middle Eastern children include the playing out of the rites of marriage, circumcision, burial, etc.

Children were eager to participate in religious feasts, to enjoy their excitement, and to raise their voices in unrestrained outcries (Matt. 21:15–16; cf. Ps. 8:3). The participation of children in religious festivals is to this day an important feature of folk life all over the Middle East. The mosques, churches, and synagogues are places of gathering where the fathers take along their sons and where even the youngest boys soon acquire a feeling of being at home and learn to take part in the proceedings.

In keeping with the general religious atmosphere of Middle Eastern life, religious education was in Biblical times, and has remained to this day, an important part of the early socialization process. This task, begun by the mother, was, in the case of boys, soon taken over by the father. In fact, the Hebrew father was commanded emphatically and repeatedly to teach his son.

In connection with the observance of the Passover is found what is probably the earliest example of ancient Hebrew religious educational methods. A religious ceremony is being performed in the home in the presence of the children: a lamb is sacrificed, and its blood is smeared on the lintel and the two side posts of the door with a bunch of hyssop. The children of the family, it is anticipated, observing the unusual ritual, will ask: "What mean ye by this service?" Once their curiosity is thus aroused, they will listen attentively to the explanation, which, at one and the same time, taught them a central doctrine of Hebrew religion and a central event in Hebrew history: "And ye shall say: 'It is the sacrifice of the Lord's passover, for that He passed over the houses of the children of Israel in Egypt when He smote the Egyptians, and delivered our houses'" (Ex. 12:21–27).

Much of ancient Hebrew religious doctrine and usage is imparted to the child in this single instructional situation: the child is, first of all, shown how to observe the ritual; then the meaning of the ritual is explained to him by a historical reference; then he is made to understand the significance of the event in the life of his people in terms of divine intervention. The seed of a religious outlook on life, on history, on the world at large is thus implanted in the child's mind.

The same pedagogical method was used in connection with another feature of the Passover ritual: the eating of unleavened bread for seven days. Here, too, the father is commanded to explain to his son, in answer to the son's inquisitive inquiry, "It is because of that which the Lord did for me when I came forth out of Egypt" (Ex. 13:8). The first person singular emphasizes for the child the direct personal nature of the experience, and thereby makes it more immediate and relevant for him as well.

In a more generalized way, the same method is recommended in Deuteronomy. Here, too, the same learning situation is presupposed: the father performs, in the presence of his son, all the religious rites. The curiosity of the child is aroused, and he asks: "What is the meaning of the signs and laws and rules which the Lord our God hath commanded you?" (Deut. 6:20). In answer to the child's question, the father then tells him about the slavery in Egypt, the redemption, the exodus, the miracles, the promise of the land, and the laws which God gave "for our good always that He might preserve us alive as it is at this day" (Deut. 6:21–25).

The father thus figures as the source of all instruction and information for the child with respect to the history of his people, and all other matters that were supposed to govern his behavior: "Ask thy father, and he will tell thee" (Deut. 32:7).

One of the basic purposes of the law in the eyes of the ancient Hebrews was to "make them known unto thy children and children's children" (Deut. 4:9). When God made His words—that is His commandments—known to the people at Mount Sinai, He did so for two purposes: "that they may learn to fear Me all the days that they live upon the earth; and that they may teach their children" (Deut. 4:10).

The confession of faith, which throughout the ages has formed the basic prayer in Judaism, consists of five verses following the pronouncement of the oneness of God, "Hear, O Israel, the Lord our God, the Lord is one." The five verses contain in essence the minimal observances required of the children of Israel. They are: to love God; to remember His commandments at all times; and to teach them diligently to the children all the time—at home, on the way, in the evening, and in the morning (Deut. 6:4–9).

The importance of teaching the laws to the children was so great that it was repeated again and again. "Ye shall teach them your children, talking of them when thou sittest in thy house, and when thou walkest by the way, and when thou liest down, and when thou risest up" (Deut. 11:19).

The patriarch, the head of the family, was supposed to use his great authority to impress his children with the need to "keep the way of the Lord, to do righteousness and justice" (Gen. 18:19). In this manner the perpetuity of the religious-moral order was assured: God gave the law to the fathers of Israel "that they should make them known to their children: that the generation to come might know them, even the children that should be born; who should arise and tell them to their children" (Ps. 78:5–6).

Sacred monuments, erected in olden times and serving as a living testimony to the great historical events which shaped the destiny of the people, were another source of instruction for the children. The monument of twelve boulders, standing in Gilgal and set up by Joshua after the tribes crossed over the river Jordan, was such a landmark: "When your children ask in time to come, saying, 'What mean ye by these stones?' Then ye shall say unto them: 'Because the waters of the Jordan were cut off before the ark of the covenant of the Lord, when it passed over the Jordan . . . as the Lord your God did to the Red Sea'" (Josh. 4:6–7, 21–22).

Another educational aim among the ancient Hebrews was to make the children obedient and loyal members of the family. The fifth commandment made it a duty for a child to honor his father and mother, and as a reward for obedience promised long and prosperous life (Ex. 20:12; Deut. 5:16). In another version, the children of Israel were commanded, not merely to honor, but to fear mother and father (Lev. 19:3). The author of the Book of Proverbs addressed himself repeatedly to the son, admonishing him that he listen to the instruction of his father and forsake not the teaching of his mother (Prov. 1:8). Only a son instructed by his father is wise (Prov. 13:1); only he who accepts reproof is prudent, while the son who despises his father's correction is a fool (Prov. 15:5). Especially when the parents grow old and feeble is it important that the son should not forget that he owes them honor and respect (Prov. 23:22).

The educational process occasionally involved the need of corporal punishment, which was regarded as a proper means of rearing children. "He that spareth the rod hateth his son, but he that loveth him chasteneth him betimes" (Prov. 13:24). "Foolishness is bound up in the heart of a child, but the rod of correction shall drive it far from him" (Prov. 22:15). "The rod and reproof give wisdom, but a child left to himself causeth shame to his mother" (Prov. 29:15). Therefore, "Correct thy son and he will give thee rest, yea, he will give delight unto thy soul" (Prov. 29:17). However, corporal punishment should be meted out in a measured way: "Chasten thy son, for there is hope, but set not thy heart on his destruction" (Prov. 19:18); and "Withhold not correction from the child, for though thou beat him with the rod, he will not die. Thou beatest him with the rod, and deliver his soul from the nether world" (Prov. 23:13–14). The central theme in an entire chapter of the apocryphal Wisdom of Ben-sirach is that a son must be educated with strictness and severity (Ecclus. 30:1ff.).

In administering bodily chastisement to his son, the father merely does what God is believed to do to his children: "For whom the Lord loveth He correcteth, even as a father the son in whom he delighteth" (Prov. 3:12). When God promised David that his son would reign after him, He said: "I will be to him for a father; if he commit iniquity, I will chasten him with the rod of men, and with the stripes of the children of men" (2 Sam. 7:14; cf. Ps. 89:31–34). In general, man must never forget that "as a man chasteneth his son, so the Lord thy God chasteneth thee" (Deut. 8:5); but, like a father's, the chastening of the Lord stops short of giving man over unto death (Ps. 118:18).

Corporal punishment has remained an accepted and valued educational method in the Middle East to this day. The Rwala Bedouins, for instance, beat disobedient children with sticks, older children even with the sword, and they believe that the rod originated in Paradise and leads men back to it. Among the Egyptian fellahin it is held that "if the child does not come up to adult expectation, it is because 'it deliberately twists its neck which should be straightened by a slap.'" Children are punished either by fulminations and curses or by corporal punishment. Beating, striking, whipping, or slapping are not uncommon. The mother administers punishment more frequently than the father, but the father's hand is heavier, and therefore it is more feared. In justification of corporal punishment they quote proverbs which sound as if they were taken straight from the Biblical Book of Proverbs. "If you don't beat the child, nothing good will come of him"; or, "The stick is for the disobedient"; or, "Those who do not feel, the stick makes them feel."

The two educational aims of obedience to the father and the acquisition from his mouth of the traditional lore, which is the framework of social existence, have remained the basic goals of socialization in the Middle East to this day. In the Upper Egyptian village of Silwa—one of the few places where a modern psychological study of socialization was carried out—it was found that "the keynote to the educational process is the eagerness of the adults to create a docile attitude in their children and thus make them acquire filial piety." The educational ideal emphasizes "subservience and obedience of the children to their parents." As among the ancient Hebrews, so in the lives of the Egyptian villagers the disciplining of children is justified by invoking the same attitude displayed by God to man. It is related that the Prophet said, "God has disciplined me and perfected by discipline."

Also the acquisition of the traditional lore of the society as the other basic aim of the educational process can be found in its full form in the twentieth-century Egyptian village. Religious tradition governs life as a whole, and as the child grows up and is taught to conform more and more to adult standards what he acquires in the process is an increasing familiarity and conformity with these traditions. "Greeting, hospitality, eating, praying, exchange of social obligations, circumcision, marriage, and dozens of items of life are shrouded with ritual and traditional prescriptions," and these precisely are the aspects of life which the child is expected to acquire in the course of his learning process. Children start to learn about God's power at an early stage, and start their religious observances by imitating the adults. The very ideal of striving to conform to the adults' standards means learning religiously sanctioned forms and norms of behavior. Also the fear of sacred objects and the belief in their blessings and dangers are inculcated during early childhood. In these and many other ways the child acquires a sense of the importance of the family and of his identification with it and self-subordination to it.

Also other examples can be adduced to show that the imparting to the child of the traditional lore of the society has remained to this day primarily the task of the father. T. Ashkenazi observed among the semi-Bedouins of northern Palestine that the fathers spend much of the day in their tents with their children, tell them stories of heroic exploits of the brave men of the tribe in the past, their wars, their fights and valiant deeds. "These recitals constitute all the social and moral instruction received by the young Bedouin."

In comparing, or rather contrasting, the educational aims of the Biblical and present-day traditional Middle Eastern family on the one hand with those of the modern Western family on the other, we find several basic divergencies. In the Western family, the educational and socializational efforts are directed toward imparting to the child an early independence. The parents take pride in the child who can do things for himself, who can cross the street at six years of age, who can find his way alone to school. Disobedience is encouraged, expression of its own will smiled upon, aggressiveness toward parents permitted. These, in the opinion of Western parents and educators are traits which are to be fostered, for they will prepare the child to take its place at an early age independently in a competitive society.

In the Biblical and present-day traditional Middle Eastern society, on the other hand, the basic educational aim pursued by the family is to mold the child into an obedient, subservient, and loyal member of the family. Independent strivings and aggressiveness are strictly limited to the area of sibling rivalry and peer-group competition. Any such tendencies in the context of the family group but outside one's own age group are powerfully discouraged. The child is taught to respect and fear its elders who can and do hit him with the rod of their tongues as well as with actual rods, sticks, and whips. What the growing child has to learn is to subordinate his wishes to those of the father, and to reach an emotional state where he actually can identify psychologically his own interests with those of the father and of the rest of the family. Only when he has learned that the interests of the family come first has he reached a stage of development recognized as mature and hence satisfactory. Only when he can govern his actions with the family point of view in mind can he hope to achieve a status of recognition and possibly even of leadership.

SIBLING RIVALRY

THE patriarchal family, with the practically unlimited powers vested in the family head, is a social environment eminently suited for the emergence of sibling rivalry, often in violent form. The sons' position, indeed their entire future, depends in such a setup on the wish and will of the father. He can make them or break them, elevate the one to a high and honored position, make him his successor, will him his material and spiritual possessions; and reject the other, cast him out, or make him subservient, and thus condemn him and his future descendants to inferior positions. What then is more natural than the rise of keen rivalry between the sons for the affection of their father?

As in many other cases, here, too, the Biblical narrative takes a situation often observed and experienced in everyday life and projects it back into the first days of mankind, thereby giving it symbolic significance.

Two sons were born—we read in the Book of Genesis—to the first human couple: Cain and Abel. Cain was a tiller of the ground and Abel was a keeper of sheep. "In the process of time," it came to pass that both brothers brought an offering to God, each from the fruits of his labor: Cain offered the fruit of the ground and Abel of the firstlings of his flock. Both were equally eager to please their divine father, to win favor in his eyes by offering up their gifts to him. But "the Lord had respect unto Abel and his offering, and unto Cain and his offering he had not respect" (Gen. 4:4–5). Why did the Lord choose to accept Abel's offering while rejecting Cain's? No explanation is offered in the text. A father's actions are often incomprehensible to the sons. He takes an excessive liking to one of his sons, nobody knows why, and deals harshly with the other or others. But it is better to resign oneself to the situation, or else tragedy may strike, as in the case of the first brotherly pair: "And Cain spoke unto Abel his brother, and it came to pass when they were in the field that Cain rose up against Abel his brother and slew him" (Gen. 4:8).

Sibling rivalry rooted in competition for the love of the mighty father, lord over life and death, over blessing and curse, was present in a more or less overt form throughout the history of the Hebrew patriarchs. It is present in the story of Noah and his three sons, two of whom, Shem and Japheth, protected their father against the disrespect of the third, Ham, and earned their father's blessing as against his curse directed to the third (Gen. 9:20–27). It is uppermost in the mind of Sarah, who, in order to safeguard the future of her son, Isaac, engineered the casting out of Abraham's first-born, Ishmael, together with his mother, Hagar (Gen. 21:10). It almost led to a tragic repetition of the first fratricide between Esau and Jacob, the twin sons of Isaac, of whom Esau was favored by his father just as God had favored Abel. It haunted Jacob himself in his later years when he loved Joseph above all his other sons and thereby caused great jealousy to stir against him in the hearts of the brethren. The unaccountable preference for one son as against the other moved Jacob even in his dying days to share out a greater blessing to Ephraim, Joseph's second son, than to Manasseh, his eldest, just as he himself in his youth received the great blessing of his father, Isaac, over his older twin, Esau, who had to be content with a smaller benediction.

Traces of sibling rivalry can be detected even between Moses and Aaron, his elder brother, who was destined to play a subordinate role in the religious leadership of his people, and who used Moses' absence on Mount Sinai to establish a new cult with himself at its head (Ex. 32:1ff.), and joined their sister Miriam in using Moses' exogamous marriage to a Cushite woman as a pretext to incite the people against him (Num. 12:1ff.).

Occasionally competition developed between the son or sons of the full wife of a man and those born to him by a concubine, or between the sons of two full wives. The Bible relates several incidents, from different periods, which illustrate this point.

Jacob's sons by Leah, Bilhah, and Zilpah all ganged up against Joseph, the son of Rachel; Benjamin, the other son of Rachel, must at the time have been a mere child. Joseph, on his part, did what he could to harm his brothers by bringing "evil reports of them to their father" (Gen. 37:2; cf. vv. 18–24).

After the conquest of Canaan, several centuries later, the situation remained the same in many patriarchal family setups. When Gideon died, he left behind seventy sons born to him by his many wives, and one more son, Abimelech, whose mother was a concubine of Gideon's from Shechem. Abimelech, too, had dwelt together with his brothers, but upon his father's death he went to Shechem and persuaded his mother's brethren there to help him kill the other sons of Gideon (Judg. 8:29–9:6).

In the patriarchal and patrilocal family half-brothers who grew up together in one household, and among whom sibling rivalry was likely to develop in an emphatic form, were always sons of one father and of different mothers. Such half-brothers were carefully distinguished from full brothers. Joseph's brothers are called "the sons of his father's wives" (Gen. 37:2). As against them, Benjamin is identified as Joseph's "brother, his mother's son" (Gen. 43:29). When Jacob in his final blessing gives pre-eminence to Judah, he says: " . . . Thee shall thy brethren praise . . . thy father's sons shall bow down before thee" (Gen. 49:8). Even in later Biblical times a difference was made between full brothers, referred to as "my mother's sons" (S. of Sol. 1:6; Judg. 8:19; Ps. 50:20; 69:9), and half-brothers, called "my father's sons" (1 Chron. 28:4; cf. Judg. 11:2). Only a full brother was regarded as being as close to a man as his own son or daughter, the wife of his bosom, or the "friend that is as thine own soul" (Deut. 13:7).

Sibling rivalry becomes closely intertwined with dynastic squabbles and fights over succession in the period of the Judges and Israelite kings. Abimelech, the son of Gideon, killed all his brothers (but the youngest one) in order to secure for himself the leadership of the people which belonged to their father before them (Judg. 9:5). Keen rivalry developed between Jephthah and his half-brothers (Judg. 11:1–3). Absalom, David's son, killed his half-brother Amnon in revenge for Amnon's rape of Tamar (2 Sam. 13:29). Adonijah, another son of David, tried to gain precedence over his half-brother Solomon (1 Ki. 1:5) and was subsequently killed by Solomon when the latter suspected that Adonijah aspired to the kingship (1 Ki. 2:24–25).

Sibling rivalry, both in its intra-familial and dynastic forms, has remained an important feature of Middle Eastern family life to this day. A proverb current in many variants in all Middle Eastern tongues contains a reference to it: "I and my cousins against the world; I and my brothers against my cousins; I against my brothers." Little love is lost, especially between half-brothers who have different mothers. According to Palestinian Arab proverbs, "They who are from one back and two different wombs do not love each other"; and, "He who has not suckled my mother's breasts is not my brother"; and, "Thy father's son is like the people who fought against thee."

A psychological study of childhood conducted in recent years in an Egyptian village established that sibling rivalry was intensive and was, moreover, used by the family as an incentive to the development of the children. Certain families in the village try to provoke sibling rivalry, if it is not manifested strongly enough between children. It is held that exposure to sibling rivalry will enable the child to stand up to its rivals upon becoming an adult. Sibling rivalry is so much a part of the cultural pattern of the Egyptian village that brothers avoid each other, especially at formal gatherings, and there is a "cultural expectation of brothers' friction and wranglings which are quite frequent amongst adults in the village." Especially the relationship between the children of one father and different mothers "is supposed to be bristling with friction and jealousy." Much of the sibling rivalry "could also be attributed to the absolute authority of the father. Jealousy of, and rivalry for, the father's power is suppressed and made acceptable by the possibility of gaining rewards of good behavior both on social and religious grounds. Hence the father-son conflict is displaced to the brothers and sisters, who are in open rivalry for the father's favour and his sanctions and rewards."

These observations made on the contemporary Egyptian scene help us to appreciate the background against which the Biblical stories of sibling rivalry must be viewed. It is possible, even probable, that also in the life of the patriarchal Hebrew family sibling rivalry figured as a consciously fostered pattern of behavior. The Biblical parents, too, might have felt that exposure to competitive stress within the family was the best way of preparing the sons for life in a social environment where, all the traditional mandatory rules of conduct notwithstanding, might meant right and a man's position and even his very life depended to such a large extent on the manner in which he was able to hold his own in the midst of his peers. The recurrent preference the Biblical patriarchs showed to their younger sons was in itself a powerful stimulus to sibling rivalry. In a society in which the oldest son was the traditional heir, in which the rights of the first-born were so highly valued, any preferential treatment of a younger son was bound to result in a keen sharpening of the relationship between the two. When Abraham preferred Isaac to the older Ishmael; when Isaac—inadvertently, it is true—gave his chief blessing to Jacob instead of the older Esau; when Jacob loved Joseph above all his older sons, and when on his deathbed in Egypt he gave a greater blessing to the younger Ephraim than to the older Manasseh—in all these cases the patriarchal preference appears as if it were purposely calculated to provoke rivalry and competition between the sons. In this light, the very story of the first fratricide—provoked by the unexplained preference of the Divine Father for the younger Abel and his rejection of the older Cain—seems as if it were a projection into the misty and mysterious days of man's infancy of a situation which was encountered with bafflement by older and younger sons alike in their actual intra-familial environment. A projection back into the past which, at one and the same time, contains an attempt at explanation: the patriarch, whose motives are almost as inscrutable as the ways of God, acts as he does, prefers the younger son as against the older, because he follows a primeval divine example whose true significance remains hidden from the sons until they themselves advance into the responsible and awe-inspiring position of the paterfamilias.

Chapter 10

INHERITANCE AND BLESSING

THE problem of inheritance is a very complicated one in the Middle East. Its laws, rules, and regulations are practically infinite in their local variations. There is only one general rule which underlies all of them in every locality and in every period. This can be summed up as follows: inheritance largely follows lines of descent within the family. From this general rule it follows that males are preferred to females as heirs, since the line of descent is patrilineal.

In the Western world a person can bequeath to his heirs property or rights. Both of these categories of inheritance existed among peoples of the ancient Near East, including the Hebrews of the Biblical period. However, a characteristic peculiarity of the Biblical story of the Hebrew patriarchs is that the main interest of the storyteller, as far as inheritance is concerned, lies, not in rights or material possessions, but in the spiritual heirloom and its devolvement in the Abrahamic family. Much of the sibling rivalry which forms a recurrent theme in the family history for three generations revolves around the issue of who gets the "blessing," that indefinable but supreme good given by God to Abraham and his legitimate heirs. This question bothers and agitates Abraham's sons and grandsons and great-grandsons to an extent which clearly demonstrates the priceless value of this spiritual heritage, compared to which the earthly goods bequeathed by father to son have little significance.

The blessing is the true first-born's right over which competition erupted between Jacob and Esau: it was this great gift which Jacob stole from his elder twin with the help of his mother—mere words to our more skeptical mind, unaccompanied even by a slightest token of material possession, and yet invaluable to the son who has unquestioning faith in the power of his father to allot both blessing and curse. As far as the material possessions of Isaac are concerned, in all probability it was Esau who inherited them, since he was the one of the two sons who remained behind to dwell, not precisely in one encampment with his old father, but certainly in his immediate vicinity, while Jacob went empty-handed to far Mesopotamia. All that Jacob took along with him were the powerful words of his father,

> "God give thee of the dew of heaven
> And of the fat places of the earth,
> And plenty of corn and wine.
> Let peoples serve thee,
> And nations bow down unto thee,
> Be lord over thy brethren,
> And let thy mother's sons bow down to thee.
> Cursed be every one that curseth thee,
> And blessed be every one that blesseth thee."
>
> (Gen. 27:27–29)

Words, mere words, and inaccurate to boot, indulging in typical Middle Eastern exaggeration, as one can easily recognize when considering that the grandiloquent plurals, "thy brethren," and "thy mother's sons" whose servitude is promised in the blessing, could refer only to the single brother of Jacob, Esau, nicknamed the Hairy One. Yet words which were worth more than flocks and which make Esau the fearless hunter cry out in agonized desperation: "Hast thou but one blessing, my father? Bless me, even me also, O my father!" (Gen. 27:38.) When Esau breaks down in tears, all that Isaac can give him are again words, words of blessing which promise him, too, a goodly share in the heritage of the father, and which hold out the promise that, when rebellious, he will be able to shake off the yoke of his brother (vv. 39–40). Little comfort is held by this promise to Esau, who is prevented from killing Jacob then and there only by the respect and fear of his father (v. 41). Similarly to this day in Upper Egypt, the blessing of the dying father is an important part of the first-born's inheritance. The father says: "If Allah wills, open the place!" that is, be generous to guests and to the poor, and, also, be in a position to be generous.

The subsequent life history of Jacob proves without fail that the paternal blessing he received was worth more than all the herds and flocks Isaac could have bequeathed him. The blessing, duly endorsed by God in a wonderful dream at Bethel, began to take effect as soon as Jacob set foot in the house of his kinsman Laban. Like his favorite son Joseph in Egypt in the house of Potiphar a generation later, so Jacob in the house of Laban was successful in everything he undertook, because the Lord was with him, and the Lord made all that he did to prosper in his hand (Gen. 39:2–3).

At a later age, after the original family of Jacob had developed into the people of the children of Israel composed of many tribes and lineages, descent from the proper ancestor through the proper line became in itself a demonstrable manifestation of divine blessing, a heritage to be proud of and to be handed down unblemished to future generations. Descent from Levi, from Aaron, from David, from other great ones blessed by God was carefully noted, its record preserved and from generation to generation committed to unfailing memory. At a still later age, in the days of the Arabian Prophet and his followers, the same mentality still prevailed, causing some of the best minds in every generation to devote their concentrated efforts to the sifting and aligning of genealogies, to the setting up of unquestionably schematic tables of descent leading back each contemporary tribe and group to remote ancestors of great fame who were assumed to have lived in the dawn of time. To this very day nothing is of greater importance to peoples of the

Middle East—with the exception of those still relatively few who have been caught in the maelstrom of deculturating Westernization—than descent, than being able to claim Muhammad, or Ali, or a companion of the Prophet, or the founder of a great tribe as one's ancestor and as the original progenitor of the family to which one belongs. Material possessions and sheer weight of numbers are relatively unimportant in comparison with noble descent in determining a tribal group's, and hence an individual member's, status in Middle Eastern society at large.

Nevertheless, rules had to be established as to the inheritance of earthly estates as well. What these rules were in the days of the Hebrew patriarchs we do not know. But from two incidents related in connection with the life of Abraham it seems that when a man died all his sons who still lived in his household were entitled to a share in his estate, while sons who had left the home received no share in his inheritance. Sarah persuaded Abraham to send away Hagar and Ishmael by referring precisely to this custom: "Cast out this bondwoman and her son," she said, "for the son of this bondwoman shall not be heir with my son, even with Isaac" (Gen. 21:10). When Abraham, upon divine instruction, hearkened to Sarah, he sent away Hagar and the child Ishmael with some bread and a bottle of water, and nothing else (v. 14). In other words, he gave his first-born son, Ishmael, no share whatsoever in his, by then extremely rich, estate. Similarly, but somewhat more generously, Abraham gave to the sons of all the other concubines he took after the death of Sarah gifts, and he sent them away from Isaac his son, and he "gave all he had unto Isaac" (Gen. 25:5-6).

One more indication as to the order of inheritance is contained in the story of the patriarchs. When Jacob's wives agree to flee with him from their father's house, they say unto him: "Is there yet any portion or inheritance for us in our father's house? Are we not accounted by him strangers? For he hath sold us, and hath also quite devoured our price" (Gen. 31:14–

15). These words, as far as they can be interpreted with any measure of clarity, seem to indicate that the ancient Hebrew and Mesopotamian custom was not to give any inheritance to daughters. On this count Rachel and Leah have no complaint against their father; they simply refer to the fact as to a known thing. What they do complain about is contained in the second half of their statement: Laban sold them to Jacob, and devoured, that is, used up for his own purposes, their bride price, instead of giving it, or part of it, to them as decent fathers would do. The bride price they refer to is, of course, the return of Jacob's labor, the great multiplication of the herds and flocks which resulted from his lucky hand.

Only from a much later age does the Bible contain any legislation as to the order of inheritance. According to the Deuteronomic law the right of the first-born son is to inherit a double portion, while all the other sons inherit a single portion (Deut. 21:17). The father is explicitly warned not to change this order of inheritance, even if the first-born be the son of a "hated" mother, and the second the son of a "beloved" wife (vv. 15–17). If a man left no sons behind, according to the original law his property was inherited by his agnates: brothers, brothers' sons, etc. This law was amended upon the request of five sisters whose father, a certain Zelophehad, died without male descendants. The new law decreed that in such a case daughters should inherit, with the added provision that such heiresses must marry within their own tribe, so as not to cause the transfer of property from one tribe to another (Num. 27:1ff.; 36:1ff.). It seems to have been an exception if a man gave an inheritance both to his sons and his daughters, as Job is recorded to have done (Job 42:15).

If a man had only a daughter and wished his line to continue, he could marry her to one of his slaves. The children of such a marriage were counted as if they were patrilineal descendants of their mother's father (1 Chron. 2:34ff.). It could also happen that a free man married a daughter of a man who had no sons and that the issue of such a marriage was regarded as the children of their maternal grandfather (Ez. 2:61; Neh. 7:63).

No rule or law is contained in the Bible as to whether a wife could or could not inherit from her husband. However, since the law of inheritance as detailed in Numbers 27:8–11 makes no mention at all of a wife or of wives, it seems probable that wives did not inherit. In fact, the very position of a wife in the patriarchal family was such that under ordinary circumstances it was unnecessary for her to inherit from her husband. If she had sons, she, of course, remained living with them or with one of them in the honored position of materfamilias. If her husband left no son, or neither sons nor daughters, she had to be taken in marriage by the brother or next of kin of her deceased husband.

All these laws of inheritance have their closer or farther parallels in Middle Eastern folk custom to this day.

Children of concubines inherit equally with children of wives, if the father recognizes them as his own. If not, they have the status of slaves. In the patriarchal era, a slave could inherit his master if the latter had no children (Gen. 15:1–5), and the same custom exists to this day among the inhabitants of southern Transjordan.

According to the Koranic law, daughters inherit half a share as against a full share of each son. This law, however, is not followed in many parts of the Muslim Middle East. Among some tribes in Morocco, for instance, only sons inherit, and among the Kababish, a Sudan-Arab tribe, property passes to a man's sons, and, if he has no sons, to his brothers, and so forth; his daughters do not inherit. Also among the Bedouins of Transjordan, daughters do not inherit. The same custom exists in northern Oman and other parts of the Middle East.

Although according to the Koranic law all sons inherit equal shares in their father's estate, the customary or 'urf law retained here and there a trace of the ancient Biblical law of the first-born's double inheritance. Among the fellahin of Upper Egypt and the semi-Bedouins of northern Palestine, for instance, the first-born son gets half of the estate, and the other half is divided up among all the other sons. Among the Rwala Bedouins, a man's camels are divided upon his death among his sons as follows: the first-born son selects two camels; then the others take one each, then again the eldest takes one, and so forth, until all are divided. If the man leaves very few camels —and most of the tribesmen are, of course, poor—this division can result in the first-born son's receiving twice as many animals as his younger brothers.

Marriage arranged between the only daughter of a man and his slave still occurred in the Middle East in the nineteenth century with the purpose of continuing the man's line in his own house.

As to widows, these inherit to this day in Middle Eastern folk societies only symbolical fractions of their husbands' estates. This is in direct contradiction to the Koranic law which prescribes that the widow or widows of a man should inherit one fourth of his estate if he dies childless, and one eighth if he leaves also children behind (Koran 4:12). In clear disregard of this regulation, the Rwala, for instance, give no inheritance at all to the widow or widows, unless specific circumstances warrant it. They follow their own specific, traditional law, called by them "tarāyez el-'arab," "Bedouin custom." According to this, if a tribesman dies, leaving two widows with little boys, his estate is temporarily divided between the two women in order to enable them to bring up their sons; whereupon the estate is divided up between the two sons, without any formal provision for the mothers. If a man dies, leaving a widow with a small daughter, his agnates take all his property and send the young mother and her daughter back to her own kinsfolk. When the daughter grows up, she returns to her father's kin. Again, no provision is made here for the widow's inheritance. Among the Qara mountain people in southern Arabia, the customary law requires that the widow get one tenth in a small estate, and generally five cows in a large estate. In Upper Egypt, the main heir (the first-born son) must take care of his widowed mother.

AGING

ONE of the basic differences in the evaluation of the human life cycle between the modern Western world and the Middle Eastern culture is in their disparate attitudes toward aging and old age. In the West, aging is regarded as a process of decline, of deterioration, painfully contrasting to youth, which is the ideal life phase and which people want to retain as long as possible. And since old age itself cannot be escaped from, they want at least to hold on to the appearance of youth, in the vain hope that the external appurtenances of young age will make them feel young and actually be young. "Be young!" is the great imperative which in our own American culture makes life more difficult than it otherwise would be for a growing proportion of our aging population. Men as well as women dye their hair, have their faces lifted, their bodies massaged, their waistlines trimmed, their midriffs girdled. Women, in addition, paint their faces with the rosy colorings of youth. Both sexes prefer to wear clothes which make them look younger, and in their behavior as well as in their attitudes and outlook try consciously and effortfully to adopt the mannerisms and to emulate the way of thinking of their younger contemporaries. To be old-fashioned is almost as lamentable as to be actually old. Our fear, even horror, of old age goes so far that we do not even like to use the word "old." A person in his fifties is referred to as "middle-aged." A man or woman in the sixties as "mature." When in the seventies, he or she is still not old but merely "aging" or "elder." In our fear of old age we simply try to ignore its existence. In our idolization of youth we try to pretend that we can remain young.

Exactly the opposite attitude characterizes the Middle East, from Biblical times down to the present day. There, childhood is regarded as an incomplete, rudimentary stage in human development, devoid of reason and understanding (Prov. 7:7).

The child is by nature foolish (Prov. 22:15). The child is ig-
norant, according to the still prevailing view of the Egyptian
villagers, and therefore inferior to the adult. The younger person must therefore be subservient to the older. A common
saying is: "He who is one day older than you is in fact wiser
by one year."

In the Biblical view, to die young was a misfortune and a
catastrophe. One of the most terrible curses that can be pronounced over a man is that he and his offspring should die
young. Early death is invoked as a punishment for the wicked
with all that it implies in the destruction of time-honored
Hebraic values:

> Let his days be few,
> Let another take his charge.
> Let his children be fatherless,
> And his wife a widow . . .
> Let his posterity be cut off,
> In the generation following
> Let their name be blotted out.
> (Ps. 109:8–9, 13)

In the terrible curse pronounced over Eli by "a man of God,"
the threat that all his descendants will die young is repeated
three times: "Behold, the days come, that I will cut off thine
arm, and the arm of thy father's house, that there shall not be
an old man in thy house. And thou shalt behold a rival in my
habitation, in all the good which shall be done to Israel, and
there shall not be an old man in thy house forever. Yet will I
not cut off every man of thine from mine altar, to make thine
eyes to fail, and thy heart to languish, and all the increase of
thy house shall die young men" (1 Sam. 2:31–33).

The wicked die young—this was an axiom of ancient Hebrew
religious belief which is referred to repeatedly in the Scripture
as a well-known truth. Elihu reminds Job that God "preserveth
not the life of the wicked . . . their soul perisheth in youth"
(Job 36:6, 14). According to the Psalmist, "men of blood and
deceit shall not live out half their days" (Ps. 55:24; cf. v. 16).

The righteous man, on the other hand, can hope to live out
the full measure of his days; or, at least, can hopefully pray to
God for this blessing:

> He weakened my strength in the way,
> He shortened my days.
> I say: O my God, take me not away in the midst of my days,
> Thou whose years endure throughout all generations.
>
> (Ps. 102:24–25)

When King Hezekiah of Judah was sick, he prayed to God
in the same vein, expressing the same thought pattern:

> I said: In the noontide of my days shall I go,
> Even to the gates of the netherworld;
> I am deprived of the residue of my years.
>
> (Isa. 38:10)

In the days to come, when all life shall be goodness and
happiness, everybody will be blessed with a long life:

> There shall be no more thence an infant of days,
> Nor an old man that hath not filled his days.
> For the youngest shall die a hundred years old,
> But the sinner being a hundred years old shall be accursed.
>
> (Isa. 65:20)

Since longevity was regarded as such a great blessing, it was
bestowed by God upon his chosen king:

> He asked life of Thee, Thou gavest it him,
> Even length of days for ever and ever.
>
> (Ps. 21:5)

> Mayest Thou add days unto the King's days,
> May his years be as many generations!
>
> (Ps. 61:7)

And it was the appropriate form of greeting a monarch: "Let
my lord king David live for ever," (1 Ki. 1:31) says Bath-sheba
to David; and similarly his presidents and satraps address Darius: "King Darius, live for ever!" (Dan. 6:7); and Nehemiah

addresses Artaxerxes: "Let the king live for ever" (Neh. 2:3).

God is, of course, the only king who actually reigns forever (Ex. 15:18), and lives forever (Deut. 32:40), and is enthroned forever (Ps. 9:8; etc.). Thus, by living long, the earthly king, and any man, for that matter, acquires something of a divine attribute.

The ideal of a long life has remained a cherished wish in the Middle East to this day. A person liked to be greeted with a prayer for long life in medieval Arab society, and the same form of greeting is still in vogue today.

In fact, the value put on old age is so great that, in sharp contrast with our own Western mores, in the Middle East a man will exaggerate his age. I can still clearly remember one such occasion when this attitude was forcefully brought home to me. In the early 1930s, in the company of a young Arab teacher, I was visiting Sheik Amīn Al-Anṣārī, the keeper of the Khālidīya Library in the Old City of Jerusalem. Sheik Amīn at the time had a long white beard which framed most impressively his finely chiseled olive-colored aristocratic features. In the course of the conversation I asked him about his age, and he answered with a modest mien that he was eighty years old. After we left him, I commented to my companion that the sheik was remarkably young and well-preserved for a man of eighty. He thereupon turned to me and said with a smile: "Did you really believe that he was eighty years old? He is in his early sixties." Such exaggerated statements about one's own age are nothing exceptional among elderly people in the Middle East, as has been noted by several investigators. Neither was it regarded by the Biblical Hebrews as bad form to inquire bluntly as to an old person's age, and, in answer to such an inquiry, to boast proudly of one's own great age and the ripe old age reached by one's forebears. When Pharaoh inquires of Jacob, "How many are the days of the years of thy life?" (Gen. 47:8) Jacob answers with apparent modesty behind which, however, it is not difficult to detect an inordinate pride: "The days of the years of my sojournings are a hundred and thirty years; few and evil have been the days of the years of my life, and they have not attained unto the days of the years of the life of my fathers in the days of their sojournings" (Gen. 47:9). Such a statement could not have failed to make a deep impression upon Pharaoh, the product of a culture whose great ambition was to prolong life on this earth as well as to secure a continued existence after death. In fact, Abraham is reported to have lived 175 years, and Isaac 180 years (Gen. 25:7; 35:28). Jacob himself died 147 years old (Gen. 47:28), and, characteristically, the account of his death is not prefaced by the phrase that he died "old and full of days" which accompanies the brief death notices of Abraham and Isaac (Gen. 25:8; 35:29).

Aging, in the Middle Eastern view, is a process of acquiring desirable qualities. As a man advances in years, he acquires experience, understanding, and wisdom. At the same time, with advancing age a man gradually rose in his social position. As his children grew, his own importance in the society increased, until finally he reached the coveted state of being one of the elders, who fulfilled various functions of civic and religious leadership. The religious commandment, "Thou shalt rise up before the hoary head, and honour the face of the old man," (Lev. 19:32), undoubtedly expresses what was the popular sentiment in ancient Israel. Job's friend, Elihu, "waited to speak unto Job because they [Job's other three friends] were older than he" (Job 32:4). Isaiah mentions the elder next to the man of rank as constituting the leadership of the people (Isa. 9:14); and in another passage he equates the child with the base, and the aged with the honorable (Isa. 3:5). The cruel enemy "shall not regard the person of the old, nor show favor to the young" (Deut. 28:50). In Lamentations the elders are equated with the priests and the princes in importance (Lam. 4:16; 5:12). Elsewhere, elders and nobles are mentioned in one breath (1 Ki. 21:11).

The most typical of the functions of the elders was to serve as judges. It seems that in the days of the Israelite monarchy any man who reached a ripe old age thereby qualified to sit at the gates and function as a judge among his peers.

Age and leadership go hand in hand in the Middle East to this day. This is indicated, in the first place, by linguistic usage. The well-known title "shaykh" (sheik) has many meanings. A tribal chief among the Bedouins is called a shaykh; the head of a family is a shaykh. Heads of dervish orders are called shaykhs. Preachers, teachers, masters, spiritual leaders, are all called shaykhs. The village head is called shaykh. The graduates of al-Azhar, the theological university of Cairo, receive the title shaykh. The original meaning of the word, however, is simply "old man."

The Biblical mores of honoring the old and paying them respect in word, deed, and behavior, such as remaining standing and keeping quiet in their presence (Lev. 19:32; Job 32:4), continue unabated in the tradition-directed sectors of twentieth-century Middle Eastern society. Among the Egyptian fellahin, when a child is introduced to a gathering in the house, he touches the older persons' hands with his lips and forehead. Even when he grows older he is expected immediately to withdraw from an adult gathering. He must walk behind and not abreast of his father or of an elder, stand up, or at least sit properly on the ground on his approach, etc. After meals, it is the boys' duty to pour water over the hands of the elders; they are allowed to be present and to listen to, but not to participate in, the talk of their elders in the guesthouse.

Similar observations were made in an Upper Egyptian small town by Dr. Klunziger in the 1860s: "Veneration is deeply, to us as it often seems almost tyrannically, impressed upon children. In the presence of a father it would be disrespectful to smoke, to sit, and to speak more than is necessary. If there are guests the son does not eat with them but serves, it is only by special desire of a guest that he joins the party. The younger brother has to behave in a similar manner towards his elder." The same customs of filial respect prevailed in the nineteenth century in Cairo and among the tribes of the Arabian Peninsula.

Since honoring the old was such an important socio-religious commandment, its transgression was punished ruthlessly. Children would occasionally mock older people, especially when the latter were not only old but also decrepit and afflicted (Job 19:18; 29:8; 30:1, 12). When the little children of Beth-el mocked Elisha and said unto him: "Go up, thou baldhead; go up, thou baldhead!" he cursed them and thereupon two she-bears came out of the wood and tore forty-two of the children (2 Ki. 2:23–24).

Thus to poke fun at old people is a mark of lack of education. However, in every age there are children who are not brought up properly, and these will go on mocking the old people. Their attitude is reflected in the Palestinian Arabic proverb which says: "The old one is not worth one piaster."

We must not assume, however, that there was no awareness in Biblical times of the feebleness often accompanying old age. An old man is "an old man and full of years" (Gen. 25:8) (The same expression is used to this day in Arabic); or referred to as "old and heavy" (1 Sam. 4:18); or "old and satisfied with days" (1 Chron. 23:1); or "old and stricken in years" (1 Ki. 1:1). These expressions may be taken as euphemisms for "old and weak." That is why the Psalmist cries out to God: "Cast me not off in the time of old age, when my strength faileth, forsake me not . . . And even unto old age and hoary hairs, O God, forsake me not . . ." (Ps. 71:9,18).

The same fear of being forsaken and lonely in old age is expressed in a modern Arabic poem:

> When my hand was shortened by age
> I found my friends no more
> I look around dismayed,
> I find only few friends.
> Many a friend said:
> I will be with thee and support thee,
> But how long ago that is.

While old age had its pitfalls and dangers, it nevertheless remained something to look forward to, the crowning period of life, during which a man becomes emotionally ready and prepared to join his ancestors in afterlife.

DEATH

EVEN death, the great mystery of not being, of ceasing to exist, could not disrupt for more than a fleeting moment the cohesion in the patriarchal family. Once the traumatic shock of the physical departure of a beloved person wore off, the belief in his continued existence restored him to the fold of his family. He continued to participate in the affairs of the family, he was around although invisible, his aura and his merits remained an integral part of the family atmosphere.

The ideal way of passing was for a man to grow old, become well satisfied with days and years (Gen. 25:8; 35:29), and then, when he felt his life force ebbing, to make preparations for his own death by putting the affairs of his house in order, by conveying his will and blessing to his sons in appropriate, measured, winged words. The last glance the dying man cast around in this world was upon the assembled group of sons and grandsons, whose very presence vouchsafed the continuation of his life and line, and testified to a fruitfully spent span of years. The truly successful life was one which went on growing and developing to the very end, which reached its last day with full mental and physical powers (Deut. 34:7), and culminated in the prophecy-like heights of poetic blessing pronounced just before passing away. Death itself was truly a mere passing, a single step over, from one's own earthly family of living descendants to one's own ancestral family of shades (Gen. 47:30). Thus death was at one and the same time also a rebirth, a re-entry into a new existence of which little was known beyond the certainty that it took place in the midst of one's reunited ancestral family.

The prospect of reunion in death, although it was void of any concrete picture of afterlife—in fact, it is doubtful whether in the patriarchal age any definite idea of afterlife existed at all—was nevertheless encouraging enough to look forward to as a great comfort in the midst of life's trials and tribulations. It meant that after death one would not be lonely, one would be again amidst those whose presence and companionship had made life worth living on this earth: one's family. It meant that—whatever else one might have to miss when one ceased to breathe—one would not miss that which was the most essential for human well-being: one's family. It meant a continuation instead of cessation, the surety of existence instead of the dread of annihilation.

The two features of the ideal end—to reach a ripe old age and to be reunited in death with one's fathers—can be traced throughout Biblical history. The Biblical patriarchs, the first fathers of the Hebrew nation, whose lives were complete in their great length and fruitful achievements, attained this two-fold ideal. When God revealed to Abraham the bitter fate that awaited his progeny in the Egyptian servitude, he held out to him the comforting promise: "But thou shalt go to thy fathers in peace; thou shalt be buried in a good old age" (Gen. 15:15). And even though Abraham had severed the relationship between himself and his fathers when, following God's command, he left his birthplace and moved to Canaan, his death was nevertheless thought of as a reunion with his fathers. When he died, a hundred and threescore and fifteen years old, "in a good old age, an old man and full of years, he was gathered to his people" (Gen. 25:7–8).

A similar phrase is used in the same figurative sense in the passage which records that God announced to Moses his impending death: "Behold, thou art about to lie with thy fathers . . ." (Deut. 31:16) whereas Moses was buried neither with his fathers nor with his descendants, but in a solitary mountaintop grave shrouded in the mystery of unknown location (cf. Num. 27:13; 31:2; Deut. 32:50; 34:6).

The great event of dying thus assumed the meaning of being gathered into the company of one's fathers and ancestors, and was thus spoken of, whether or not the ingathering was capable of being expressed symbolically in the act of burial in an ancestral grave. When Abraham's first-born Ishmael died—where, we do not know—"he was gathered unto his people" (Gen. 25:17). Jacob died in Egypt, far from the ancestral burial place of the cave of Machpelah, but his passing had the same meaning; he "was gathered unto his people" (Gen. 49:33) even before his sons brought him to burial in the cave. When Aaron died and was laid to rest in a solitary grave on Mount Hor, he, too, was nevertheless "gathered unto his people" (Num. 27:13; Deut. 32:50).

In the case of others, death meant actual, physical reunion with the ancestral group. From the time of the patriarchs down to the very end of the Biblical period, family sepulchers were the ideal burial places for all those who could afford them. In the cave of Machpelah were buried Sarah and Abraham, Isaac and Rebekah, Leah and Jacob (Gen. 49:31). The kings of Judah had their family graves in Jerusalem, and the greatest promise they could receive, the greatest ambition they could achieve, was to "lie with their fathers" or to "go with their fathers" or to be "gathered to their fathers" (2 Sam. 7:12; 2 Ki. 22:20; 1 Chron. 17:11; 2 Chron. 34:28).

Reunion with the fathers was thought of in the first place in physical terms. To be buried in one grave, or in one cave, with one's fathers was a prerequisite for attaining that state of grace. This is why it was such a dreadful threat to say to a man, "thy carcass shall not come unto the sepulchre of thy fathers" (1 Ki. 13:22). This is why even a nomad, who had no permanent fixed abode while alive, strove to acquire a burial ground which could be his and his progeny's after him, "made sure" as an everlasting possession, and a place for ultimate reunion (Gen. 23:17–20). Once one member of the family was buried in a place, there was no more question but that those who died after him had also to be buried there. Thus, when Abraham died, several years after he had buried Sarah in the cave of Machpelah in Hebron, it was a matter of course that his sons Isaac and Ishmael buried him in the same place (Gen. 25:9–10).

To be buried in the family grave was a prerogative of the son who carried on the main line of the family, who received the "blessing," while the son who in his lifetime severed the family ties was buried elsewhere by his own progeny. Thus, of the two sons of Abraham, only Isaac, but not Ishmael, was buried in the cave of Machpelah, again by his two sons, Esau and Jacob (Gen. 35:27–29). When Jacob felt his death near in Egypt, he charged his sons: "I am to be gathered unto my people; bury me with my fathers in the cave that is in the field of Machpelah which is before Mamre, in the land of Canaan, which Abraham bought with the field from Ephron the Hittite for a possession of a burying place. There they buried Abraham and Sarah his wife, there they buried Isaac and Rebekah his wife, and there I buried Leah. The field and the cave that is therein, which was purchased from the children of Heth" (Gen. 49:29–33).

What a loquacious, repetitious way of informing his sons of his last wish! How many superfluous details, facts of family history known only too well to all the sons of Jacob! Yet they a.e not the babblings of an old, senile, dying man. That Jacob was in full possession of all his faculties is amply testified by the foregoing long blessing in which his winged words apportioned the fates of his twelve sons in unstumbling fluency, in a sequence of outpouring purple passages. The heaping of detail over detail, the repetitions must therefore have a different reason. They manifest the extraordinary importance Jacob attached to being buried in the cave of Machpelah. By repeating the story of Abraham's purchase of the cave, by reiterating the details of its location, by recounting the names of the deceased ancestors of the family already buried there, Jacob in fact says to his sons: this is of the greatest importance to me; do not fail me in this my last request! And neither did his sons fail him. All his descendants, with the exception of the little ones, went up from Egypt to Hebron, accompanied by a huge Egyptian retinue, and buried Jacob in the ancestral cave (Gen. 50:7–9, 13).

The importance of being buried in the ancestral grave remained the same throughout the centuries of the Hebrew monarchy. The Biblical historian is quite emphatic about King Saul and his son Jonathan having been buried in the sepulcher of Kish, Saul's father (2 Sam. 21:14); and does not tire of repeating the statement in connection with the burial of several kings (1 Ki. 14:31; 15:24; 22:51; 2 Ki. 15:38, etc.).

The value of being buried in the grave of one's fathers was so great that when a man had to face death he would betake himself to the place where his ancestral grave was located in order to die there and be buried with his fathers. When Ahithophel decided to commit suicide, he "saddled his ass and arose and got him home unto his city and set his house in order and strangled himself, and he died and was buried in the sepulchre of his father" (2 Sam. 17:23). When Barzillai was eighty years old, he asked leave from King David to "turn back, that I may die in mine own city, by the grave of my father and my mother . . ." (2 Sam. 19:38).

The humanly understandable desire to be buried in one's home town is the emotional expression of the mystical idea that a man's life is truly complete, his life cycle fulfilled, when he returns in death to the place where he was born. This is implied in the generalized statement, "Dust thou art and unto dust shalt thou return" (Gen. 3:19); but is expressed more specifically when it is said that each man returns to *his* dust, that is to say, to the place whence his dust was taken. Even the animals complete their life cycle in this manner: "Thou withdrawest their breath, they perish, and return to their dust" (Ps. 104:29). Similarly man: "His breath goeth forth, he returneth to his dust" (Ps. 146:4).

The very same idea still forms part of the traditional Middle Eastern outlook on life. "Until the very moment of death a human being must wander and seek the place from which his clay was taken . . . From whatever place the dust is taken to make a man, in that place he must die . . ." This is the view held by the South Palestinian Arab villagers of Artas.

BURIAL AND MOURNING

THE culturally conditioned response to a death in the family was expressed among the ancient Hebrews in largely the same ritualized forms which can still be found in the Middle East.

When a man died, it was the duty of his son to close his eyes (Gen. 46:4). Overcome by emotion, a son may fall upon his dead father's face and kiss him (Gen. 50:1), as is still done in some parts of the Middle East. In the days of the Hebrew monarchy the dead were buried in the clothes they wore at the time of death. When the ghost of Samuel is brought up for Saul, the witch of En-dor describes him as "an old man . . . covered with a robe," whereupon Saul recognizes that it must be Samuel (1 Sam. 28:14). In a prophecy of Isaiah, the king of Babylon is threatened with being cast forth from the grave "in the raiment of the slain, that are thrust through with the sword, that go down to the pavement of the pit . . ." (Isa. 14:19). Warriors seem to have been buried with their weapons (Ezek. 32:27).

In later times, the deceased was washed (Acts 9:37), anointed with sweet spices (Mark 16:1; Luke 24:1) and costly, sweet-smelling ointments (John 12:3–7), and his body wound in fine linen clothes (John 19:40; Matt. 27:59; Mark 15:46; Luke 23:53). It was also customary to tie his hands and feet with graveclothes, and to wrap a napkin around his face (John 11:44; 20:7), the latter probably in order to prevent his chin from falling down. Each one of these ministrations to the dead is still being performed in many parts of the Middle East, e.g., in Persia, Arabia, Egypt, Sudan, the Sinai Peninsula, Transjordan, Palestine, Tunisia, Morocco.

Part of the burial ceremony of kings and other notables was to burn, probably spices, before them (Jer. 34:5; 2 Chron. 16:14; 21:19); or to fill his grave "with sweet odours and divers kinds of spices prepared by the perfumers' art" (2 Chron. 16:14). Although the Hebrews were acquainted with the Egyptian art of embalming the dead (Gen. 50:2–3, 26), they do not seem to have practiced it.

Only in exceptional cases was the body cremated. This was done to the bodies of Saul and his sons, and thereafter the remaining bones were buried under the tamarisk tree in Jabesh (1 Sam. 31:12–13). Also according to a somewhat obscure passage in Amos, the burning of a dead body was followed by, or connected with, the burying of the bones (Amos 6:10). Especially execrable sex crimes, such as the taking of a woman with her mother (Lev. 20:14), or the self-profanation of a priest's daughter in harlotry (Lev. 21:9), or, in earlier times, the adultery of a woman married or promised in marriage to a man (Gen. 38:24) were punished by burning with fire. This, however, has nothing to do with cremation as a method of disposing of the dead body.

The accepted method of disposal was burying in the ground or in a cave (Gen. 23:19; 25:9; Judg. 2:9; 8:32). Where natural caves were not available, sepulchers were hewn out in the rocks (Isa. 22:16; 2 Ki. 23:16ff.). Sometimes a person was buried under a prominent tree (Gen. 35:8; 1 Sam. 31:13); or a pillar (stone monument) was erected over the grave (Gen. 35:20). Such tombs under a tree, or under a small dome-capped building, still adorn the countryside in many Middle Eastern lands and are shrines venerated by the people of the neighborhood.

Occasionally the deceased was buried in his own house (1 Sam. 25:1; 1 Ki. 2:34), or in the garden of his house (2 Ki. 21:18, 26). House burial was an old Canaanite custom as attested by numerous skeletons found under the floors and thresholds of excavated houses.

No direct statement is contained in the Bible as to the time which was allowed to elapse between death and burial. However, there is reason to believe that the rule was to bury the dead as soon as possible, generally the very day on which death occurred. In connection with the execution of a criminal by hanging, the Biblical law commands: "His body shall not remain all night upon the tree, but thou shalt surely bury him the same day; for he that is hanged is a reproach unto God; that thou defile not thy land which the Lord thy God giveth thee for an inheritance" (Deut. 21:23). From this it can be concluded that other dead as well were buried on the very day they died. This is the prevalent custom to this day all over the Middle East.

Apart from the question of the time of burial, to bury the dead was regarded as a sacred duty by the ancient Hebrews. To remain unburied, to have one's carcass devoured by the fowl of heaven and the beasts of the earth, was regarded as the most terrible of all fates that can overtake a man (1 Ki. 13:22; 14:11; 16:4; 21:24; 2 Ki. 9:10; Jer. 7:33; 9:21; 14:16; 16:4; Ezek. 29:5; Ps. 79:2–3). A terrible form of post-mortem punishment was to have one's bones removed from the grave and spread out under the open sky, "like dung upon the face of the earth" (Jer. 8:1–2).

The same ideas were shared by peoples of the classical antiquity, and are current to this day in the Middle East. Even in the desert, where people are satisfied with digging a shallow grave for the dead, they cover the body, not only with earth, but also with stones to serve as a protection against hyenas, jackals, and other wild animals.

In Biblical times it was customary to provide the dead with food and drink which they were believed to need in their continued existence in the grave or the "pit." This is attested clearly by a Biblical passage the purport of which is that it was forbidden to give to the dead from that part of the crop which was to be distributed as a special tithe among the poor (Deut. 26:14). There is, however, no prohibition in the Bible of giving food to the dead in general. On the contrary, the accepted custom was to hold a funeral repast (Jer. 16:7) in which the deceased was supposed to participate. Ben Sirach ridicules the custom of placing food and drink on the tombs of the dead (Ecclus. 7:33; 30:18; cf. Tob. 4:17). That the custom was widely prevalent in Biblical days among all the inhabitants of Palestine is known from the evidence of archeological explorations. To this day in many parts of the Middle East, food and water are offered to the dead in ceremonies which take place either immediately following the funeral or at stated intervals thereafter. The deceased is believed to need food and drink and to partake in the ceremonial meals which are eaten by his relatives and friends, whether at the grave or in his old home. In many cases these food offerings to the dead take the form of an animal sacrifice, the meat being distributed among the friends of the family.

Simultaneously with these administrations to the deceased, the traditionally prescribed mourning rituals were also commenced.

When the dying person breathed his last, his relatives, assembled around him, rent their clothes (Gen. 37:34). The same gesture served as the ritual expression of the upsurge of pain and despair upon receiving news of the death of a relative or of a prominent person (2 Sam. 1:11; 3:31). Thereupon the mourner girded his loins with sackcloth (Gen. 37:34; Isa. 3:24, etc.), which was the standard symbol of mourning (Amos 8:10; Jer. 6:26, etc.). The third gesture of mourning was to strew ashes or dust upon one's head (Jer. 6:26; Ezek. 27:30).

A more violent but still ritually sanctioned expression of despair over a bereavement was to roll or wallow oneself in ashes (Ezek. 27:30; Esth. 4:1) and in dust (Mic. 1:10), and to lay bare part of the body (Mic. 1:8). It was also customary to make oneself "utterly bald" (Ezek. 27:30; Jer. 16:6; 47:5) or to make a baldness between one's eyes (Deut. 14:1) or on the head (Amos 8:10; cf. Isa. 3:24; 22:12), and to cut oneself, or one's hands, as a sign of mourning (Jer. 16:6; 41:5; 47:5;

48:37), although these two customs were forbidden by Levitical (Lev. 19:28) and Deuteronomic (Deut. 14:1) laws.

The mourners also loosened their headtire, covered their
heads or their faces or their upper lips, clipped their beards,
and took off their shoes (2 Sam. 15:30; Jer. 14:3; 48:37; Ezek.
24:17; Esth. 6:12).

Crying and weeping, of course, were general (Gen. 37:35,
etc.). It was even customary to collect the tears in small bottles
(cf. Ps. 56:9). Dissatisfied with these half-spontaneous and
amateurish manifestations of grief, the family employed the
services of professional male and female mourners (Amos
5:16; Jer. 9:16). The loud cries of these skilled professionals
stimulated the vociferous expression of grief also among the
members of the bereaved family (Jer. 9:17; cf. Mark 5:38).
Especially audible was the shrill tone of pipes (Jer. 48:36;
Matt. 9:23) which seem to have been the traditional instru-
ments accompanying the cries of the mourners, their dirges
and lamentations.

Those who were gifted with poetic ability, like a King David
or a Jeremiah, or many anonymous "singing men and singing
women," lamented their dead with moving elegies and threno-
dies they composed for the occasion (2 Sam. 1:17–27; 3:33–34;
19:1; Amos 5:1; 8:10; 2 Chron. 35:25). Others were satisfied
with a few traditional words, such as, "Alas, my brother!"
(1 Ki. 13:30); or, "Ah, sister!" "Ah, Lord!" "Ah, his glory!"
(Jer. 22:18), which, in all probability, were repeated many
times with increasing frenzy and self-intoxication.

All these customs were not confined to mourning over the
dead, but were also the expression of any deep grief, despair,
shame, and confusion. If something terrifying happened to a
person, if he underwent what we would call today a traumatic
experience, he reacted with one or more of these traditional
manifestations of mourning. After Tamar was raped by
Amnon, she "put ashes on her head and rent her garment of
many colors that was on her head, and she laid her hand on
her head and went her way crying aloud as she went" (2 Sam.

13:19). Jeremiah calls upon the symbolic daughter of Zion whose doom he foretells: "Gird thee with sackcloth, and wallow thyself in ashes, make thee mourning as for an only son, most bitter lamentation, for the spoiler shall suddenly come upon us" (Jer. 6:26). The downfall of Tyre, according to Ezekiel, will be mourned by all the mariners and pilots of the sea in the same way. They "shall cause their voice to be heard over thee, and shall cry bitterly, and shall cast dust upon their heads. They shall roll themselves in ashes, and they shall make themselves utterly bald for thee, and gird themselves with sackcloth. And they shall weep for thee in bitterness of soul, with bitter lamentation" (Ezek. 27:30–31). Mordecai, in anticipation of the destruction of his people, "rent his clothes, and put on sackcloth with ashes, and went out into the midst of the city, and cried with a loud and a bitter cry" (Esth. 4:1).

Mourning customs very similar to those recorded in the Bible continued to be practiced in the Middle East down to the present day. Among the pre-Islamic Arabs, the bereaved women used to scratch their faces with their fingernails and beat their faces with their sandals; they opened up and shook their hair, and cut it off; they put on a sack or hair blouse and a black headcloth. They also used to rend their clothes and to uncover their faces and to forego the use of eye paint.

In spite of the official disapproval of Islam, the same customs are still followed. Among the women of Artas, for instance, Miss Granqvist noted that no amount of teaching, persuasion, and even threats could make them abandon these age-old customs. She describes that she was present when the village women gathered around the deathbed of a dying person, and they were admonished by the village priest "not to strike their faces, wail and shriek, not to rend their garments and loosen their hair when the dying one expired. But scarcely had this happened before the women did all that the village priest had forbidden them to do, although he had expressly said that it was sin and was forbidden by the Muhammadan law. They knew well enough, they said, that they would be punished for

it in the other world, but not even the fear of the everlasting
fire could keep them from performing the duties laid upon
them by a custom older than Muhammad."

Among the Arabs of Transjordan the same violent expression is given by the women to their grief. They scratch their
bodies until blood flows, rend their clothes to the waist, put
earth or ashes on their heads, and utter fierce cries and shrieks.

Similarly in Morocco "generally the women of the family
cry and shriek, moving their bodies and arms like maniacs,
rub their faces with ashes and earth mixed with water and
fresh cow dung, and scratch and tear their cheeks till they
bleed." In some places in Morocco, in addition, the women
also cut off their hair, blacken their kerchiefs with soot, gird
themselves with ropes, and bare their breasts and scratch them.
All these customs are done by the women in spite of the disapproval of the men, who, with a few exceptions, are not supposed to give vent to their grief.

The composition of poetic laments over the dead by both
professionals and laymen is still practiced in many Middle
Eastern societies. Some of these poets can reel off uncounted
verses, composed on the spur of the moment, for two hours
every day during the mourning week.

Also the brief painful outcry is still heard. The very words
reported by Jeremiah (22:18) in Hebrew, "Ah Lord!" and, "Ah
his glory!" were still heard, in Arabic, by Lane in Egypt in the
1830s: "O my lord!" and, "O my glory!" as well as other similar
cries such as, "O my camel!" "O my lion!" "O my resource!"
"O my father!" and the like. Also the wailing women are still
called in, but instead of the pipe they accompany their laments
with a tambourine from which, however, the usual tinkling
metal plates are removed to give it a more somber tone.

While death and mourning thus take place in largely the
same atmosphere as they did in Biblical times, there is one
important development which must not be overlooked. From
the Biblical sources it does not become apparent whether there
was any difference in the expected and customary mourning

behavior between men and women. All the information concerning the mourning customs seems to apply equally to men
and women. That, nevertheless, there must have been a tend-
ency among men and women to behave differently in expressing their grief can be assumed on the basis of the extremely
sharp differentiation which characterizes the mourning behavior of the two sexes in the traditional sectors of the present-day
Middle East. This differential behavior must be the end result
of a long and slow development which may well go back in its
origins to Biblical times.

The difference consists, to put it briefly, in the almost complete self-control expected of the male mourners, as against the
almost complete lack of control and the abandoned hysterical
behavior expected of the female mourners. This is the general
rule in the Middle East today, but it is subject to local modifi-
cations. Among the Rwala Bedouins, for instance, while the
men are allowed no overt manifestations at all of their grief,
even the women are restricted in their freedom to express their
pain. Only the first-degree female relatives of the deceased
(mother, wife, sister, or daughter) are supposed to mourn the
dead, and even they are allowed only one quiet cry in the tent,
and thereafter they may go outside the camp and there "lament
twice more, tear their dress at the breast, scratch their faces,
throw dust all over themselves, wind a white band around
their forehead, weep, and then return to the camp. Only the
sister and daughter may cut off their hair, which they either
hang over or lay on the grave. There is no other mourning. The
white band is worn by the women until the third night . . ."

Among the Egyptians, Lane observed in the nineteenth century that the female relations would beat their own faces, di-
shevel their tresses, rend their clothes, bare their breasts, cry
and shriek, tie a strip of linen or cotton or muslin, generally
blue, around their heads, and occasionally twirl a blue kerchief
over their shoulders or before their faces. Women of the lower
classes even besmear their faces and their head coverings with
mud. They also dye their shirts, head veils, face veils, hands,

and arms up to the elbows, and the walls of their rooms, with a dark-blue indigo dye. The Biblical sackcloth is found again in the rope girdle, made of coarse grass, which the Upper Egyptian peasant women tie around their waists as a mourning garb. As to the tear bottles, these were found in great numbers in ancient tombs in Egypt and in Syria and were still in use in Persia in the nineteenth century.

Chapter 11

THE RELEVANCE OF IT ALL

AT THE conclusion of this hasty trip through the remote world of sex and family in the Bible and in the Middle East, one more point remains to be raised: Do the conditions and attitudes as described and analyzed in the foregoing pages have any relevance to our own lives in the midst of this modern Western world, in the impatient, change-fraught second half of the twentieth century? After satisfying our intellectual curiosity, beyond our desire to reach a fuller understanding of the main ultimate fountainhead of our ethical value system, is there something we can learn from a scrutiny of the life patterns of the Biblical and the Middle Eastern family? Can we put to use the Biblical examples in our baffled groping for a solution of some of those problems which beset the newly emerged constellation of our own family life?

The problems of the modern Western family are many, and their harassing nature is becoming more and more evident. Leaving aside those traumatic occurrences which grip only some of our families, such as divorce and juvenile delinquency, there are problems which must be faced by each and every family and which seem to defy solutions within the framework which circumscribes our lives.

There is the problem of the young. As has been pointed out earlier in this book, modern Western culture, and the culture of these United States in particular, is a youth-oriented culture. More recently, some sociologists and students of the American scene have begun to speak—some semi-facetiously, some in earnest—about America as a child-dominated society. The typical parent-child relationship is clearly heading into the direction of a pattern in which the child does what it wants and the parents, too, do what their child wants. Advertisers, who are especially sensitive to new trends in socio-cultural values which can be exploited commercially, have already begun to capitalize on this pattern and to recommend consumer goods which can be used by parents without interfering with the uninhibited self-expression and the often destructive tendencies of their children. Typical of this type of advertising is the television cartoon which shows a small child, with the fanatic eyes and evil grin recurring in many ads of this type, jumping wildly up and down with his dirty shoes on a kitchen floor while a booming voice reassures us that the advertised floor wax resists "child scuffing." The advertisers seem to take it for granted that the other solution to the problem, namely the prevention of "child scuffing" by child scolding or child spanking, would occur to nobody. In fact, disciplining has to all practical purposes receded beyond the horizon of the admissible in child-rearing practices.

The child and the adolescent who are the typical products of the modern American educational and socializational system grow up with the conviction that the parents and the parental home are there for one purpose only: to serve them and to fulfill all their whims and wishes. No feelings of mutual responsibility develop in the young, because they are not given any responsibility or duty in the home. At an early age they become oriented away from the parental home and integrated into the peer group. The domination of the peer group is expressed in the necessity to conform, the need to be alike, the compulsion to behave, talk, and think like all the others, to share likes and dislikes. Thus, far from being truly unrepressed, the adolescent in fact suffers (subconsciously, of course) from peer-group domination from which he seeks reprieve in uninhibited behavior in the extremely permissive atmosphere of the parental home.

At the same time, the permissive as well as submissive attitude of the parents, coupled with the general tenor of the youth-oriented culture, creates a feeling of superiority in the adolescent in relation to older people in general and his own parents in particular. The desire soon develops in him to dissociate himself from the parents, who, in spite of all their efforts to understand him, appear to him as old-fashioned; and to put a distance between himself and the parental home in which he has neither duties nor responsibilities and in whose mechanics he has no share. To live with the peer group, notwithstanding all its pressures for conformity, or possibly precisely because of them, is the great aspiration of the adolescent.

This desire is achieved by a great number of eighteen-year-old boys and girls when they leave home for the out-of-town college campus. The main incentive for this move is, not the type of study they want to engage in, but the openly stated wish to get away from home and to live with the peer group. And woe to the parents who cannot afford the economic sacrifice required, and whose child must consequently remain at home during his college years. They are failures, in the eyes of their child as well as in their own, because they are unable to live up to those expectations which they themselves, in cooperation with their social environment, inculcated in their child.

Once the sons and daughters are in college, for all practical purposes they cease to be members of the family of their parents. They still come home, it is true, for vacations, but these assume the character of holidays, of visits with distant relations during which both sides are careful to behave tactfully and considerately. Once the college studies are concluded, the next step is to find a job and to rent a room or an apartment, anywhere but with the parents.

Marriage among young people brought up in this type of family is usually entered into on the basis of romantic love.

After a number of friendships or affairs of shorter or longer duration, the boy and girl are expected to fall in love and marry. The notion of romantic love is irresistibly impressed into the minds of the adolescents by novels, magazine stories, movies, television, radio plays, and many other influences. Although one out of every three marriages in the United States ends in divorce, the illusion that romantic love must be *the* basis for marriage is clung to with pathetic irrationality. The idea that the parents could have anything to say in connection with the marriage of their children is probably the most abhorred of any other forms of parental interference.

As far as residential arrangements are concerned, it is a matter of course that the young couple must have a house or apartment of their own. The presence of the parents would be felt as a serious disturbing and irritating factor by the couple which was conditioned by upbringing to an independent and self-centered outlook on life. It is an inevitable consequence of the educational methods whose products they are that they should regard the establishment of a separate household as a precondition for their own married life. The situation of the parental couple is thereby—typically—not considered at all. That the parents have to remain alone after the children fly the coop is regarded as just as natural and inevitable as to grow old with the passage of years.

And indeed, to remain alone in a middle-aged or elderly twosome is not at all the worst that awaits parents who have conscientiously fulfilled the duties of bringing up the new generation in accordance with the unwritten but none the less mandatory laws of our society. Worse is yet to come when one of the parental couple dies and the other remains completely alone. Due to the difference in life expectancy and to the prevalent marriage customs, the average American married woman can look forward to a period of ten to fifteen years of widowhood. By the time this stage of life is reached, the living patterns have become so much a part of the thinking processes of both the older and the younger generation that the question of moving in with a married son or daughter either does not arise at all or is rejected by the widowed parent. What ensues then is a concluding period of life beset with loneliness.

Thus the generally prevalent living arrangements dovetail with the relative evaluation of youth and old age: youth is valued and idolized and at the same time made by the social conditions into as pleasant a life period as possible. Old age is deprecated and, in actuality, social conditions make it an increasingly unpleasant and, indeed, painful period of life. The life curve in the Western world reaches its peak at a very early age, and then begins to decline continuously, through a life span that is being prolonged by medical science, until it fades away into death.

In sharp contrast to this depressing picture the Biblical outlook places the peak of the life curve at its very end. As long as a man lives he has something to look forward to; the older he gets the more respected he is, the greater his prestige, the higher his standing. Far from meaning increasing loneliness, aging means continued living in a family whose numbers grow as years pass. Instead of moving out as soon as they can stand on their own feet, the sons bring their wives under the parental roof and bring up their own children in the parental home. Needless to say that in this family setup marriages arranged with circumspection by the parents are inevitable and, in fact, the rule. The basic goals of the educational and socializational process are not early independence and self-centeredness, but unceasing loyalty to the family and obedience to one's elders. The parents do what they think is best for the children, and the children, in turn, obey their parents and do their bidding. The competitive and aggressive drives of the young are directed away from the family and into the peer group. There is an uninterrupted continuity in family tradition as well as in the physical and biological sense. In the Middle Eastern world, where this traditional family still survives, juvenile delinquency, old age loneliness, and many of the other problems incidental to Western family life are practically unknown.

The relevance of our analysis of Biblical family life to our own life now becomes clear. Let us ask ourselves, first of all, a few concrete questions: are our children really better off, being exposed as they are to the leveling force of peer-group pressure, than they would be if they were instead disciplined, that is, exposed to socializing influences which would make them willing to submit to their own, more experienced, and wiser elders? Are early separation from the parents and the setting up of independent residence indeed values so high that it is worth paying for them a few years later by the penalty of loneliness and unhappiness? Could the Biblical example not be followed instead and the entire atmosphere of the home be changed to such an extent that the children should be made to realize that from the point of view of the total human life span it is more rewarding to remain living in a cohesive household, in an undisrupted family?

Generally, it would be a highly worth-while project to undertake a feature by feature comparison of the modern Western and the Biblical-traditional family, concentrating all the time on the purely subjective criterion: which of the two patterns seems to be more conducive to happiness? If the findings should show us—as I believe they will—that the Biblical family pattern is superior from this point of view to the modern one, then, of course, the next step should be to see whether some of the features of the Biblical family pattern could not be reintroduced into our lives, and whether a reformulation of our entire educational philosophy in the light of the Biblical example would not be feasible.

The concluding chapter of a historical-anthropological study is not the place to give prescriptions or blueprints as to how such a major reshaping of our educational goals and of the parent-child relationship could be brought about. It can be anticipated, however, that the first reaction to these ideas of today's young parent generation will be that they simply cannot be implemented. How can the established pattern, firmly fixed into our lives, be changed, they will ask. The fact, of course, is that the family pattern only seems fixed and firmly established to those who are caught within it. From a perspective it becomes readily visible that the structure and functioning of the family are changing—constantly and at an accelerating rate. Witness, for example, the rapid reduction in the average age of young people getting married that has taken place since the end of World War II. Or the spreading custom of marrying before achieving economic independence which has quite radically changed the pattern of early married life. It should therefore be self-evident that the family pattern is far from being rigid or unchanging. It is, quite on the contrary, flexible, malleable.

Once the task of convincing is accomplished, the mechanics of the change can be worked out. As it is, our lives are subject to directed change to a much greater extent than most of us are aware. We are directed to accept, and actually do accept, changes in fashions, in car styles, in our habits of crossing streets, and many other facets of our everyday lives. Why should it not be possible to implement a directed change in our family life in the direction of the much abused but nevertheless superb American ideal of better living?

Sources and Notes

SOURCES AND NOTES

The following notes consist almost exclusively of references to sources. They are arranged according to the text pages to which they refer.

Page 18

Louis Ginzberg, *The Legends of the Jews*, Philadelphia, 1909, I: 108.
H. A. Winkler, *Bauern zwischen Wasser und Wüste*, Stuttgart-Berlin, 1934: 47.

Page 23

Egypt: Ayrton, Curelly, and Weigall, *Abydos*, III: 44; Pausanias, *Descriptio Graeciae*, I: 7:1; Johannes Nietzold, *Die Ehe in Aegypten zur ptolemäisch-römischen Zeit*, Leipzig, 1903: 12 ff.; Hastings, *Encyclopaedia of Religion and Ethics* (ERE), VIII: 444; Adolf Erman, *Life in Ancient Egypt*: 153; E. Westermarck, *The History of Human Marriage*, London, 1925, II: 91; Diodorus 1:27.

Iran: Herodotus III: 31; Fr. Spiegel, *Eranische Altertumskunde*, Leipzig, 1878, III: 678 f.; Rapp, *Zeitschrift der deutschen morgenländischen Gesellschaft* (ZDMG), XX: 112 f.; Hubschmann, *ib.*, XLIII: 308 ff.; ERE VII: 457; Westermarck, *op. cit.*, II: 86–87; Darab Dastur Peshotan Sunjana, *Next-of-kin Marriages in Old Iran*: 16 ff.; West, "The Meaning of Khvetuk-das or Khvetudad," *Sacred Books of the East*, XVIII: 427 f.: Moulton, *Early Zoroastrianism*: 207.

Page 24

William Robertson Smith, *Kinship and Marriage in Early Arabia*, Cambridge, 1885: 163.

Page 26

Bertram Thomas, *Arabia Felix*, New York, 1932: 219–20; Rizkallah, *Heshr el-litham*, §167.

Page 28

Cf. Raphael Patai, "Cousin Right in Middle Eastern Marriage," *Southwestern Journal of Anthropology*, Vol. 11, No. 4, 1955: 371 ff.

Page 30

Westermarck, *Wit and Wisdom in Morocco*, New York, 1931: 72.

Page 31

Chapple and Coon, *Principles of Anthropology*, New York, 1942: 303.

Page 36

G. Wyman Bury, *The Land of Uz*, London, 1911: 278; Fulanain, *The Marsh Arab*, Philadelphia, 1928: 251–73.

Page 37

E. Bräunlich, "Zur Gesellschaftsordnung der heutigen Beduinen," *Islamica*, VI, 1934: 186–87; Alois Musil, *Manners and Customs of the Rwala Bedouins*, New York, 1928: 136–37, 139; H. R. P. Dickson, *The Arab of the Desert*, London, 1949: 140–41, 602; Père Antonin Jaussen, *Coutumes Palestiniennes I: Naplouse et son district*, Paris, 1927: 65–67; Musa Kazem Daghestani, *Étude Sociologique sur la Famille Musulmane Contemporaine en Syrie*, Paris, 1932: 17–19; Leonard Bauer, *Volksleben im Lande der Bibel*, Leipzig, 1903: 86; Thomas, *Arabia Felix*: 67; Bury, *Uz*: 278.

Page 38

Hilma Granqvist, *Marriage Conditions in a Palestinian Village*, Vol. I, Helsingfors, 1931: 192 ff.

Page 39

A. C. Jewett, *An American Engineer in Afghanistan*, Minneapolis, 1948: 262; Horace Miner, *The Primitive City of Timbuctoo*, Princeton, 1953: 180.

Page 40

Granqvist, *Marriage Conditions in a Palestinian Village*, Vol. II, Helsinki, 1935: 180, 186, 190, 194, 202, 209; Koran 4:128–29; Yosef Meyouhas, *Hafellahim*, Jerusalem, 1937: 56 ff.; Jaussen, *Naplouse*: 95; Musil, *Arabia Petraea*, Wien, 1908, III: 207 f.; id., *Rwala*: 230.

Page 43

William M. Thomson, *The Land and the Book: Lebanon, Damas-*

cus and Beyond Jordan, New York, 1886: 90; Edward William Lane, *An Account of the Manners and Customs of the Modern Egyptians*, London, 1871, I: 232; Granqvist, *Marriage*, II: 191–93.

Page 45

Musil, *Rwala:* 230–31; *id.*, *Arabia Petraea*, III: 207 f.

Page 47

Bury, *Uz:* 273, 276; Granqvist, *Marriage*, I: 60 ff.; II: 114, 170, 202.

Page 48

Musil, *Rwala:* 135.

Page 49

G. Robinson Lees, *Village Life in Palestine*, London, 1905: 120.

Page 52

Bury, *Uz:* 277; George W. Murray, *The Sons of Ishmael: A Study of the Egyptian Bedouin*, London, 1935: 183; W. H. Ingrams, "The Hadhramaut: Present and Future," *Geographical Journal*, 1938, 92: 298. Thomas, *Arabia Felix:* 98; Lees, *The Witness of the Wilderness*, London, 1909: 120–21.

Page 53

Ibn Battuta, ed. Defremery II: 168; Sir Richard F. Burton, *Personal Narrative of a Pilgrimage to al-Madinah and Meccah*, London, 1913, II: 84; Lane, *Modern Egyptians*, I: 370; Granqvist, *Marriage*, I: 46 ff.

Page 56

Granqvist, *Marriage*, II: 10–11; C. T. Wilson, *Peasant Life in the Holy Land*, London, 1906: 108.

Pages 58–59

Musil, *Rwala:* 140, 445; Philip J. Baldensperger, *The Immovable East*, London, 1913: 120; Mülinen, "Beiträge zur Kenntnis des Karmels," *Zeitschrift des deutschen Palästina-Vereins* (ZDPV), XXX, 1907: 170; Klein, "Mittheilungen über Leben, Sitten und Gebräuche der Fellachen in Palästina," ZDPV, VI, 1883: 90; Ermete Pierotti, *Customs and Traditions of Palestine*, Cambridge, 1864: 179 ff.; Elihu Grant, *The People of Palestine*, Philadelphia and London, 1921: 54; H. J. Van Lennep, *Bible Lands: Their Modern Cus-*

toms and Manners, New York, 1875: 540; Granqvist, *Marriage*, I: 124; John Lewis Burckhardt, *Arabische Sprüchwörter*, Weimar, 1834: 173; Lane, *Modern Egyptians*, I: 121 ff., 202 f.; Westermarck, *Marriage Ceremonies in Morocco*, London, 1914: 74 f.; Thomas, *Arabia Felix*: 96, 191; Patai, "Marriage Among the Marranos of Meshhed," *Edoth*, Jerusalem, II, 1947: 173; Granqvist, *Marriage*, I: 128; E. Übach and E. Rackow, *Sitte und Recht in Nordafrika*, Stuttgart, 1923: 37; Snouck Hurgronje, *Mekka*, The Hague, 1889, II: 158; H. St. John B. Philby, *Sheba's Daughters*, London, 1939: 46; Eugen Mittwoch, *Aus dem Jemen: Herrman Burchardt's letzte Reise*, Leipzig, no date: 57; Thomas, *Arabia Felix*: 191; *id., Alarms and Excursions in Arabia*, London, 1931: 276; A. M. Goichon, *La Vie Feminine au Mzab, Étude Sociologique Musulmane*, Paris, 1927: 75.

Page 61

Granqvist, *Marriage*, I: 108–9.

Pages 63–64

Musil, *Rwala*: 228–29; J. G. Wetzstein, "Sprachliches aus den Zeltlagern der Syrischen Wüste," ZDMG, 1868, XXII: 69 ff.; Smith, *Kinship*: 169.

Page 65

Henri Massé, *Persian Beliefs and Customs*, New Haven, 1954: 59; Winkler, *Bauern zwischen Wasser und Wüste*: 124; S. H. Leeder, *Modern Sons of the Pharaohs*, London, 1918: 115 ff.

Page 67

Hurgronje, *Mekka*, II: 185 ff.; Leo Africanus, *History and Description of Africa*, London, 1896, II: 450.

Page 68

Westermarck, *Marriage Ceremonies in Morocco*: 267 ff.; Burckhardt, *Arabic Proverbs*, London, 1830: 117 f.; Lane, *Modern Egyptians*, I: 218 f.; Dickson, *The Arab of the Desert*: 205; Erich Brauer, *Yehudē Kurdistan*, Jerusalem, 1947: 116; Massé, *Persian Beliefs and Customs*: 60; Patai, "Marriage among the Marranos of Meshhed," *Edoth*, 1947: 186.

Page 69

Burckhardt, *Notes on the Bedouins and Wahábys*, London, 1830,

I: 15; H. Ayrout, *Fellahs d'Egypte*, Cairo, 1952: 145; Burckhardt, *Arabic Proverbs*: 117; Winkler, *Ägyptische Volkskunde*: 204 ff.

Page 70

E. Neufeld, *Ancient Hebrew Marriage Laws*, London, 1944: 100; Pierotti, *Customs and Traditions of Palestine*: 188; Jaussen, *Naplouse*: 83; Spoer and Haddad, "Volkskundliches aus el-Qubebe bei Jerusalem," *Zeitschrift für Semitistik*, Vol. 1, Leipzig, 1927: 130; Schmidt und Kahle, "Volkserzählungen aus Palästina," *Forschungen zur Religion und Literatur des Alten und Neuen Testaments*, Heft 17, Göttingen, 1918: 259; Wetzstein, ZDMG, 1868: 106; *id.*, "Die syrische Dreschtafel," *Zeitschrift für Ethnologie*, V, Berlin, 1873: 290 ff.; Burckhardt, *Arabic Proverbs*: 117 f.; Bastian, *Zeitschrift für Ethnologie*, 1873: 287 ff.; Delitzsch, *Commentar zum Hohenlied*: 165 f.; Niebuhr, *Beschreibung von Arabien*: 35 ff.; Klein, ZDPV, VI, 1883: 100; Wetzstein, "Die syrische Dreschtafel": 291; Musil, *Rwala*: 240; Dickson, *The Arab of the Desert*: 205.

Page 75

Granqvist, *Marriage*, II: 166–67.

Page 76

Patai, "Jewish Folk-Cures for Barrenness," *Folklore*, London, Vol. LV, Sept. 1944: 177–78; T. Canaan, *Mohammedan Saints and Sanctuaries in Palestine*, London, 1927: 108, 118.

Page 77

Canaan, *op. cit.*: 182–83; Samuel Ives Curtiss, *Primitive Semitic Religion Today*, London, 1902: 157–58.

Page 78

Chardin, *Voyages*, Paris, 1811, IV: 441; Neufeld, *Ancient Hebrew Marriage Laws*: 125–26.

Page 79

Patai, "Birth in Popular Custom," *Talpioth*, New York, Vol. IV, 1953: 244–45; Jaussen, *Coutumes des Arabes au pays de Moab*, Paris, 1908: 16; Granqvist, *Marriage*, II: 211–12.

Page 83

Genesis Rabba 45: 4, ed. Theodor-Albeck, Berlin, 1912, I: 451; *ibid.*, 54: 2, p. 577; cf. also *Midrash Hagadol* 1: 346 f.; Grant, *The*

People of Palestine, Philadelphia and London, 1921: 63 f.; Granqvist, *Marriage*, II: 211; C. G. Seligman, ERE, IV: 709.

Page 86

Yer. Taan. 66c mid.; cf. Patai, *Man and Temple in Ancient Jewish Myth and Ritual*, Edinburgh, 1947: 146, 149–50.

Page 87

Patai, *Man and Temple*: 156–61; Burckhardt, *Travels*, II: 378–79; *id.*, *Notes on the Bedouins*, I: 179–80.

Page 90

Mishnah Sōṭāh 4: 3; *Tos. Sōṭāh* 2: 3, ed. Zuckermandel: 294; *Babylonian Talmud, Tractate Sōṭāh* 25b–26a; *Ber.* 31a; *Sifrē Num.*, *Nāsō* §19; *Num. Rab.* 40: 41; *Yalquṭ Shimōnī* 200: 704; *Yer. Sōṭāh* 19c mid.; *Num. Rab.* 9: 15.

Sir James George Frazer, *The Worship of Nature*, London, 1926, I: 415, quoting I. Spieth, *Die Religion der Eweer in Süd-Togo*: 58.

Page 91

Smith, *Lectures on the Religion of the Semites*, ed. Cook, London, 1927: 568 f.; Ploss-Bartels-Reitzenstein, *Das Weib*, Berlin, 1927, II: 330; Hovorka-Kronfeld, *Vergleichende Volksmedizin*, Stuttgart, 1909, II: 520; Reuben Levy, *The Social Structure of Islam*, Cambridge, 1957: 120–21.

Page 96

Bab. Yebamoth 39b; Neufeld, *Ancient Hebrew Marriage Laws*, 49 ff.; Al-Biruni's *India*, transl. Sachau, London, 1888, I: 109 f., as quoted by Louis H. Gray in ERE, V: 745–46; Tabari, as quoted by Smith, *Kinship*: 87.

Page 97

Jaussen, *Coutumes des Arabes au pays de Moab*: 53; Burckhardt, *Notes*, I: 264; Granqvist, *Marriage*, I: 126–27; II: 303, 304–6; Musil, *Arabia Petraea*, Wien, 1908, III: 426; cf. Josef Henninger, "Die Familie bei den heutigen Beduinen Arabiens," *Internationales Archiv für Ethnographie*, Vol. 42, Leiden, 1943: 119, on levirate in Transjordan, the Sinai Peninsula, the semi-nomads of northern Palestine, etc.

Page 98

Burckhardt, *Notes*, I: 112–13; H. C. Armstrong, *Lord of Arabia*,

Penguin edition: 118; Elphinstone, *Account of the Kingdom of Caubul*, London, 1815, I: 236, as quoted in ERE, I: 159; W. H. R. Rivers in ERE, VIII: 431; George A. Barton in ERE, VII: 471; T. Ashkenazi, *Tribus semi-nomades de la Palestine du Nord*, Paris, 1938: 69.

Page 99

Smith, *Kinship*: 89.

Page 104

Musil, *Rwala*: 240.

Page 105

Charles M. Doughty, *Travels in Arabia Deserta*, New York, 1937, II: 132–33.

Page 112

Neufeld, *Ancient Hebrew Marriage Laws*; David R. Mace, *Hebrew Marriage*, New York, 1953.

Page 113

C. H. Gordon, *The World of the Old Testament*, New York, 1958: 229–30.

Page 116

Dickson, *The Arab of the Desert*, London, 1949: 144.
Doughty, *Travels in Arabia Deserta*, I: 272 ff.

Page 117

Ayrout, *Fellahs d'Egypte*: 148; Murray, *Sons of Ishmael*: 225–26; Winifred Blackman, *The Fellahin of Upper Egypt*, London, 1927: 90; Granqvist, *Marriage*, II: 258, 259–66.

Page 118

Josephus Flavius, *Antiquities* IV: viii: 26. *Babylonian Talmud Sanh.* 71b.

Page 119

Mace, *Hebrew Marriage*: 252 ff. *Mishnah Ketubboth* 1: 2 ff.

Page 121

Philo Judaeus, ed. Yonge III: 312; Amram, *Jewish Law of Divorce*: 99; Granqvist, *Marriage*, II: 166; Dickson, *The Arab of the Desert*: 147.

Page 125

Patai, *The Kingdom of Jordan*, Princeton, 1958: 172–73.

Page 129

H. Gunkel, *Genesis*, 4th ed., Göttingen, 1917: 241–42.

Page 133

Musil, *Rwala*: 240; Jaussen, *Coutumes des Arabes au pays de Moab*: 38–39; Thomas, *Arabia Felix*: 98; Ayrout, *Fellahs d'Egypte*: 148; Blackman, *The Fellahin of Upper Egypt*: 36.

Page 134

Winkler, *Bauern zwischen Wasser und Wüste*: 126; Fulanain, *Marsh Arab*: 251–73; Jaussen, *Moab*: 19.

Page 135

Lane, *Modern Egyptians*, I: 69.

Page 136

Wellhausen, *Die Ehe bei den Arabern*: 433; Smith, *Kinship*: 291 ff.; Payne, *The Child in Human Progress*: 171; George Sale, *Introduction to the Koran*: 93; Henninger, "Familie": 102; Georg Jacob, *Altarabisches Beduinenleben*, Berlin, 1897: 212; Levy, *The Social Structure of Islam*: 91; Wensinck, *Early Mohammadan Tradition*, Leiden, 1927: 43; Musil, *Arabia Petraea*, III: 215; id., *Rwala*: 240; Canaan, "The Child . . ." *Journal of the Palestine Oriental Society*, VII, 1927: 162 ff.

Page 139

Yaqut, *Geographical Dictionary*, ed. Wüstenfeld, IV: 481–82. Also quoted by Carlo Comte de Landberg, *Études sur les Dialectes de l'Arabie méridionale*, Leiden, 1909, II/2, and by Wilken, *Matr.*: 31–32.

Page 140

Landberg, *Études*, II/2: 909–10.
Kitab al-Aghani, XIX: 131; Wellhausen, *Die Ehe bei den Arabern*: 462; el-Mubarrad, *Kāmil*: 288; Landberg, *Études*, II/2: 916.
Burckhardt, *Travels in Arabia*, London, 1829, II: 378–79.

Page 141

Id., *Notes*, London, 1831, I: 179–80.

Page 142

Landberg, *Arabica*, Vol. IV, Leiden, 1897: 25–26; *id.*, *Études*, II/2: 203–4, 944, 972.

Page 143

Landberg, *Études*, II/2: 908; *id.*, *Arabica*, IV: 27–28, 33.

Page 144

Bury, *Uz*: 135.

Lane, *Modern Egyptians*, I: 365; A. Bergrugger "La polygamie musulmane, ses causes fatales et le moyen de la detruire," *Revue Africaine*, Alger, III, Avril 1859: 254–58; Count Byron Khun de Prorok, *In Quest of Lost Worlds*, New York, 1935: 42–46; Sir Denys Bray, *Census of India 1911, Report*, Vol. IV: 104.

Brenda Z. Seligman, "Studies in Semitic Kinship," *Bulletin of the School of Oriental Studies*, III, 1923–25: 275.

Page 147

Mace, *Hebrew Marriage*: 238–39.

Smith, *Kinship*: 143; Levy, *The Social Structure of Islam*: 118–19.

Page 151

Levy, *op. cit.*: 118–19; Wilken, *Matr.*: 21, quoting Hurgronje, *Het Mekkaanische Feest*: 111 f.; Henninger, "Familie": 42.

Page 152

Lane, *Modern Egyptians*, II: 90, 91, 149; Winkler, *Bauern zwischen Wasser und Wüste*: 116.

Dickson, *The Arab of the Desert*: 162; Hamed Ammar, *Growing Up in an Egyptian Village*, London, 1954: 73.

Page 154

Matthews, *Mishkat*, I: 97, as quoted by Granqvist, *Birth and Childhood among the Arabs*, Helsingfors, 1947: 221; Dickson, *The Arab of the Desert*: 162; Musil, *Rwala*: 231.

Page 155

St. H. Stephan, *Journal of the Palestine Oriental Society* (JPOS), VIII: 216; Dickson, *op. cit.*: 173; Doughty, *op. cit.*, I: 515; Granqvist, *Birth*: 104–5; Westermarck, *Ritual and Belief in Morocco*, London, 1926, II: 398; Wensinck, *Early Muhammadan Tradition*: 76; Hurgronje, *Mekka*, II: 140 f.

Page 156

Mishnah Oholoth 7: 4; Bab. Shabbath 129a.

Page 157

Mace, Hebrew Marriage: 198.

Page 162

Lane, Modern Egyptians, I: 372; Blackman, The Fellahin of Upper Egypt: 43–44; Dickson, The Arab of the Desert: 162–63; Ayrout, Fellahs d'Egypte: 146 f.; Granqvist, Child Problems Among the Arabs, Helsingfors, 1950: 187.

Page 163

Ammar, Growing Up in an Egyptian Village: 97, 159, 185–86, 190–92.

Page 164

Patai, Man and Temple: 71, 141; Ammar, Growing Up: 75.

Page 166

Jacob, Altarabisches Beduinenleben: 51–53; Musil, Rwala: 140–98.

Pages 167–68

Musil, Rwala: 430.

Page 168

Musil, Rwala: 240.

Page 169

Dickson, The Arab of the Desert: 204; Hurgronje, Mekka, II: 64; Daghestani, Étude Sociologique: 132; Henninger, "Familie": 47.

Pages 170–71

Alfred von Kremer, Kulturgeschichte des Orients, Wien, 1875–77, II: 85–86; Jewett, Afghanistan: 166.

Page 171

Landberg, Études, II/2: 937; von Kremer, Kulturgeschichte, I: 45–46.

Page 172

Lane, Modern Egyptians, II: 92; I: 375; II: 100.

Page 173

Burton, *Arabian Nights*, X (Terminal Essay): 205 ff.

W. P. and Zelda K. Coates, *Soviets in Central Asia*, London, 1951: 78; Baldensperger, "Orders of Holy Men in Palestine," *Palestine Exploration Fund Quarterly Statement*, London, 1894: 38; cf. also Frederick J. Bliss, *The Religions of Modern Syria and Palestine*, New York, 1912: 254.

Page 174

C. G. Campbell, *Tales from the Arab Tribes*, New York, 1950: 23 ff.; Ammar, *Growing Up in an Egyptian Village*: 192; Levy, *Sociology of Islam*, Cambridge, 1931, I: 130; Westermarck, *Wit and Wisdom in Morocco*: 86 ff.

Pages 175–76

Robin Maugham, *Journey to Siwa*, London, 1950: 80, 120; Prorok, *In Quest of Lost Worlds*: 64, 67; Walter Cline, *Notes on the People of Siwah and el-Garah in the Libyan Desert*, General Series of Anthropology, No. 4, Menasha, Wis., 1936: 43.

Page 176

Lees, *Witness of the Wilderness*: 102; Doughty, *Travels in Arabia Deserta*, I: 308–9; Ammar, *Growing Up*: 192.

Philby, *The Heart of Arabia*, London, 1922, II: 146; Henninger, "Familie": 41; Musil, *Rwala*: 473; Westermarck, *Ritual and Belief in Morocco*, London, 1926, II: 289.

Page 177

Cod. Hitt. §§187–88; Gordon, *The World of the Old Testament*, New York, 1958: 99; Barton, ERE, XI: 672.

Page 178

B. *Yebamoth* 63a; S. H. Hooke, *The Origins of Early Semitic Ritual*, London, 1938: 41.

Page 179

Granqvist, *Birth*: 33, 40; Canaan, JPOS, VII: 166.

Page 180

Babylonian Talmud Ket. 60b–61a.

Page 183

Granqvist, *Birth*: 36–37; Ayrout, *Fellahs d'Egypte*: 147.

Page 184

Ammar, *Growing Up:* 90; Granqvist, *Birth:* 52–56, 61 f., 233; *id., Marriage,* I: 23; Patai, "Birth in Popular Custom," *Talpioth,* New York, 1953, Vol. VI: 267.

Granqvist, *Birth:* 61 f., 233; *id., Marriage,* I: 23.

Granqvist, *Birth:* 56; Baldensperger, "Birth, Marriage and Death among the Fellahin of Palestine," *Palestine Exploration Fund Quarterly Statement,* London, 1894: 127; Ammar, *Growing Up:* 90.

Pages 185–86

Granqvist, *Birth:* 64 f.; Doughty, *Arabia Deserta,* I: 514 f.; Musil, *Arabia Petraea,* III: 214; Thomas, *Arabia Felix:* 98.

Page 186

Musil, *Arabia Petraea,* III: 215.
Ammar, *Growing Up:* 91.
Granqvist, *Marriage,* I: 32; *id., Birth:* 93 ff.; Canaan, JPOS, VII: 165; Musil, *Arabia Petraea,* III: 215.

Page 187

Canaan, JPOS, VII: 165; Granqvist, *Birth:* 101.
Smith, *Religion of the Semites:* 594; S. Reich, *Études sur les Villages Arameens de l'Anti-Liban,* Paris, 1938: 73 f.; Musil, *Arabia Petraea,* III: 215; Westermarck, *Ritual and Belief in Morocco,* II: 380.

Pages 187–88

Granqvist, *Birth:* 98; Canaan, JPOS, VII: 163; Jaussen, *Naplouse:* 31; Ashkenazi, *Tribus semi-nomades de la Palestine du Nord:* 70; Baldensperger, *Palestine Exploration Fund Quarterly Statement,* 1894: 127; Westermarck, *Ritual and Belief in Morocco,* II: 379; Ammar, *Growing Up:* 90; *Babylonian Talmud Shabb.* 129b.

Ammar, *Growing Up:* 90.

Granqvist, *Birth:* 74, 100, 243; Ammar, *Growing Up:* 90.

Page 188

Grant, *The Peasantry of Palestine,* Boston, 1907: 73.

Page 191

Musil, *Rwala:* 243; Granqvist, *Birth:* 11; *id., Child:* 12; Musil, *Rwala:* 243–44.

Page 193

Rich source material is listed in Granqvist, *Birth*: 247–48; cf. also Dickson, *The Arab of the Desert*: 506.

Page 194

Canaan, JPOS, VII: 171; Jaussen, *Naplouse*: 39; *id.*, *Moab*: 20 f.; Pierotti, *Customs*: 191; Granqvist, *Birth*: 110.
Granqvist, *Birth*: 112 f.
Dickson, *The Arab of the Desert*: 163.

Page 195

Schubert, *Reisen*, II: 48, as quoted by Wilhelm Nowack, *Hebräische Archäologie*, Freiburg I. B. und Leipzig, 1894, I: 171; Jaussen, *Moab*: 29.

Page 199

Granqvist, *Birth*: 207; Ammar, *Growing Up*: 121.

Pages 201–2

Sale, *Introduction to the Koran*: 89.
Granqvist, *Birth*: 208; Ashkenazi, *Tribus*: 72; Hurgronje, *Mekka*, II: 141; Ammar, *Growing Up*: 117, 122; Murray, *Sons of Ishmael*: 176; Doughty, *Arabia Deserta*, I: 385–87; Thomas, *Arabia Felix*: 72; *id.*, "Anthropological Observations in South Arabia," *Journal of the Royal Anthropological Institute*, XLII, 1932: 87.
Philby, *Arabian Highlands*, New York, 1952: 449–50.

Pages 202–3

Eldon Rutter, *The Holy Cities of Arabia*, London and New York, 1928, II: 55–56.
Thomas, *Arabia Felix*: 71–72.

Page 203

Origines, *Ad Gen.* I: 16; Eusebius, *Praep. Ev.* VI: 293b; Dillmann, *Genesis*: 264; Philo, *Quaest. in Genesim*, III: 47; Gunkel, *Genesis*: 272.
Paul Volz, *Die biblischen Altertümer*, Calw and Stuttgart, 1914: 229.
Granqvist, *Birth*: 208.

Page 204

Thomas, *Arabia Felix*: 71; Ammar, *Growing Up*: 116, 121; Smith,

Kinship: 76; Musil, *Arabia Petraea,* III: 219; Jaussen, *Naplouse:* 40 f.; *id., Moab:* 35 f.; Hurgronje, *Mekka,* II: 142.
Ammar, *Growing Up:* 118–21.
Thomas, *Alarms and Excursions:* 163.

Page 205

Granqvist, *Birth:* 123–24; Canaan, JPOS, VII: 173; Jaussen, *Moab:* 17; Lane, *Modern Egyptians,* I: 67.
Canaan, JPOS, VII: 174; Béchara Chémali, "Naissance et premier âge au Liban," *Anthropos,* Vol. 5, Vienna, 1910: 1085 f.; Granqvist, *Birth:* 124.
Ammar, *Growing Up:* 144–56; Granqvist, *Birth:* 127–30, 135–37, 267.

Page 210

Musil, *Rwala:* 256; Ammar, *Growing Up:* 128.

Pages 210–11

Ammar, *Growing Up:* 126–27, 130, 133, 137–38, 139.

Page 211

Ammar, *Growing Up:* 78, 132, 134, 188.
Ashkenazi, *Tribus:* 73.

Page 216

Granqvist, *Child:* 170.

Page 217

Ammar, *Growing Up:* 54, 110.

Page 221

Winkler, *Bauern:* 138.

Page 224

Musil, *Arabia Petraea,* III: 349; Jaussen, *Moab:* 126; Henninger, "Familie": 125.
Levy, *The Social Structure of Islam:* 146; Thomas, *Alarms and Excursions:* 193; Henninger, "Familie": 124.

Page 225

Musil, *Rwala:* 664; Winkler, *Bauern:* 130; Henninger, "Familie": 124; Ashkenazi, *Tribus:* 96.
Musil, *Rwala:* 663; Thomas, *Arabia Felix:* 56–57; Winkler, *Bauern:* 138.

Page 227

Ammar, *Growing Up*: 125, 127.

Page 229

Lane, *Arabian Nights Entertainments*, I: 380, as quoted by Granqvist, *Child*: 275.

Schmidt and Kahle, *Volkserzählungen aus Palästina*, Göttingen, 1918: 18–19; Granqvist, *Child*: 274; C. B. Klunzinger, *Upper Egypt: Its People and Its Products*, London, 1878: 170.

Page 231

Ammar, *Growing Up*: 129–30; Granqvist, *Birth*: 142.
Klunzinger, *Upper Egypt*: 170.

Page 232

Lane, *Modern Egyptians*, I: 91; Burckhardt, *Notes*, I: 201 f.
Granqvist, *Child*: 188–89; *id.*, *Marriage*, I: 37.

Pages 237–38

Granqvist, *Birth*: 37.

Page 238

Westermarck, *Ritual and Belief in Morocco*, II: 45.

Sykes, *The Glory of the Shia World*, London, 1910: 110; Von Wrede, *Reise in Hadhramaut*, Braunschweig, 1870: 234; Lane, *Modern Egyptians*, II: 253–54; C. G. and Brenda Z. Seligman, *The Kababish, a Sudan Arab Tribe*, Harvard African Studies, II, Cambridge, 1918: 168; Murray, *Sons of Ishmael*: 191; Musil, *Arabia Petraea*, III: 423; Pierotti, *Customs & Traditions of Palestine*: 242; Loir, "Usages et coutumes au moment de la mort chez les Tunisiens," *Revue scientifique*, Ser. IV, Vol. XIV, Paris, 1900: 237; Westermarck, *Ritual and Belief in Morocco*, II: 434 ff., 491 ff.; Doughty, *Arabia Deserta*, I: 498; Burton, *Personal Narrative of a Pilgrimage to Al-Madinah and Meccah*, II, London, 1898: 32.

Page 239

Cf. e.g., Canaan, *Mohammedan Saints and Sanctuaries in Palestine*; Josephus Flavius, *Wars of the Jews*, I: xxxiii: 9, translated by William Whiston, London, 1870: 606.

Page 240

A. Bertholet, *Kulturgeschichte Israels*, Göttingen, 1919: 140.
Lane, *Modern Egyptians*, II: 253; Musil, *Rwala*: 670 f.; Doughty,

Arabia Deserta, I: 498; Murray, *Sons of Ishmael:* 191; Westermarck, *Ritual and Belief*, II: 451.

Page 241

Doughty, *Arabia Deserta*, I: 498; Murray, *Sons of Ishmael:* 191; Westermarck, *Ritual and Belief*, II: 530.

Barton, *Archeology and the Bible*, Philadelphia, 1937: 223; Westermarck, *Ritual and Belief*, II: 530–36; Musil, *Rwala:* 671–72.

Page 243

Jacob, *Altarabisches Beduinenleben:* 139–41.
Granqvist, *Birth:* 153–54.
Jaussen, *Moab:* 96.

Page 244

Westermarck, *Ritual and Belief*, II: 437–39, 440, 442. Cf. also p. 493, note 2, where rich literature is cited to show that these customs are followed all over the Muslim world.

Nowack, *Hebräische Archäologie*, I: 196; Wetzstein, *Zeitschrift für Ethnologie*, 1873: 270 ff., 294 ff.; Niebuhr, *Reisen*, I: 186; Shaw, *Reisen:* 211 f.; Wellhausen, *Skizzen*, III: 160.

Lane, *Modern Egyptians*, II: 252–53.

Page 245

Musil, *Rwala:* 671.

Pages 245–46

Lane, *Modern Egyptians*, II: 253, 257–58, 271; H. Clay Trumbull, *Studies in Oriental Social Life*, Philadelphia, 1894: 145–46, 156–57.

Index of
Scriptural Passages

INDEX OF SCRIPTURAL PASSAGES

A13